Kenneth Burke

and the

Conversation

after

Philosophy

Rhetorical Philosophy and Theory
A Series Edited by David Blakesley

Kenneth Burke

and the

Conversation

after

Philosophy

Timothy W. Crusius

Southern Illinois University Press
Carbondale and Edwardsville

Copyright © 1999 by the Board of Trustees,
Southern Illinois University
All rights reserved
Printed in the United States of America

02 01 00 99   4 3 2 1

Library of Congress Cataloging-in-Publication Data
Crusius, Timothy W., 1950–
    Kenneth Burke and the conversation after philosophy /
Timothy W. Crusius.
        p.   cm. — (Rhetorical philosophy and theory)
Includes bibliographical references and index.

    1. Burke, Kenneth, 1897– . I. Title. II. Series.
B945.B774C75 1999
191—dc21
ISBN 0-8093-2206-4 (alk. paper)   98-21997
ISBN 0-8093-2207-2 (pbk. : alk. paper)   CIP

The paper used in this publication meets the minimum requirements of
American National Standard for Information Sciences—Permanence of Paper
for Printed Library Materials, ANSI Z39.48-1984. ∞

For Bill Rueckert,
friend and colleague,
who inspired and guided an
entire generation of Burke scholars

Contents

Acknowledgments

I wish to thank Robert Hunter, past chair of the English department at Southern Methodist University, and James L. Jones, formerly dean of Dedman College, for arranging a leave of absence during which most of this book was composed.

Both Bill Rueckert and Sam Southwell read the manuscript chapter by chapter in first draft and had many helpful suggestions. In a later stage, the careful and insightful reading of Anthony Cascardi made the book much better than it otherwise would have been. Finally, for the last version, the work of David Blakesley and Jack Selzer is much appreciated.

I wish to acknowledge as well all the work of all the people at Southern Illinois University Press, especially Tracey Sobol. Everyone claiming rhetoric as our special concern owes a deep debt of gratitude to SIUP.

Finally, mindful of everyone on whom I have inflicted my thirty years of Burke-obsession—my talks, lectures, seminars, articles, phone calls, emails, half-intoxicated late night ramblings in improbable places—may this book show that your patience and tolerance had issue. Thanks especially to Kenneth Burke and his family, who put me up and put up with me on more than one occasion over these years and made me feel welcome.

Grateful acknowledgment is made to the following for permission to reprint previously published materials:

University of California Press and Michael Burke for material in *Language as Symbolic Action: Essays on Life, Literature, and Method* by Kenneth Burke, copyright © 1966 by The Regents of the University of California.

Michael Burke for two untitled poems ("Here are the steps" and "If, to seek its level") in *The Rhetoric of Religion: Studies in Logology* by Kenneth Burke, copyright © 1961 by Kenneth Burke, and for selected lines from "Dialectician's Prayer" in *Collected Poems, 1915–1967* by Kenneth Burke, copyright © 1970 by Kenneth Burke.

MIT Press for material in *After Philosophy: End or Transformation?* edited by Kenneth Baynes, James Bohman, and Thomas McCarthy, copyright © 1987 by the Massachusetts Institute of Technology.

Abbreviations of Burke's Works

ATH	*Attitudes Toward History*
CP	*Collected Poems*
CS	*Counter-Statement*
GM	*A Grammar of Motives*
LASA	*Language as Symbolic Action*
PC	*Permanence and Change*
PLF	*The Philosophy of Literary Form*
RM	*A Rhetoric of Motives*
RR	*The Rhetoric of Religion*

Kenneth Burke

and the

Conversation

after

Philosophy

Introduction:
The Question of Kenneth
Burke's Philosophy

Kenneth Burke's international reputation as a literary and rhetorical critic
and theorist seems secure. His influence on most fields in the humanities
and social sciences is a matter of record. However, despite the philosophical dimension of his work, detectable from *Permanence and Change*
(1935) on, no one has offered a full-length assessment of him as a philosopher. Nor has his impact on philosophy been significant thus far: Of the
contemporary philosophers I read, only Paul Ricoeur refers to him, in passing, in one book (*Ideology and Utopia* 11, 82, 256, 323). In the hope of
getting him into a conversation from which he has been excluded, I propose to expound and interpret his thought in the context of current philosophical issues and questions.

The Argument in Brief

My argument depends on reading both Burke and recent philosophy in
a certain way. I offer the following synopsis:

1. By 1935 Kenneth Burke already understood the intellectual situation that Jean-Francois Lyotard has called the "postmodern condition,"
part of which is a resolve to work "after Philosophy," without a foundation in epistemology or metaphysics, without even the aspiration for certain and comprehensive Truth that drove modernism, especially in the
Cartesian tradition. That is, "early Burke" (which I define as Burke in the
thirties) was already our contemporary. He was a postPhilosophical thinker.

Drawing on four books from the thirties, I attempt to confirm his
contemporaneity by exploring his views of the subject or agent, of reason, and of language. In brief, Burke rejects the Cartesian *cogito* and the
strong claims for reason one finds in Kant and Hegel; he takes language
as irreducibly metaphorical and rhetorical. For Burke subjectivity or con-

sciousness is not the key category of philosophy, nor reason its privileged, reliable instrument, nor literal truth, faithful correspondence of word to "reality," its end or purpose.

I also demonstrate that Burke made the much-discussed "turns" to language, society, and rhetoric in the thirties and made them not piecemeal but in an integrated, uncompromising way. Burke's philosophy was already language-centered; he held that philosophy could not claim an objective position above or apart from culture or society but was itself caught up in both; and he acknowledged, and thought that philosophy should acknowledge, the will to power inseparable from claims to truth, from the passion to persuade.

2. For some influential postPhilosophical thinkers (e.g., Lyotard, Michel Foucault, and Jacques Derrida), the end of Philosophy means the end of philosophy. In place of philosophy, such postphilosophical thinkers advocate doing something else instead—cultural criticism, historiography, the study of language games, deconstruction, and so forth. Burke also did and defended doing other things besides philosophy. For him, however, the end of Philosophy did not mean the end of philosophy. Rather the "postmodern condition" is the setting of a problem, a challenge to find a way of doing philosophy in an intellectual environment fortified to resist "grand theory" or "master narratives."

In the conclusion to Part One, "Being Without Metaphysics," I discuss how Burke formulated the problem of doing philosophy in postmodern culture. Can we cease to be scandalized by the "scandal of philosophy," its failure to secure univocal truth? Can we opt out of Philosophy's struggle for *the* metaphysic or *the* epistemology—the final, preemptive synthesis—without bringing thought to a close in skepticism or nihilism?

Burke thought we could. His solution is summed up in the oxymoron "skeptical groundings" and in the intention to work "through [the study of] symbolism to a philosophy of being." His approach is hermeneutical, especially in aiming to retrieve or refurbish (rather than refute or dismantle) past thought. Burke belongs to the movement to *transform* philosophy rather than to abandon it. In this important respect, he is closer to, say, Hans-Georg Gadamer, or Alasdair MacIntyre, or Charles Taylor, than he is to Lyotard, Foucault, or Derrida.

3. In the work of the thirties Burke set out to practice philosophy within postmodern conditions. "Later Burke," which I define as everything from A *Grammar of Motives* (1945) on, offers an innovative humanism capable of withstanding the most corrosive contemporary critique.

Another way to characterize Burke's mature philosophy in general is to describe it as a continuation of practical philosophy. Rather than by deduction from abstract metaphysical or epistemological principles, practical philosophy develops by reflection on human behavior and achievement, trying to make explicit for analysis and contemplation that which is only implicit in human behavior and achievement itself. Dedicated to the ancient quest for self-understanding, practical philosophy and humanism obviously belong and work together.

Part Two's four essays explore Burke's approach to hermeneutics, human being, dialectic and dialogue, and *praxis*. My basic contentions are as follows:

Hermeneutics. In what he called "discounting," Burke practices both positive hermeneutics (the hermeneutics of tradition or trust) and negative hermeneutics (depth hermeneutics or the hermeneutics of suspicion). Paul Ricoeur has argued that these two historical antagonists should function as complements ("Hermeneutics" 63–64); in Burke they actually do so function.

Human being. Burke overcomes the conflict between pre-Darwinian and post-Darwinian views of human being. Burke defines us as "the typically symbol-using animal." As an animal we are a species among species, barely distinguishable in biological terms from other hominids. But as a symbol or language-using animal we are apparently unique; through us nature has found a way to talk about itself. We are, then, both special and not special, part of nature and apart from nature.

The contemporary problem is not so much deciding whether we are special or not but rather in coping better with what makes us special. Language enables a creative exuberance, but it also drives us toward war and ecological disaster. Can we understand our symbol-driven motivations better and through increased understanding achieve greater self-control? If not, Burke thinks our very specialness will be our undoing.

Dialectic and dialogue. Burke integrates partitive (analytical, dialectical) thought with relational (dialogical) thought, fusing the long tradition of interest in the logic of natural language with the recent renewal of interest in dialogue and dialogics (e.g., George Herbert Mead and Mikhail Bakhtin). The result is a "conversation of many voices," a dialectical pluralism, as exemplified in the metahermeneutic of *A Grammar of Motives*.

Praxis. Burke reaches beyond Marx and his followers to a nonrevolutionary, therapeutic praxis, the end of which is "ecological balance." Burke advocates an ecology of thought and action at every level: in self-construction, in the social and political arena, and in the relation of human societies to the biosphere.

In sum, then, I am contending that Burke *began* where philosophy now is—self-consciously at work "after Philosophy." Rather than turning away from philosophy, as many postmodern writers have done, Burke sought to edify without foundations. The result is a philosophy of high contemporary interest and importance, which we are only now prepared to examine with the care it deserves. Perhaps the time is right for assessing Kenneth Burke as a philosopher, in part because the way to Burke is also one way to cope constructively with our own postPhilosophical condition.

The Problem of Identity

Writing in 1950 about *A Grammar of Motives* and *A Rhetoric of Motives*, Malcolm Cowley claimed that "[i]t is an error to approach him [Burke] as a critic primarily. In his latest books one finds that his interest in human relations is leading him more and more toward general philosophy" (249). Clearly there is nothing new in claiming Kenneth Burke for philosophy. Whatever Burke may be primarily, his critics have never been able to take him as a literary critic only. As far back as 1935, in an essay-review of *Permanence and Change*, Austin Warren offered what may be the first label for Burke's thought, skepticism (54), a characterization echoed by Charles Glicksburg two years later (77). In a hostile review of *Attitudes Toward History* (1937), Sidney Hook grudgingly credited Burke with "develop[ing] independently of technical philosophical thought a kind of home-baked objective relativism" (91). Having identified him four years earlier as "a master of Marxist 'dialectic'" ("Address" 143), in 1946 John Crowe Ransom claimed that Burke was "of all our [American] critics . . . philosophically the subtlest," beyond any easy labeling ("Dialectic" 160). Also in 1946 Max Black began the long association of Burke with Aristotle: Dramatism, Black decided, "is an alias for neo-aristotelianism" (168).

As these few citations indicate, the problem has never been recognizing the philosopher in Kenneth Burke. Friend or foe, many have seen it and found it worth commentary. Rather the problem, which persists to the present—indeed, intensifies as we encounter more recent criticism—is that there is no agreement whatsoever about the philosophy itself. Skeptic, objective relativist, Marxist, neo-Aristotelian: These are but four of a host of descriptive designations applied to Burke's thought. As yet his philosophy has no settled identity. In saying "Burke" we do not invoke a philosophy and philosophical traditions as we do by saying "Marx" or "Heidegger." This lack of an established identity makes the question of Burke's philosophy especially interesting, but it has also kept him out of most philosophical conversations. Names without definite associations are just not invoked.

What I mean, then, by "the question of Burke's philosophy" is the question of Burke's philosophical identity. This study is an attempt to answer that question in the context of postPhilosophy, explicitly or implicitly the context of most recent interpretations of Kenneth Burke as well. We shall take now a brief look at both.

PostPhilosophical Culture

> This [postPhilosophical] culture would be a culture in which
> neither the priests nor the physicists nor the poets nor the Party
> were thought of as more "rational" or more "scientific" or
> "deeper" than one another. . . . *A fortiori*, such a culture would
> contain nobody called "the Philosopher" who could explain
> why and how certain areas of culture enjoyed a special rela-
> tion to reality. Such a culture would, doubtless, contain spe-
> cialists in seeing how things hung together. . . . They would
> be all-purpose intellectuals who were ready to offer a view
> on pretty much anything, in the hope of making it hang to-
> gether with everything else.

> —Richard Rorty, "Pragmatism and Philosophy"

> O let me be as much of a disgrace
> as I can risk
> and still pay the taxes.
> Let me run afoul
> but not too much
> of every specialty.

> —Kenneth Burke, "Apostrophes Before Desisting"

When we compare the early reception of Burke's philosophy with recent
criticism, we encounter sharply different climates of opinion. By and large
the early critics found something philosophical about Burke, but found
him wanting as a Philosopher—which indeed he was, since Philosophy
for him was no longer what William James called a "live option." They
were applying criteria for Philosophy to a thinker already at work after
Philosophy. (See William Rueckert's *Critical Responses to Kenneth Burke*,
especially 26–29, 71–79, 89–96, 109–21, 222–34, 247–50).

With few exceptions, Burke's recent critics simply take his work as
philosophy without debate and without hesitation. For example, in *Criticism and Social Change*, Frank Lentricchia calls Burke a Western Marxist (23) and identifies him in passing with such counter-hegemonic figures
as Antonio Gramsci and Michel Foucault. In *The Culture of Criticism
and the Criticism of Culture*, Giles Gunn associates Burke (as Cowley
did before him [248]) with American pragmatism (66–79). In *Kenneth
Burke and Martin Heidegger*, Samuel Southwell not only links Burke's
name with Heidegger and the hermeneutic project but also contends that

"if the complementarity of the two writers is to result in synthesis, it may do so only by requiring a revision, not of Burke, but of Heidegger" (82).

Recent critics no longer pose the question implicit or explicit in the early criticism: Can we call what Burke is doing philosophy? Several of them are so far beyond this question that, like Southwell, they find more in Burke's philosophy than they do in the work of thinkers whose status as philosophers has never been in question. For instance, Fredric Jameson argues that "Burke's notion of the symbolic act is . . . a privileged expression of current notions of the primacy of language," as well as being "a critique of the more mindless forms of the fetishism of language" ("Symbolic Inference" 69–70). How do we account for this about-face in the reception of Burke's philosophy?

No doubt many factors come into play. Perhaps the most important is the virtual disappearance of any meaningful distinction between textual criticism and philosophy. Textual criticism has become philosophical reflection on textuality itself and the process and function of criticism; philosophy—whatever else it may, a collection of texts read as philosophy—is now often seen as textual interpretation. In an era of philosopher-critics, Burke is no longer an oddity presenting special problems of assimilation.

As disciplinary boundaries have come to mean less, so cultural barriers are not as formidable as they once were. In 1950 one could still discriminate sharply between Anglo-American and Continental thought. Now we find, for instance, Jurgen Habermas writing with insight and sympathy about American pragmatism and American philosophers (Richard Bernstein is a good example) devoting careers to interpreting Continental philosophy to the English-speaking world. From the outset Burke worked with American, English, and Continental traditions, drawing on all three about equally and without apparent prejudice. The overcoming of intellectual provincialism, therefore, is another of the many cultural developments that has helped make Burke more accessible.

Another way to put this point is to say that Anglo-American philosophy had to move beyond its constriction to positivism and analytics before even the potential for listening to Burke could exist. As we will see in Part One, by 1935 Burke's rejection of positivism is fully articulate, his break with the dominant philosophy of his time and place decisive. Continental philosophy is only partly responsible for this, as it is only one of the intellectual influences on writers such as Michael Polanyi and Thomas Kuhn, who prepared the way for more consciously hermeneutical philosophy in the contemporary English-speaking world. Without its influence, however, Burke would have had far less to work with and positivism might have avoided serious challenge much longer.

Positivism, however, is but one strain in Philosophy. The way to

Burke's philosophy could not open fully until the development of a post-Philosophical conversation. But what exactly is postPhilosophy?

Noting that the term "philosophy" itself is highly ambiguous, Richard Rorty contrasts two meanings it has had historically:

> "[P]hilosophy" can mean simply what Sellars calls "an attempt to see how things, in the broadest possible sense of the term, hang together, in the broadest possible sense of the term." . . . In this sense, Blake is as much of a philosopher as Fichte, Henry Adams more of a philosopher than Frege. No one would be dubious about philosophy, taken in this sense. But the word can also denote something more specialized, and very dubious indeed. In this second sense, it can mean following Plato's and Kant's lead, asking questions about the nature of certain normative notions (for instance, "truth," "rationality," "goodness") in the hope of better obeying such norms. The idea is to believe more truths or do more good or be more rational by knowing more about Truth or Goodness or Rationality. I shall capitalize the term "philosophy" when used in this second sense, in order to help make the point that Philosophy, Truth, Goodness, and Rationality are interlocked Platonic notions. Pragmatists are saying that the best hope for philosophy is not to practice Philosophy. (28)

Behind Rorty's explication of the difference between Philosophy and philosophy is a story about how the former became the latter. But before retelling this now familiar story, some commentary on the P/philosophy distinction might be helpful.

Sellars's comically vague "definition" of philosophy deflates the pretension and undermines the ritual seriousness of traditional Philosophy. Method, system, "rigor" in the "scientific" sense, academic "purity"—in sum, all the signs of the hubris of mastery and the drive to have an exclusive club—all have no special privilege in philosophy. Anyone capable of thinking beyond a speciality, anyone interested in contemplating life more than casually or occasionally, in the hope of somehow making sense of it (to a degree), of achieving an articulate and coherent understanding of it (more or less), can lay claim to or be claimed by philosophy. The "definition" also implies: Resist the temptation to ask, What does philosophy "really" mean? The question is a Philosophical question. It has no single answer, any more than the question, What is Truth? has a single answer. We have philosophies. Sometimes we even have truths. Be content with this, and get on with philosophizing.

"The best hope for philosophy is not to practice Philosophy"—from

Kierkegaard and Nietzsche on, many modern philosophers have been saying this, if not exactly in these words. You don't have to be a pragmatist to hope that Philosophy is over. What little remains of it is confined mainly to the Carnap-Frege analytical tradition, which has its origin in Kant's concern with Rationality. Analytics is precise; analytics is professional. But the price for these advantages is much too high. Philosophy becomes only another speciality, just another constricted arena of expertise, too arcane to matter to anyone who is not a professional logician.

"Henry Adams," Rorty claims, is "more a philosopher than Frege." This claim is not merely a swipe at the analytical tradition. It represents, rather, a transvaluation of values—not an abandonment of norms but the substitution of one set of values for another. Adams and his education matters, even to professional logicians insofar as they are humans and not specialists. Philosophy should embrace the human struggle with concrete situations. It should be thought not only thought but *lived*, as it was among classical philosophers. It should be, in Kenneth Burke's words, "a *rationale of art*—not . . . a performer's art, not a specialist's art for some to produce and many to observe, but an art in its widest aspects, an *art of living*" (PC 66, his emphasis).

What happened to Philosophy? How did we come to envision a postPhilosophical culture?

The last Philosophical "theory of everything" was Hegel's. Although Hegel's thought is still very influential, his synthesis did not long survive his death. Absolute idealism ceased to be a live option in philosophy long ago. But Hegel's understanding of philosophical thought as unfolding in time, as historical rather than, in the classical sense, theoretical (contemplation of the eternal, of transhistorical Truth), not only survived but became normative. Most significant philosophy after Hegel views philosophy in dynamic, historical terms, as always "on the way," permanently open ended.

Hegel, then, is the beginning of the end of Philosophy. For when philosophy understands itself as historical (when, as in Heidegger, being becomes a function of time), it can no longer be Philosophy. And once it sees itself in time, it is not far from interpreting itself as many contemporary philosophers (including Kenneth Burke) do—as a social, cultural, and linguistic phenomenon, distinguishable by the sort of questions it asks, but not by being first, special, purer, higher, and so forth, than other intellectual work.

After Hegel, the whole foundationalist rationale driving Philosophy slowly erodes away. Beginning with Kierkegaard, philosophy increasingly stresses human finitude, a sense of limitation akin to tragic conceptions of human existence. Although heir to Enlightenment Philosophy and the ideology of endless progress toward human perfection, modern science has contributed mightily to a new understanding of the vanity of human wishes. Only a species amid species, new on the scene and hardly assured of surviving much longer, we inhabit a universe unimaginably vast and unimaginably old—more unfathomable than it ever was, and seemingly much more indifferent to our existence, not to mention our projects. A theory of everything becomes a monstrosity or a joke whose source of humor is irony. At a time when we have far more information in every field than we can possibly digest, we have so much trouble getting anything to hang together with anything else—modest philosophical quests for a little connectedness and coherence—that grand theories and master narratives necessarily become part of an immodest Philosophical past.

Then Freud took away the central category of Cartesian epistemology, consciousness or the Subject, and with it the normative notion of Reason. Consciousness (*Bewusstsein* in German) becomes, as Gadamer memorably put it, "more being (*Sein*) than consciousness (*Bewusst*)" ("Scope" 38), more absent than present, more forgetting than remembering, more a social and rhetorical fabrication than a faithful mirror of the world. The Subject cannot know itself and cannot be autonomous. The mind functions for the most part unconsciously or preconsciously, forever beyond our grasp, and we are utterly dependent on "the given," on nature, social arrangements, and tradition, also forever beyond total understanding. Our motives are at least as much arational or nonrational as rational, so that even if a complete account of Reason were possible, it could not be normative even for human being, much less for all existence. The "I" of Descartes's "I think" is no longer "in itself," isolated, punctual, self-transparent, and thinking is no longer reducible to categories and propositions. In short, the way Philosophy used consciousness, the subject, and reason is no longer open to us; Husserl's phenomenology was its last gasp.

Even more than Kierkegaard, or Darwin, or Freud, it was Nietzsche who administered the blows to Philosophy that would prove fatal. From Plato to Kant, Philosophy defined itself by contrast with rhetoric. Against rhetoric's probabilities and verisimilitudes, its concern was Truth. Against rhetoric's involvement in public life, its venue was private, withdrawn, contemplative, conversational rather than oratorical. Against rhetoric's tropes, its language was plain and literal. Philosophy knew itself, maintained its identity, its sense of purity, by not acknowledging its own passion to persuade, the will to power implicit in any claim to truth. Mercilessly, Nietzsche exposed Philosophy as rhetoric and the pursuit of Truth, Goodness, and Rationality as not just one instance of the will to power but the supreme example of it. For the very desire to impose order and fixity on a contingent, decentered, dynamic world is the common denominator of all manifestations of the will to power.

After Nietzsche, Philosophy is increasingly vulnerable to the charge of self-deceit—or still worse, bad faith. Now philosophy is turning to rhetoric, in part as a way of understanding itself, of creating an identity not dependent on the untenable polarity of Philosophy/rhetoric. After Heisenberg, after Godel—that is, after loss of faith in the complete formal coherence of mathematics (Philosophy's inspiration, both at the source and typically thereafter)—philosophy has little choice but to recognize what Hans Blumenberg calls "the axiom of all rhetoric," "the principle of insufficient reason" (447), and therefore the need for rhetorical argumentation. Demonstration ceases to be either the norm or the ideal of philosophy.

Closely related to Nietzsche's frontal attack on Philosophical identity is the rejection of traditional Philosophical aims. Among others, utilitarians, Marxists, and American pragmatists all want to know not What is Truth? but rather, What is philosophy good for? What difference does it make in the concrete quality of life? By this reversal of value, *praxis* takes precedence over theory and theory itself becomes not contemplation of the eternal but rather the product of reflection on *praxis* itself. *Theoria* (literally, "a looking at") survives as the kind of "seeing" or "insight" that can result from making explicit what is implicit in human activity. But the point, as Marx said, is not theory, understanding in itself; the point, to borrow the title of Kenneth Burke's novel, is to move "towards a better life."

Of course, the pragmatic test of usefulness is itself very problematical, but the turn to *praxis* is nevertheless one of the defining characteristics of postPhilosophy. The focus on *praxis* moves philosophy away from the contemplative ideal and toward the public arena—toward, that is, rhetoric. Loss of faith in Rational sufficiency and the focus on *praxis* work together to undermine any hard-and-fast distinction between Philosophy (or philosophy) and rhetoric.

So far, in fact, has this undermining gone that some recent philosopher-critics in the Nietzschean tradition (e.g., Foucault, Derrida, de Man) state or imply that there is no meaningful way to distinguish philosophy from rhetoric. Against what has been called the "assimilation hypothesis" (Cooper 193–94), less radical postmodern philosophers hold out for a rough, practical distinction but seek to explore philosophy in rhetorical terms or rhetoric in philosophical terms. For instance, inspired by the work of people such as Chaim Perelman and Stephen Toulmin, the "rhetoric of inquiry" movement studies P/philosophy and science as discursive practices, as communities of discourse. Interest in philosophies of rhetoric, including Burke's *A Rhetoric of Motives* (1950), has never been higher, and the neglected tradition of rhetorical philosophy (the line extending from the Sophists and Isocrates to Cicero and, through the Latin Renaissance generally, to Vico, and beyond to such recent figures as Ernesto Grassi) is at last getting some attention. None of this opening up, this cross-fertilization of philosophy and rhetoric, could have happened if Philosophy still held sway.

But Philosophy is, finally, over. To be sure, pockets of resistance to full acceptance of the end of Philosophy still exist here and there. Mostly outside of contemporary philosophy, one can still detect sometimes the kind of hand-wringing about centers that will not hold and fragments shored against ruins we recall from modernist poets like Yeats and Eliot. For the most part, however, contemporary thinkers have indeed, as Lyotard says, "lost the nostalgia for the lost narrative" (87). Many hope that if the falcon cannot hear the falconer, perhaps the doves will fare better. In any case, the appearance of volumes like *After Philosophy: End or Transformation* (1987) marks a definitive change of topic. Philosophers are no longer debating the future of Philosophy. The question now involves the apparent either/or of end or transformation: Does the end of Philosophy mean the end of philosophy? If so, what will or should take its place? If not, what will/should philosophy be?

Critical Appropriations and PostPhilosophical Alternatives

By "the conversation after Philosophy," I mean, then, the ongoing debate about end or transformation. Many schools of thought belong to this discussion, and many shades of opinion may be discerned within the schools. We shall be concerned with only three such discourse communities, the ones that have thus far claimed Kenneth Burke for their own viewpoint and projects: Hermeneutics (e.g., Southwell, Damrosch), Critical Theory (e.g., Lentricchia, Gunn), and Radical Postmodernism (e.g., Williams, Nelson). The point of this discussion is to share a context and to locate Burke in a rough but (I hope) useful way within the conversation after Philosophy—not to offer an adequate account of recent Burke criticism or of the three schools in question. Our purpose being thus so limited, we shall pretend that the schools are more uniform than they are, opting for dominant colors rather than shades of opinion.

In general, then, we have the following:

Hermeneutics. This school is represented by Gadamer, Ricoeur, Blumenberg, Charles Taylor, among others. All are to some degree indebted to the Heidegger of *Being and Time*. For this group, human being is always human-being-in-the-world (*Dasein*), "thrown" by the circumstances of birth into a time and place—a tradition, a history, a culture, an array of social and economic practices, and so forth—it can never fully comprehend. For hermeneutics, language is disclosure, the way parts of our world (our being in it) comes to presence. The task of philosophy is interpretation, "reflection . . . [on] the opaque, contingent, and equivocal signs scattered in the cultures in which our language is rooted" (Ricoeur, *Freud* 47).

Critical theory. This school derives from Nietzsche, Marx, and Freud and is associated with the Frankfurt School, whose most influential contemporary representative is Habermas. A critical theory is "a reflective theory which gives agents a kind of knowledge inherently productive of enlightenment and emancipation" (Geuss 2). Critical theory resembles hermeneutics in its view of human thrownness and in taking the function of language as primarily disclosure. But whereas hermeneutics stresses understanding traditions and practices as the source of our being, critical theory stresses exposing traditions and practices as the source of bondage. Philosophy is a continuation of the Enlightenment project to liberate human being from error, superstition, neurosis, and various forms of economic and political oppression.

Radical postmodernism. Admittedly this school's "family resemblances" are much harder to specify. Among others, Rorty, Foucault, Derrida, and Lyotard belong to radical postmodernism. Call it "French poststructuralism plus," the plus designating an assortment of minds all over the world who for one reason or another resist assimilation to hermeneutics or critical theory. Radical postmodernism shares with hermeneutics belief in the primacy of interpretation. But whereas hermeneutics stresses a common understanding shared by interpreters and the goal of consensus in interpretation, radical postmodernism celebrates diversity, difference, and the search for dissensus. Consequently, although usually sympathetic with the emancipatory goal of critical theory, radical postmodernists are skeptical of theory itself and wary of the totalitarian temptations of people who think they know something "inherently productive of enlightenment and emancipation." If anything unites a group of thinkers suspicious of unity itself, radical postmodernists share a "neocartesian vision." That is, what they seem to want is as clean a break with Philosophy as possible, "to change terrain," as Derrida put it ("Ends" 151). But whereas Descartes sought certainty via method, radical postmodernists are Cartesians-in-reverse, underminers of claims to certainty secured by method. The task of philosophy is to do away with itself. Some form of cultural criticism is to take its place.

Our question is, Can Burke be assimilated successfully to any one of these three schools? Or does he remain "other," a distinctive voice in the conversation after Philosophy?

In linking Burke with Heidegger, Southwell places Burke within the general region occupied by hermeneutics. So does David Damrosch, who argues that Burke and Gadamer are the two "major dramatistic theoretician[s] of interpretation" (224).

Certainly there are strong affinities between Burke and the hermeneutic tradition. "Intellectually," Southwell observes, "Burke and Heidegger are united by descent from a common ancestor: Friedrich Nietzsche." He goes on to specify in seventeen propositions the "common profile" of Nietzsche, Heidegger, and Burke. I offer below a selection from his list:

- The dominant forces of modern thought are inimical to human wholeness.

- Determinism is a fiction.

- The concepts of "progress" and "liberalism" must be rejected.

- There is no subject-object dichotomy.

- The subject is a multiplicity.

- The power of language pervades and largely controls all human thought and all human perception.

- All human thought and perception are necessarily interpretation (hermeneutics).

- Art is a more reliable guide to reality than is reason, and the rational (scientific-intellectual) paradigm of the world must be replaced by an artistic paradigm. (4–5)

Even reduced to only eight propositions, Southwell's argument for linking Burke with Heidegger via Nietzsche is strong. When we add to this Damrosch's key point, that both Burke and Gadamer "find a natural grounding for . . . dramatism in religious experience" (225), we have a *prima facie* case for bringing Burke into the hermeneutical branch of the conversation after Philosophy.

Here and there throughout this study I will call attention to homologies between Burke and hermeneutics. However, simply appropriating Burke for hermeneutics would be almost as great a distortion of his thought as the once common association with the New Critics. Nietzsche's impact on Burke is as great as Southwell says it is but diminishes after *Permanence and Change*. When Dramatism emerges in the forties, Marx and Freud are more important to Burke than Nietzsche is. I can imagine a fruitful dialogue between Burke and hermeneutics as part of the conversation after Philosophy, but anything more than this, anything that would synthesize Burke with hermeneutics (or vice versa), can only succeed in deforming both.

I will mention only a few of the more salient differences. Heidegger has much to say about human "second nature," cultural being, language, but he ignores the human body, biology, second nature's dwelling within nature. For Burke, human being is the *symbol-using* animal, but also the symbol-using *animal*. Consequently, whereas Heidegger cannot locate human being in nature, Burke can and does.

More fundamentally, Heidegger takes all definitions of human being as humanisms caught up in the conceptual language of metaphysics. Heidegger wanted to overcome metaphysics. But Burke holds that metaphysics is always implicit in any interpretation of motives and, therefore, a recurrent if undecidable issue that we can never pass beyond. (Burke would agree with Rorty that we can change the subject, talk about something else instead of metaphysics. But overcoming it—passing beyond the question—is not open to us.)

The gulf between Burke and Heidegger is very wide indeed. With Gadamer it narrows appreciably, but bridge-building ("pontificating," as Burke punningly designates such feats of intellectual engineering) remains problematical. They share the dramatistic-dialogical view of language. Both are fascinated by dialectic, Plato's and Hegel's. Both see their philosophies as belonging to the tradition of practical philosophy and as constructive gestures for current *praxis*. However, American pragmatism and Marx stand between Burke and Gadamer. Gadamer is vulnerable to Habermas's charge of idealistic reluctance to engage the domain of work and political struggle ("Review" 272–73). Burke may not be Marxist enough for some Marxists, but his many-sided reflections on capitalism and technology make any Habermas-style critique of his philosophy unconvincing.

It is true that Burke shares with Gadamer—and with Ricoeur, Taylor, Iris Murdoch, Alasdair MacIntyre, and others with affinities for the hermeneutic tradition, such as Bakhtin—a strong interest in religion and theology. But whereas the hermeneutic tradition since Schleiermacher has tended to be religious in the ordinary sense of the word, Burke consistently approaches religion from outside faith itself. An agnostic who writes prayerful poems to the "Big Shot" he cannot quite believe in, Burke studies religion with a mixture of affection and suspicion. His quip that he is "respectful of primates, both simian and ecclesiastical" (*CP* 101) captures his comic ambivalence well.

Burke belongs and does not belong to the hermeneutical conversation after Philosophy. There is common ground enough for good dialogue and difference enough to make the conversation interesting. But what about critical theory? Nietzsche's "art of distrust" links him more to the hermeneutics of suspicion than to Gadamer's hermeneutics of tradition. If, as Southwell maintains, Burke owes so much to Nietzsche, why not follow Lentricchia, who reads Burke as a kind of American Habermas? We have Burke's own wry observation that he could "find no difference between suspicion and love of knowledge" (*CP* 103). He once described himself as an "anti-Faust," whose motto is "No flight! I will each year dig down deeper" (*CP* 25). Doesn't this archaeologist of the word belong to "depth hermeneutics," Habermas's term for critical theory?

Another *prima facie* case can be made for Burke as a critical theorist, a case at least as strong as the one for Burke and hermeneutics. It has its origin in the conversion narratives that try to make sense of what happened in the twenties and thirties. I here insert the relevant details from Burke's life. His career began just after the First World War and centered in the brilliant artistic and intellectual life of New York City in the twenties. It was a fairly conventional literary career: Burke published poetry and short stories, did some translating and reviewing, and worked as an editor for *The Dial*. Then came the Depression and the rise of fascism, which transformed some of the best literary minds of an entire generation from aesthetes to social and political critics and activists. At first sympathetic toward both the agrarians and the Marxists, Burke was moved by events decisively toward the latter, toward, that is, depth analysis of economic and social ills inspired by the ideas and methods of Marx and Freud. In the mid-thirties Burke participated in the communist-controlled meetings of the American Writers Congress; in *Attitudes Toward History* (1937) he advocates a social-centered criticism and hopes to see capitalism displaced by socialism.

The tale's frame is indeed familiar; plug in the appropriate details, and it can tell the story of many American intellectuals of Burke's generation. In Part One I shall tell the story somewhat differently: In my view, the crises of the thirties made Burke a philosopher. Philosophy was his way of coping with the tensions and contradictions of this painful decade and with his own disorientation "at a time when there was a general feeling that our traditional ways were headed for a tremendous change, maybe even a permanent collapse" (*PC* xlvii). Instead of turning to social activism, Burke chose to examine and evaluate both traditional dogma and the dogma of its critics. He used Marx and Freud, but he never became a Marxist or a Freudian. The conversion narrative imperfectly applies to Burke because his own hermeneutic of suspicion was from the outset suspicious of conversions (Crusius, "*Auscultation*" 362, 364–65). Nevertheless, Burke can *converse* with "liberation philosophy" quite as well as he can with philosophical hermeneutics.

Assimilating Burke to critical theory, however, works about as well as assimilating him to hermeneutics—not very well. Let's recall Geuss's definition of depth hermeneutics: "a reflective theory which gives agents a kind of knowledge inherently productive of enlightenment and emancipation." For Burke a reflective theory, any reflective theory, can only be a "terministic screen" (*LASA* 44–50), a hermeneutical vocabulary that directs our attention to some aspects of whatever we are trying to interpret while ignoring other aspects. In other words, a reflective theory is only "inherently productive" of the kinds of insights it was designed to achieve. It discloses the world selectively, partially, with an intense spotlight that throws much more into darkness than it illumines. We can learn much from such concentrations of attention, but the claim to special, authoritative insight—the claim to have "depth" when everybody else has only "surfaces"—is indefensible.

The need to substantiate some special claim to depth insight drives Habermas's concern with legitimation in general as well as his effort to secure his own critical theory in particular (see *Legitimation*). In sharp contrast, Burke sees no possibility for securing claims to depth and cannot see what we would gain if it were possible. Given certain contexts and purposes, one hermeneutical vocabulary may be more appropriate or useful than another. But the best general strategy is to use an array of critical theories in an organized and principled way—exactly what Burke does, while also developing a critical theory of his own designed to expose and criticize motives peculiar to symbol-using. So far as critical theory is concerned, Wayne Booth was right to take Burke as a pluralist (*Critical Understanding* 99–124). Burke's aim is "a dialectic of many voices" (*CS* xi), not a dialogue restricted to Marxists or Freudians, and certainly not a monologue in behalf of a single depth hermeneutic.

Burke is skeptical about any claim to Truth advanced for a depth hermeneutic. He is also skeptical about critical theory itself insofar as it would advance an unqualified claim to "enlightenment and emancipation." Burke certainly believes that we can understand our own motives better—that is, he is committed to reflection and reflective theories— and that greater enlightenment can result in a degree of control over our motives, even sometimes liberation from thoughtless bondage to tradition. He is no pessimist. However, as Southwell noted in formulating the stances common to Nietzsche, Heidegger, and Burke, he is also no progressive liberal either. When others speak of progress, Burke only recognizes the inevitability of change, a mixed bag of gains and losses. When others speak of conversions, new ages, and liberations, Burke calls attention to the persistence of the "old self" in the "new self," to cultural lag, and wants to know, Liberation for whom? From what exactly? And most importantly, *to* What? Are we really better off? By what measure are we better off?

Somewhat like Freud or Foucault, Burke puts more stock in coping than liberating. Some psychic states are healthier than others, but there is something about human being that makes us at best permanently neurotic. Some regimes of power are less oppressive and destructive than others, but regimes of power there will always be, and they will be, always, oppressive and destructive to an extent. Dreams of liberation, therefore, are at best utopian goads to meliorism, persistent effort to make things better. Burke has no investment in golden ages, turnings, omega points, or final, end-time fruitions in the Kingdom of God or absolute spirit or the withering away of the State. Consequently, his claims for critical theory in general and for his theories in particular are quite modest, designed more for coping than liberating, and meant self-consciously to avoid both idealism and its devastating reflex, cynicism.

At bottom Burke is not the sort of "true believer" who becomes a critical theorist—a committed Marxist, Freudian, feminist, New Historian, or whatever. He is suspicious of liberators, while not foreclosing on the possibility of some enlightenment, some emancipation. In short, critical theory is part of Burke's ways and means but not equivalent to his philosophy as a whole.

We turn, then, to the end-of-philosophy school, the radical postmodernists. Of all the figures that could be associated with radical postmodernism, Rorty is the one closest to Burke in general outlook and attitude. They share American pragmatism; they are both levellers, undercutting traditional genre distinctions and undermining traditional hierarchies that elevate some disciplines over others; Rorty's postPhilosophical culture can hardly be realized without Burke's open or comic attitude; Burke exemplifies Rorty's "all-purpose intellectual."

Burke's recent critics, however, have not emphasized Burke's connections with Rorty and postPhilosophical culture; they have instead linked him with Derrida and deconstruction. John Freccero was the first to do so, alleging that "Burke's interest in theology is the reverse of the theologian's and is essentially deconstructive of the theological edifices of the past" (52–53). David Cratis Williams explored the "margins of overlap" between Burke and Derrida, "especially in their respective analyses of the antinomies of dialectics." For both the concept of margin itself is important; both "problematize knowledge and truth"; both focus "on language itself, on its fundamental duplicity, its siren song of certitude, and, ultimately, its potential to annihilate itself and obliterate all meaning" (197, 199, 200).

Williams finds only margins shared by Burke and Derrida; he sets them apart in an important way we shall consider in a moment. But first let's listen to Cary Nelson, whose "Writing as the Accomplice of Language: Kenneth Burke and Poststructuralism," is frankly intended "to offer a counter-Burke to the humanistic Burke" so dominant in all criticism so far (157).

"The issue," Nelson says, "is whether one sees the symbol-using animal in Burke as an independent agent or as a figure occupying the role of agency within a verbal drama that is in a sense already written for us."

Nelson argues that Burke moved back and forth between these two positions until recently, when he "comes to believe that language is *all* there is, that no material world exists for us":

> Burke suggests . . . first, that we see always through terministic screens; second, that language is an independent source of human motivation; and third, more deeply, that anything we can see or feel is already *in* language, given to us *by* language, and even produced *as us* by language. (169, his emphasis)

"It is with poststructuralism," Nelson concludes, ". . . that Burke's work finds its true homology and its most fitting basis for comparison and contrast" (171).

Beyond any doubt, what we now call deconstruction is part of Burke's hermeneutical repertoire. Even Southwell, who uses Burke to bolster his argument against Derrida and de Man, admits to finding "a kind of deconstructionism" in Burke (1). So also does Lentricchia, who, for different reasons, is just as unfriendly to deconstruction as Southwell is: According to Lentricchia, Burke deconstructs such key terms as "agent," but without "destroy[ing] the humanistic impulse of his dramatism" (71).

It is one thing to find deconstructive acts in Burke, quite another to identify him with poststructural (anti/non)philosophy. Burke differs from Derrida fundamentally in his view of language: Far from being a self-contained system of signs, language is for Burke action in a scene, and this scene includes much that is not language, most notably the neurological and muscular equipment of the body upon which utterance or inscription depends. Even if, as Nelson says, "anything we can see or feel is already in language"—an assumption shared by most postPhilosophy— this assumption need not lead us to hold, with Derrida, that "there is nothing outside the text" (*Grammatology* 158). Burke would never make such a claim. Quite the contrary, he assumes that everything he calls "nonsymbolic motion"—that is, nature—existed before the symbol-using animal and will go on existing after we're gone. Moreover, nature and the human body are not merely passive enablers of language use; they have ways of "making assertions" of their own, which we feel most acutely when they "resist" our desires or expectations. Albeit always mediated by symbols, human experience includes experience with the extratextual, the nonsymbolic.

Burke understands language pragmatically, not in the semiotic way Derrida conceives it. Burke also differs from Derrida in offering something close to (but as we will see, also different from) what Philosophy understands by ontology. In Williams's words,

> [D]ramatism . . . tells us who we *are* in a substantial, constitutive sense. We *are* the symbol-using animal . . . we inhabit,

enact, dramatize the problematics of language, the duplici-
ties of dialectic . . . [W]hether we succumb to deterministic
impulses, reify difference, and initiate war or whether we retreat into inhabitation of the ironic, enacting the paralysis of
action characterized by Hamlet, we nonetheless affirm our
very nature as symbol-using animals. (216)

Derrida, of course, rejects all such claims. He does so, Williams believes,
to ward off the "dangerous certitude" that leads to war. The price he pays
is "to embrace the openness of indeterminacy," equivalent to "the emptiness of the nihilistic abyss" (209). Burke's object is also to avoid war—
"to purify war" (GM, epigraph), to confine it to verbal conflict—precisely
by affirming our being as symbol-using animals. If we think of ourselves
this way, our proper study becomes our own symbol-driven motives.

Burke shares enough with deconstruction to permit useful dialogue.
However, dialogue between them seems unlikely for at least two reasons. First, deconstruction takes dialogue as phonocentric, caught up in
the illusion of presence created by the human voice. Consequently, when
Derrida sat down with Gadamer in Paris, the result was correctly described as an encounter, not a dialogue (Michelfelder and Palmer 2). Had
it been a dialogue, especially a successful dialogue—that is, a discussion
that clarifies differences and discovers common ground, shared understandings—then Derrida's commitment to indeterminacy and undecidability would have been compromised and Gadamer's faith in dialogue
affirmed. Burke's understanding of dialogue is more agonistic than
Gadamer's, but his commitment to dialogue is no less strong. Burke and
Burkeans enter dialogue in good faith; Derrida and Derrideans do not,
for they have no faith in dialogue.

The second reason for doubting that any useful interchange between
Burke and Derrida could occur is that deconstruction would find itself
in an untenable, self-refuting position. Williams notes that "one may
question or deconstruct Burke's privileging of his unique ontological perspective" (217). But if one questions or deconstructs Burke's contention
that people are typically symbol-using animals, one must in so doing
perform as the symbol-using animal. To deconstruct Burke's definition
is, unavoidably, to affirm it. The only other response is not to respond,
to say nothing. Outside the law, silence may or may not imply assent,
but it certainly would preclude dialogue.

Burke's Otherness

What can we conclude from this brief exploration of Kenneth Burke's
place or places in the conversation after Philosophy? Burke's recent critics have been trying to locate him in or claim him for hermeneutics,
critical theory, or deconstruction. In other words, something of a con-

sensus exists already that Burke belongs to postPhilosophy. The broader framework of this study can reveal a shared understanding hard to detect in the divergent readings themselves.

So far as these readings are concerned, all are stimulating, but none convincing. They certainly confirm Burke's "uncanny contemporaneity" (Lentricchia 71) but they also reveal his equally uncanny Otherness. Assimilations of Burke just do not quite come off.

My approach, therefore, is not the way of appropriation. My concern throughout this study is Burke's philosophical identity. My goal is to engage this stubborn Otherness as Other rather than reduce it to some more comfortable and established position.

If we can come to understand what Burke represents, then dialogue with the various postPhilosophical "schools" becomes a more realistic and fruitful possibility. The best potential for dialogue, I believe, is between Burke and hermeneutics, Burke and critical theory, Burke and neo-pragmatism, represented here by Richard Rorty.

With this general idea of Burke's place or places in the postPhilosophical conversation in mind, we turn now to his most prolific decade, the thirties, whose crises and conflicts had much to do with his turn to philosophy.

Part One

From "Poststructuralism" to Dramatism:
The Early Philosophy

1

Skeptikos: The Postphilosophical Phase

> When in Rome, do as the Greeks—when in Europe, do as the Chinese.
>
> —Kenneth Burke, *Counter-Statement*

> We advocate nothing, then, but a return to inconclusiveness.
>
> —Kenneth Burke, *Counter-Statement*

As noted in the introduction, the standard account of Burke's career begins in the late teens and twenties with aestheticism, when Burke was devoting most of his time to fiction and literary criticism. Compared with his work in the thirties, this earliest period may seem almost prephilosophical. I read it, however, as postphilosophical, as a set of attitudes and stances denying the very possibility of any stable viewpoint. In places it is even specifically poststructural in implication. That is, Burke's version of aestheticism is comparable to the stances we now associate with Derrida or Lyotard.

Burke published *Language as Symbolic Action*, his last major work, in 1966, one year before three of Derrida's works were translated into English, inaugurating poststructuralism in the English-speaking world. Consequently, Burke has had little to say (in print, at least) about it. One morning in the summer of 1979 I decided to find out what Burke thought about Derrida, Foucault, Barthes, and company. He listened politely as I talked about poststructuralism and made a few connections with his own work. But after about half an hour, I could see his attention begin to wane, and so I asked, in effect, "What do you think?" He shrugged and said, "We were doing that in the twenties."

At the time, I dismissed the comment as typical of an older generation's response to the "innovations" of a younger one. (Burke was thirty-three when Derrida was born.) But I never forgot the comment and began to take it more seriously as the intellectual antecedents of poststructuralism became clearer to me. The route to Derrida, Lyotard, and Foucault begins with Nietzsche, and as we have already had occasion to notice, Nietzsche strongly influenced Burke's thought at least through 1935, the date of *Permanence and Change*. Burke not only read Nietzsche with care and sympathy, he also encountered Nietzsche through other authors influential in this early period, writers Burke himself wrote about and, in some cases, even translated—most significantly Thomas Mann but also Andre Gide, Remy de Gourmont, and Oswald Spengler. Burke was more nearly a Nietzschean than anything else in the twenties: Whether or not, then, "we" were doing poststructuralism in the twenties, perhaps it is not so implausible to say that Burke was—or at least doing something postphilosophical akin to it.

Plausibility increases when we look closely at Burke's first collection of essays, *Counter-Statement* (1931). In the midst of formalism and "art for art's sake," Burke was reading literature as rhetoric, and because as rhetoric, inseparable from ethics and politics. In other words, he turned to rhetoric as an alternative to Kantian aesthetics and the compartmentalized, "scientific" philosophy we now associate with modernism and which Kant exemplified so well. Decades later, also driven in part by resistance to modernism, poststructuralism would likewise draw on rhetoric's broad and ancient tradition, especially on its concern with the arts of language, or style, particularly with tropes. So Burke not only shared Nietzsche and his tradition, itself self-consciously rhetorical, with poststructuralism, but also the rhetorical tradition itself, which modernism generally despised and attacked through neglect or abuse, but never quite succeeded in rooting out. We need not, then, read Burke's early "poststructuralism" as a historical anomaly. In context it is quite explicable.

The Cult of Conflict

Jack Selzer has recently offered a modernist reading of Burke in the twenties. Selzer's main interest—the poetry, fiction, and literary criticism—may well be best understood against a modernist backdrop. If so, Burke's thought ranged far beyond his aesthetic practice. I shall confirm this contention by considering a few key passages from *Counter-Statement*, where the philosophy is most explicit.

"These essays," Burke claims in the preface to the first edition, "elucidate a point of view" that is "negativistic, and even antinomian" (viii), dedicated to what he calls the "cult of conflict" (102). As Burke explains in an extended commentary on Thomas Mann (Mann being for Burke in this period roughly what Dostoevsky was for Bakhtin), the cult of conflict involves "sympathy with the abyss," "the morally chaotic."

> Aschenbach [the central character of *Death in Venice*] is committed to conflict: whatever policy he decides upon for his conduct, he must continue to entertain disintegrating factors in contemplation. That practical "virtuous" procedure which silences the contrary is not allowed him. (101)

The abyss is the void that opens with the realization that any moral or intellectual order is imposed by us to discipline the flux of sensation and the clamor of our own competing motives. There is no transcendental standard against which to gauge our exercise of the will to power; there is nothing solid upon which our principles and concepts rest. A collective inheritance from the past, they just are; we have thrust them upon experience, that there may be experience rather than chaos. Hence, the Nietzschean-Mannian ironist, "essentially *impure*, even in the chemical sense of purity, since he is divided. He must deprecate his own enthusiasms, and distrust his own resentments" (102, Burke's emphasis). "To the Rooseveltian [Theodore!] mind he is corrosive"—an outsider, "corrupting," "dissolute"; this Rooseveltian mind stimulates in him "nostalgia . . . a kind of awe for [its] fertile assurance, even while remaining on the alert to stifle it with irony each time he discovers it growing in unsuspected quarters within himself" (102–3).

What is the point of this cult of conflict Burke admires so much in Thomas Mann? Speaking of both Mann and Andre Gide, he asks:

> Are not these men trying to make us at home in indecision, are they not trying to humanize the state of doubt? . . . Perhaps there is an evasion, a shirking of responsibility, in becoming certain too quickly, especially when our certainties involve reversions to an ideology which has the deceptive allurement of tradition. To seek the backing of the past may be as cowardly as to seek the backing of the many. (105)

Here are the tonalities of the Enlightenment, a fearless Nietzsche contemptuous of all comfort and scornful of safe haven from intellectual quest. Dancing on the edge of the abyss, we must learn to think for ourselves, without supports.

Without supports? Actually there is always a reservoir of certainty.

"The body is dogmatic," Burke observes, always sure of what it needs to sustain itself. Must we, then, Burke asks, also acquiesce to "social forces," to what Foucault would later call "regimes of truth"? (131)

> Society might well be benefited by the corrective of a disintegrating art, which converts each simplicity into a complexity, which ruins the possibility of ready hierarchies, which concerns itself with the problematical, the experimental, and thus by implication works corrosively upon those expansionistic certainties preparing the way for our social cataclysms. An art may be of value purely through preventing a society from becoming too assertively, too hopelessly, itself. (105)

The idea of "humanizing the state of doubt" is tantamount to Lyotard's "losing the nostalgia for the lost narrative." "A disintegrating art" that "works corrosively," that undermines "obvious truths" and dissolves or inverts schemes of value, all in the cause of guerrilla warfare against the "expansionistic certainties" that lead to repression and war: Allowing for differences in historical circumstances, what significant aspect of poststructural motivation did Burke lack in the twenties? We should now be able to understand his *deja vu* experience with poststructuralism half a century later. He had long ago earned the shrug and the dismissive comment.

And yet we do not have simple identity here. Burke's cult of conflict is deconstructive; it cannot, from our perspective, fail to remind us of poststructuralism. For all the resemblances, however, the differences are at least as numerous and probably more significant.

First, Burke's concern is not in any direct way with Philosophy, or the metaphysics of presence. He is not urging us, as Derrida put it, "to read philosophy in a certain way" ("Structure" 967). Rather he is reading culture, the culture of what we would now call "late capitalism," still in its colonial phase. Of course, capitalism and colonialism have their Philosophical collaborators, but Burke's target is the popular culture that associates its own self-respect with "expansionistic certainties." About this culture he is anything but undecided: He rejects it totally. The nostalgia he speaks of is not a pining for the narrative of white, European, capitalist supremacy—why pine for something still triumphant, available for the taking all around him?—but rather for the "fertile assurance" that comes from solidarity, lost forever by any determined practitioner of negative dialectic.

Second, Burke does not share Derrida's view of language. For Derrida the duplicity of language resides in the code itself. Even philosophical language, which often tries to be as unliterary and unrhetorical as possible—literal, consistent, precise—upon examination reveals its dependency on that which it would exclude, on tropes, especially metaphor. Univocal meaning, therefore, becomes impossible, which means that Philosophy becomes impossible.

For Burke the duplicity of language resides in ideological reification. Viewed pragmatically, in context, language, whether spoken or written, seldom deconstructs itself, as Paul de Man says poetry does (10). Quite the contrary, meanings are shared all too readily, all too univocally, so that, as Burke will put it later in *Permanence and Change*, people can be conned into "hat[ing] as [our] deepest enemy a people thousands of miles away" (6). The duplicity of language has less to do with traces and absence than with the unthinking presencings of ideology, which converts every complexity into a simplicity, provides for ready hierarchies, and disciplines and punishes anyone who would play the gadfly. Language inscribes much more than itself, its web of self-referentiality; it inscribes regimes of power.

From this difference in viewpoint toward language alone, we can see how far Burke is from Derrida's kind of poststructuralism. Even as early as *Counter-Statement*, Burke takes language as action-in-the-world: pragmatically, not semiologically. Consequently, I would link Burke's cult of conflict to the most contextual thinker among the poststructuralists— to Foucault rather than Derrida.

The resemblances are quite striking. For example, whereas Derrida writes "under erasure," retreating endlessly from stable assertion, Burke and Foucault prefer the dialectical strategy of checking assertions or lines of thought by opposing assertions or lines of thought. (This is what Burke means by calling his essays a counter-statement, his point of view "negativistic" or "antinomian.") The idea is to assist in the return of the suppressed, the very suppressions required by ideological reification or regimes of power. One cannot throw a monkey wrench into the machine by Derrida's strategy (as old as the ancient skeptics) of refusing to take a stance. One only avoids thereby all dogma—and opts out of dialectic itself. Anyone who hopes to make trouble for the current order of things must enter the dialectic, asserting the claims of those marginalized or excluded by the dominant rationale of human effort.

Mention of the marginalized or the excluded helps to explain why Burke is so attracted to Mann's locating of the ethical in "the repellent, the diseased, the degenerate" and of art in "the forbidden, the adventurous" and in "self-abandonment" (101)—and why, twenty years later, in the 1952 preface to the second edition of *Counter-Statement*, Burke is still extolling "the cultural value of fear, distrust, and hypochondria" (xii). Like Foucault, Burke is drawn to the forbidden, to self-abandonment, the difference being that Burke sought the marginalized and excluded in the imaginative possibilities of art, whereas Foucault sought it, notoriously, in sexual excess and sadism. More in keeping with our time, Foucault "acted out"; more in keeping with his, Burke remained, like Mann, under control, more or less conventional in behavior, adventurous in mind.

A more significant difference separating Burke from both Foucault and Derrida lies in the purpose of opposition itself. For Burke a "disintegrating art" has value *only* in "preventing a society from becoming too assertively, too hopelessly itself" (105). Its role is Socratic, gadflyish, not deconstructive in the sense of a wholesale assault on Western metaphysics as incoherent or Western culture as corrupt and exploitive. As Burke explains in *Counter-Statement*'s "Program" section, the aesthetic, the cult of conflict,

> is defensible because it could never triumph. Certainties will always arise, impelling men to new intolerances. (Certainty is cheap, it is the easiest thing of which a man is capable. Deprive him of a meal, or bind his arms, or jockey him out of his job—and convictions spring up like Jacks-in-the-box.) Thus, we can defend the aesthetic as anti-practical, anti-industrial, anti-machine because the practical, the industrial, the mechanized is so firmly entrenched. Did distrust kill all believing, did sloth kill all efficiency, then the aesthetic as here defined would be simply suicide. But we may depend upon it that even a world rigorously schooled in doubt will be dogmatical enough. (113)

It is only in the context of certainties that skepticism has anything to do. Its function is partly "timeless" in that there is always "a large reservoir of physical unquestioning" (105), partly historical in that each regime of power must be called into question according to its own pattern of suppressions. In any event, however, it could never triumph; if somehow it did, it would cease to exist, just as the "loyal opposition" ceases to exist when it wins an election.

Philosophy as Resistance

What can we conclude from this inquiry into Burke's thought in the twenties, summed up in the notion of "a cult of conflict"? We can call his position both philosophical and postPhilosophical. It is philosophical because it belongs to a long philosophical tradition, skepticism. It is post-Philosophical in that, unlike Descartes (for instance), Burke is not seeking some ground or foundation that will allow him to pass beyond doubt to certainty. Quite the contrary, he wants to "humanize the state of doubt," cooperate with losing the nostalgia for the lost narrative. Burke's position is closer to classical (rather than modernist) skepticism: That is, skepticism is not part of science, part of a method for attaining truth; rather, as ancient skeptics held, Truth is not accessible in any complete or final way at all. (PostPhilosophy is hardly only postmodern. It is at least as old as the skeptics that dominated the Academy after Plato's death.) We must accept our finitude, which means accepting the permanent elusiveness of Truth. The ideal is to become a *skeptikos* in its original meaning, that is, an inquirer, for whom philosophy is an interplay of voices in a perpetually open-ended dialogue, or in a series of inconclusive ones.

According to Burke himself, *Counter-Statement* leads toward "a dialectic of many voices" (xi). Such a dialectic is implicit in his exempting of art from an otherwise antinomian stance. As he explains, his attitude is "not antinomian as regards art because . . . art is naturally antinomian. Art's very accumulation (its discordant voices arising out of many systems) serves to undermine any one rigid scheme of living" (viii). In a way similar to Bakhtin, Burke is attracted to the dialogical potential of literature, especially fiction.

However, the stress in *Counter-Statement* is "against custom," anti-*nomos*, not on dialogue with tradition, or among traditions, but rather on countering the ideology of industrial and colonial capitalism. In hoping for a future in which "not vacillation, but assurance" will become "the first sign of mental decay" (203), Burke shares a generally skeptical stance with poststructuralism. But what lends his thought in the twenties its contemporary, poststructual flavor is that the target of his aggressive skepticism is not only the current ideology—which Burke sees as tending toward Fascist efficiency (114)—but also structure itself—the "ready hierarchies" of all ideology, "the deceptive allurement of tradition," any tradition (105). Because "the body is dogmatic" (never uncertain about what it needs to sustain its own structural integrity) and because most people seek the comforts of a thoughtless solidarity ("Our fellows want the seasoned stocks and bonds of set beliefs . . . hoping to enrich themselves in these securities as rapidly as possible" [106]), structure can and will take care of itself. What always requires nurturing is the repressed, the suppressed, the marginalized, the excluded, the experimental, the deviant—everything, in short, that each regime of power creates as a reflex of its own existence. Possessing a content and character specific to an age, counter-hegemonic activity is nevertheless permanent, as "eternally recurrent" as the skeptical Other that has always disturbed the dogmatic slumbers of Philosophy.

In construing what we now call poststructuralism as a dialectical function, as the anti-*nomos* resisting the current regime of power, Burke understood poststructuralism better than many of its adherents and critics do today. Poststructuralists sometimes write as if their viewpoint can come to prevail, as if they are harbingers of a new age—and cultural conservatives sometimes attack poststructuralism as if they fear it has or will prevail. At most, antinomianism can at times dominate a segment of an intellectual elite, a tiny minority whose impact on the culture as a whole is far less than broader, more diffuse forms of resistance—the Bohemians of the nineteenth century, the aesthetes of the twenties, the beatniks of the fifties, or the flower children of the sixties. This role can nevertheless be significant, especially in encouraging tolerance, in holding open a cultural space for expression of the otherwise off limits and out of bounds. But it can never "win." Structure of some kind, regimes of power, will always "win." One structure can be replaced by another, but human societies can never be "poststructural." We are always already structured. To recall Burke's words, "even a world rigorously schooled in doubt will be dogmatical enough" (113).

It follows that "a disintegrating art," a corrosive skepticism, a deconstructive criticism—in themselves, at least, unaligned with some structural alternative to existing structures—can only help to "prevent a society from becoming too assertively, too hopelessly, itself" (105). Anyone who thinks s/he can depose or dispose of an established order by deconstructing one of its key texts or even all of its key texts is almost pathologically self-deceived. Anyone who fears that poststructuralism will "take over" is no less out of touch with social realities. Burke understood the limitations of all cults of conflict quite early in his career. The modest role he conceives for his own is one of its most attractive features. Also appealing is his clear recognition of complicity in the order whose certainties he would undermine. The ironist must turn his irony on him/herself, or descend to mere caricature of the Other, to a paranoid "us" versus "them" construction of social life. We may be able to lose the nostalgia for the lost narrative, the master story that makes everything comprehensible, ordered to human desires, but awe for the "fertile assurance" of the true believer, the fundamentalist, whether capitalist, Christian, Marxist, or whatever, can go unacknowledged but not unfelt. The power certainty has over the minds of most people is too great to forego without regret—and self-interference, though indispensable to the ethical and examined life, is deeply painful, frequently humiliating, not least because it doesn't socialize very well. The state of doubt, as Burke says, is "an athletic norm" (106), in part because it must struggle with obvious rhetorical disadvantages.

Skepticism Revised

Had Burke remained an antinomian skeptic, we would now be talking about him as an American version of Theodor Adorno, as someone who holds a quite respectable view of the limitations of post-metaphysical thought: Postphilosophy is "negative dialectic," capable of critique, but not of affirmation, a philosophy of its own. But Burke does affirm; he does eventually articulate a philosophy of his own, Dramatism, with which his name will always be linked. Clearly something happened to the antinomian skeptic of *Counter-Statement*.

Something did happen, but it would be wrong to say that Burke rejected or overcame skepticism. As we will see in the following chapter, Burke's views toward the subject, toward reason and logic, and toward language all have strongly skeptical implications. Skepticism of some kind is also implicit in the linguistic, social, and rhetorical turns discussed in Chapter 2. Indeed, if Burke is not a skeptic of some kind, my argument for Burke as a postPhilosopher is in trouble, for Philosophy and skepticism are necessarily at odds. If there is Truth, if we can know it, if it can be articulated in propositions, then the Philosophical quest must go on; if any of these conditions do not obtain, then skeptical postPhilosophy of some kind is the alternative.

Burke does discard the antinomian skepticism of *Counter-Statement*. He does so in part because he revises his view of *nomos*. As we have seen, *nomos* in *Counter-Statement* is "the deceptive allurement of tradition." By *Attitudes Toward History* Burke is saying something quite different: "A man is necessarily talking error unless his words can claim membership in a collective body of thought" (172). The earlier and the later statements are not flatly contradictory, but the difference in attitude does indicate that Burke is no longer seeing tradition in Enlightenment terms, as the repository of error, ignorance, and superstition. He has moved to a position closer to Romantic hermeneutics, with its respect for the past. Tradition has become more inclusive, itself a cult of conflict, a polyphony of voices that provides both the supports propping up the current regime of power and the demolition equipment required to remove them. What we are is so much a social, collective inheritance that without talking error, we can be antitraditional only in traditional ways.

Burke also discards antinomian skepticism because he comes to see it as unlivable and ineffectual. The classic refutation of skepticism is to assert that it is self-contradictory: If we say that nothing warrants assent, then we are claiming certainty about uncertainty. This argument never concerned Burke very much because he assumes that skepticism only functions within a vast reserve of dogma. We cannot actually suspend all beliefs, only some of them. How we live, our choices, our actions, will continue to "assert" what we believe. The problem with the oppositional stance is practical, not logical, and constitutes an objection often and rightly raised against contemporary poststructuralism. We can refuse to affirm simply by not uttering truth claims at all, but if we do, if we restrict ourselves to critique of the truth claims of others, we leave the current order of things prevailing by default, by not providing an alternative. In practical terms, if we deconstruct we must reconstruct, or the deconstructive act itself is without consequence and empty.

Burke would affirm an alternative to the capitalist rationale that seemed to be collapsing as he assembled *Counter-Statement*—and a little later and more broadly, an alternative to the complete dominance of scientific-technical reason. In being so certain about the value of socialism and the inadequacy of instrumental reason as a norm for reason itself, what happens to his skepticism?

To the end of his career Burke remains, from the standpoint of traditional metaphysics and traditional epistemology, a skeptic. He never affirms a metaphysical or epistemological theory. He is also a skeptic in a neo-Hegelian sense similar to Charles Taylor or Hans-Georg Gadamer. Truth is the whole, the totality of all viewpoints or perspectives we acknowledge as having some share in truth; but we do not have and can never have the whole, the totality, that is Truth. We can learn more. We can see better. There is no end to enlarging and adjusting our horizons of understanding. But claims to the fully adequate, the complete, the finalized, the theory of everything—toward these Burke remains relentlessly skeptical. He will say in *The Philosophy of Literary Form* that Spinoza's "adequate idea" could only reside "in an infinite, omniscient mind" (*PLF* 7). Since Burke leaves the question of God's existence open, Truth for him may not exist at all. If it does exist, our finite minds certainly could not grasp it. Surely this position is skeptical enough, without falling into the extreme, self-contradictory, and impractical skepticism of denying even the possibility of claims to truth warranting provisional assent.

I have devoted considerable space here to Burke's skepticism because skepticism is a fixture of his thought from *Counter-Statement* to his last essays in the 1980s. If we fail to grasp his skepticism, we fail to grasp his philosophy as well as its postPhilosophical setting. I dispute, therefore, a common reading of Burke's development as a thinker. William Rueckert refers to "the transient skepticism which marked Burke's development through the thirties and on into the late forties when the dramatistic system set. This skepticism is a form of openness . . . and remains as a characteristic even of dramatism" (*Responses* 60). Burke's thought certainly manifests openness, but his skepticism is not transient. Instead, the function of skepticism changes—changes, in fact, from *Counter-Statement* to *Permanence and Change*. As we have seen, Burke uses skepticism in *Counter-Statement* as much philosophical interpretation does now, as a corrosive to traditional certainties, as an undermining of ideological reification. In *Permanence and Change* skepticism becomes part of the assumptions of his thought so that, in effect, Burke is asking, "Granting everything we cannot know, what can we find good reasons to affirm?" It is this shift in the role of skepticism that permits Dramatism to emerge. But Dramatism always entails skepticism in the post-metaphysical and neo-Hegelian senses described above.

2

PostPhilosophical Themes: On Identity, Reason, and Figurative Language

In his "General Introduction" to *After Philosophy: End or Transformation?* Thomas McCarthy claims:

> In undercutting the "Platonic conception" of reason, truth, and language, post-Nietzschean philosophers have stressed their lowly origins in struggle and conflict, in arbitrariness and contingency, in a *will* to truth that is essentially involved with power and desire. (11, his emphasis)

If McCarthy is right about post-Nietzschean contemporary philosophy, if we really have learned to accept "human finitude and fallibilism" (12) as permanent and ineluctable, then we ought to find Burke's philosophical *persona* very appealing. He has never been reluctant to acknowledge the "lowly origins" of his quests for truth. For example, Burke would recall in 1953 that *Permanence and Change*

> was written in the early days of the Great Depression, at a time when there was a general feeling that our traditional ways were headed for a tremendous change, maybe even a permanent collapse. It is such a book as authors in those days sometimes put together, to keep themselves from falling apart. (xlvii)

Burke's stance is close to the opposite pole of Habermas's "master thinkers" ("Philosophy" 296)—that is, Descartes, Kant, Hegel, and so forth. Instead of philosophy as Truth, or system, or method, or grand synthesis, for Burke it is a "salvation device," one way among many of "saving one's soul, saving one's hide, saving one's face" (*ATH* 218).

That is, philosophy offers, in Richard Rorty's phrase, "a tool for coping" (30)—in the case of *Permanence and Change*, intellectual strategies for coming to terms with a concrete, historical situation Burke found profoundly unsettling.

> Not knowing quite where he was, this particular author took notes on "orientation." Not being sure how to read the signs, he took notes on "interpretation." Finding himself divided, he took notes on division. . . . In sum, being in a motivational quandary, he wrote on "motivation." The result is a kind of transformation-at-one-remove, got by inquiry into the process of transformation itself. (xlvii)

The times demanded transformations, individual and collective changes of identity. Before the Depression, in the relatively halcyon days of the twenties, Burke knew who he was—a dissenter, a skeptic whose target was the dogmas of capitalism and colonialism. But now, with the system in massive disarray, his old identity no longer worked because it had no work to do. The failure of the order of things called the order into question far more than any disintegrating art or criticism could.

Even as he was feeling his way toward a new identity, he was studying the process of reorientation and reinterpretation itself. This is truly philosophy *Sitz im Leben*, what Burke would later decide all significant language use amounts to, symbolic action, "strategies for the encompassing of situations" (*PLF* 1).

But why philosophy? With so many means of coping, why did Burke write *A Treatise on Communication*, the working title of the manuscript that became *Permanence and Change*?

"All told," Burke says, "concerned with words above all, when things got toughest he thought hardest about communication" (xlviii). What he thought was basically this: Community is in trouble. Occupational diversification, lack of deep and permanent ties to place, family, and tradition, capitalist overemphasis on competition rather than cooperation, boom and bust economies—such anti-structural forces have fragmented society and impaired ordinary language, the collective sense of shared meaning and value upon which art depends for its appeal. Rather than a community, we have become a patchwork of interest groups, which leaves the poet (in a broad sense, any artistic "maker") without many resources for broad appeal. The *sensus communis* has been eroding since the rise of industrialism and scientific-technical reason, leaving a cultural topsoil so thin that it can sustain only art with very shallow roots.

Serious art is too socially marginal to provide an alternative to the juggernaut of "free" enterprise allied with science and technology. Poetry alone cannot do the counter-structural job Burke allotted it in *Counter-Statement*. And yet, as Burke observes in the first section of *Permanence and Change*,

> A corrective rationalization must certainly move in the direction of the anthropomorphic or humanistic or poetic, since this is the aspect of culture which the scientific criteria, with their emphasis on dominance rather than upon inducement, have tended to eliminate or minimize. . . . [Since] the poetic . . . is weakened by the fact that the poetic medium itself is weakened, [it follows that] the center of authority must be situated in a philosophy . . . of poetry, rather than in a body of poetry. (65–66)

Clearly Burke did not drift into philosophy; the choice of philosophy as a means of coping was quite deliberate. In an age without a broad and strong *sensus communis*, whose assets and deficits both require analytical-interpretative *terminologies*, painstakingly worked-out conceptualization, Burke's opting for philosophy makes good sense. He could gain the prestige of precise formulation, part of the prestige of science itself, while resisting the culture of technical manipulation, "dominance rather than inducement." Burke turned to philosophy, then, for rhetorical reasons, for strategic advantage, fully aware of his own will to power. He wanted "to revise the productive and distributive patterns of our economy to suit our soundest desires, rather than . . . revise our desires [to] suit the productive and distributive patterns" (*PC* 66). His work was still the work of cultural resistance. But the tactics have changed. Moreover, the turn to philosophy was partly driven by his own motivational quandary. If the times demanded painful transformations, they also demanded reexamination of certain long-established philosophical themes. We shall examine Burke's views on three of them, all still vigorously debated in the conversation after Philosophy: the subject (or the self, or the agent, or the problem of identity), the nature and function of reason and logic; and language, specifically the literal/figurative distinction, traditionally one of the ways Philosophy tried to distinguish itself from rhetoric and literature.

On the Subject

> The so-called "I" is merely a unique combination of partially conflicting "corporate we's."
>
> —Kenneth Burke, *Attitudes Toward History*

Although very much alive in popular culture as bourgeois individualism and indispensable to legal rationales defending the rights of individuals against the state, Descartes's "sovereign rational subject—atomistic and autonomous, disengaged and disembodied . . . ideally self-transparent"— is dead in contemporary philosophy. The self is not atomistic because of the "intrinsically social character" of consciousness; it is not autonomous or self-transparent because of "the influence of the unconscious on the conscious," which conditions behavior in ways that elude awareness, much less assessment or control. It is not disengaged because subjects are always "practically engaged with the world," with "purposes and projects, passions and interests." And it is not disembodied because minds and consciousness depend on the human brain, the human brain on the human body. In sum, "subjectivity and intentionality are not prior to but a function of forms of life and systems of language; they do not 'constitute' the world but are themselves elements of a linguistically disclosed world" (McCarthy 4). In contemporary philosophy, language occupies the place once held by the "I am."

So much seems beyond serious dispute. But as is usually the case in postPhilosophy, consensus ends with agreement about what we reject. What remains after the demise of the Cartesian *cogito* is far more controversial. Language remains, certainly—but has "the epistemological and moral subject . . . been definitively decentered" (McCarthy 4) so that all talk about it is anachronistic, wholly the illusion of a discredited ideology?

For poststructuralism the answer seems to be yes, the subject has been decentered beyond retrieval:

> From Barthes to Foucault, from Lacan to Derrida, the wholeness, uniqueness, intentionality, and generative power of individual human beings, generally phrased as "the problem of identity," has been thrown into question. . . . A common thrust that links these various approaches . . . [is] a view of the individual as "constructed" rather than "constructing," that is, determined by forces, whether environmental or linguistic, which are impersonal and universal, and hence, nonproductive of uniqueness or "identity." (Oravec 176)

We will consider Burke's approach to the problem of identity in the context of the rejection of the Cartesian subject and the "constructed" view of the self characteristic of poststructuralism.

Burke's "I" has the following characteristics:

1. "It" exists only in human bodies.

2. Identity is not an essence but a process, a social, symbolic, linguistic process.

3. The self is normally multiple and conflicting.

4. The self is "poetic," integrative, synthetic.

5. The self is dynamic, always "on the way."

Although each clause is entangled in the others, I will attempt to draw out the implications of each in itself, before commenting on Burke's position as a whole.

From *Counter-Statement* to the last essays written in the 1980s, the human body has figured centrally in Burke's philosophy. Burke's emphasis on the body (and therefore on biology and nature) distinguishes his thought from figures such as Heidegger and Wittgenstein and links him to Bakhtin and Merleau-Ponty. So far as the self or "I" is concerned, to hold that it exists only in human bodies is enough by itself to show how thoroughly Burke rejects the Cartesian *cogito*. There is no mind/body dualism in Burke. In *Permanence and Change* he mentions this distinction as a source of pseudoproblems and argues for resisting the traditional dualism by speaking always of a mind-body merger (94). For Burke, however, there is no separate entity "mind" that somehow "merges" with body, or vice versa. The "I" is a bodily "I" and has no existence apart from the body.

But the "I" is not only or merely body, an epiphenomenon of the brain. In *Attitudes Toward History* Burke takes up the problem of identity as such. He criticizes "bourgeois naturalism" for its "blunt distinction" between the individual and the environment, which leads "bourgeois psychologists" to classify "all collective aspects of identity under the head of pathology and illusion."

> That is: they discovered accurately enough that identity is *not* individual, that a man "identifies himself" with all sorts of manifestations beyond himself, and they set about trying to "cure" him of this tendency. It can't be "cured," for the simple reason that it is *normal*. (263, Burke's emphasis)

It is normal because "one's participation in a collective, social role cannot be obtained in any other way" (266). The self is the sum of our social roles, made possible by identification with "some corporate unit (church, guild, company, lodge, party . . .)" (267). These identifications with corporate units are the "corporate we's" comprising Burke's "I."

It follows that identity cannot be an essence in the sense of a fixed, perduring substance—for instance, "the soul" of Greek conception. It can only be a process. If I can claim a relatively stable sense of self over time, this relative stability resides in a pattern of identifications, not in some given, mystical essence that is me. What stability I have, that is, resides in corporate units, in collective meanings, with which I associate or dissociate myself.

Because we identify with many corporate units and perform many social roles, "the self" is necessarily multiple, taking on one role or set of roles to write a book, another to interact with a spouse, another to chair a committee, another to teach a class, and so on. Furthermore, as Burke remarks, "for various reasons"—say, chemical changes in the body from one day to the next—"one has many disparate moods and attitudes. These may be called sub-identities, subpersonalities, 'voices'" (*ATH* 184). The self is not sole or whole. There are many of us "in here."

And conflict among our "selves" is normal. The world we experience on a bad day cannot be aligned with the world of a good day. An "old self" asserts its identifications against those of a "new self." A corporate unit makes conflicting demands on us. One unit demands one kind of action; another, equally important to us, demands something else not reconcilable with the first. And so on. The self is not a neat hierarchy of naturally cooperating subunits. Disintegration continually threatens all sense of "my me."

Consequently, to cope with our many, sometimes conflicting subpersonalities, "the poet [the maker in all of us] seeks to build the symbolic superstructures that put them together into a comprehensive 'super-personality'" (*ATH* 184). Here is the Nietzschean dimension in Burke's concept of the self. The self is not simply a given, analogous to, say, the seed of a plant, which, falling into conditions propitious for growth, must produce whatever its genetic "instructions" call for. Rather, the self must be fabricated, fictionalized. To be sure, the material arises spontaneously from our bodily experience and from socialization. In this sense, the "self" is a given: We just "have" subpersonalities and identifications. But, to whatever degree we can claim coherence and integrity, they are achievements, not givens; it requires effort, partly conscious and critical effort, analogous to the making of a work of art. Burke's "I" is active, not only constructed but also constructing.

However, the materials are not like a jigsaw puzzle, which can be assembled into a single representation. There are too many pieces to bring under control, and they tend to change shape and significance relative to one another. They also vie for the same places in the "total picture," which alters even as we assemble it. And some of the pieces are missing—"forgotten" or not yet available, "over the horizon." The image is therefore always partial, intuited as a whole, rather than present as a whole. The "symbolic superstructures" are always under construction, never finished. And yet, short of death or psychic disintegration, we cannot cease working on it. Burke's "I" is dynamic, always "on the way."

What conclusions can we draw from this exploration of Burke's views about the subject and the problem of identity? As radically as any contemporary philosopher, including Foucault and Derrida, Burke rejects the Cartesian subject. Burke's "I" is not atomistic because it is made of otherness and therefore multiple—we cannot be otherwise than self-divided, self-different. It is not autonomous because we cannot choose our body's chemistry or the "corporate we's" of our time and place. We are dependent on natural and social dispensations. It is not disembodied because Burke's "I" is not some essence distinct from the body that can take up residence in a body—that is, be "embodied" in the first place. It is not self-transparent because the self is never fully present to be "seen" or "seen through." And it is not disengaged because the problem of identity is our existential problem, not an abstract P/philosophical one. Among other practical tasks, we are engaged in making ourselves.

According to my reading, then, Fredric Jameson is mistaken to take Burke's view of the self as entangled in bourgeois individualism ("Symbolic Inference" 86–87). In fact, as we have just seen, Burke explicitly distinguishes his view of the subject from "bourgeois naturalism" and "bourgeois psychology." When Frank Lentricchia claims that "the strongest political case" that can be made against Burke is to take him as "modernism's cagiest champion" (93), we can safely conclude that the political case must not be very strong. So far as the Cartesian subject is concerned, Burke is no champion of modernism at all.

And yet his view of the subject is not exactly poststructural either. In rejecting the modernist subject and critiquing bourgeois individualism, Burke did not seek to erase "the individual" altogether. On this point he is quite explicit: "To be sure, there *is* the individual. Each [person] is a unique combination of experiences, a unique set of situations, a unique aggregate of mutually re-enforcing and conflicting 'corporate we's'" (ATH 289, Burke's emphasis). From Burke's point of view, the poststructural contention that an individual (a unique identity) cannot result from impersonal and universal forces must be in error. Identification is one of those impersonal and universal forces. Yet, no two individuals will have exactly the same pattern of identifications. Even when two people identify with the same corporate unit, on a micro level their identifications will be at least subtly different. As members of the same faculty, for instance, we might identify our interests (or some of them) with those of our university. But even faculty in the same field have experiences and face professional situations not exactly the same. Shaped by forces beyond our control and quite impersonal in the sense of "transpersonal," we will nevertheless be individuals, with distinct identities and roles. In this limited sense we can speak in a Hegelian way of "identity in difference" or "difference in identity."

A paradoxical or dialectical logic of "contradictions" does apply to the concept of the individual. Recall the family portrait gallery Wittgenstein used to illustrate the notion of "family resemblance" (66–67). Perhaps every feature of "my" face is shared by some relative of mine—but the peculiar combination of shared features remains uniquely mine. So it is with individual identity; it can because it must be both unique and collective, like the combination of genes no one else has but me, both mine and not mine.

Discarding the Cartesian subject, Burke "saves" the individual. He does so, however, by deconstructing what he calls the "blunt distinction" between the individual and the environment characteristic of bourgeois individualism. We can then say that he saves the individual while undermining individualism—or better, that he replaces bourgeois individualism with a "social individualism" having obvious socialistic implications. In any case, neither authors nor agents disappear. They are reconceived in a way strikingly like Bakhtin's self (Clark and Holquist 64–68)—that is, nonexistent without the other and dialogical in the making-never-made. Like Bakhtin's, Burke's self is polyvocal, both an inner dialogue of voices and a potential for dialogue with other individuals whose identity is also both collective and unique.

Burke also departs from poststructuralism and draws near to Bakhtin in stressing an active self. Dependent on the prestructured—on the body, on society, on language and symbols—Burke's individual is clearly more constructed than constructing. Burke recognizes the condition that Heidegger calls "thrownness" (Being and Time 416). Furthermore, as we have seen, Burke does not take the self as self-possessed, its workings transparent to consciousness, fully available for assessment. Nevertheless, in our thrownness, in our being caught up in transpersonal forces beyond our control and mostly preconscious, unconscious, or nonconscious, we still do act. Burke's individual is an agent. Constructed, s/he also constructs. Part of what we construct is the "poem" of our self, the fictionalized superpersonality that struggles to integrate all of our subpersonalities into a workable (but never "worked out") self-conception (cf. Wess, especially pp. 136–85).

In Attitudes Toward History, Burke emphasizes changes in identity as much as he does the synthetic process by which identities are "composed" out of collective materials. Picking up on this emphasis, William Rueckert claims that for Burke "the most fundamental process of all living" is "the drama of the self in quest,"

> an extraordinarily complex life-long ritual of death and rebirth, rejection and acceptance, purification and change, disintegration and reintegration . . . the drama of moral choice. Confronted by such problems as evil, unchangeable brute realities, the trackless maze of unresolved and even undefined

personal and social conflicts, and by an always fundamentally chaotic world, the self attempts to build its individual character and adopt its proper role by constructing . . . a "more or less organized system of meanings" [*ATH* 5]. (*Drama* 45)

The key phrase is "the drama of moral choice," Burke's version of Nietzsche's will to power. We impose a degree of order and significance on "an always fundamentally chaotic world," a world to which the self belongs, within which it must organize itself, despite its own internal chaos.

So far as the conversation after Philosophy is concerned, Burke's active self, his drama of moral choice, is the most significant aspect of his reflections on the self. What does it have to say to us now?

In *Attitudes Toward History* Burke describes a condition he calls "being driven into a corner" (220–24). One of the ways an orthodoxy sustains itself is to charge anyone who dissents a little with rejecting an entire outlook. A Catholic who doubts papal infallibility will be charged with being a "bad Catholic" or perhaps with being no Catholic at all and may even come to see him/herself this way. The advantages for keeping people in line are obvious. "Being driven into a corner" is among the major strategies of "discipline and punish."

The philosophical equivalent is to persuade one's self or be persuaded that in rejecting some key idea from the past one must go on, compulsively, to reject everything associated with it. The usual outcome is to deprive ourselves needlessly of concepts that we require for what Charles Taylor calls the "best account" or "BA" principle (*Sources* 58–59). That is, we find ourselves discarding concepts that we employ on an everyday basis to explain ourselves or the conduct of others. Assuming that we want to be consistent and candid, clearly anything we require for the BA principle must find a place in our philosophy.

Poststructuralism has driven itself into a corner where the subject or agent or self is concerned. Beginning with rejection of the Cartesian subject, it concludes with Derrida's "end of Man," rejection of the entire humanistic tradition, including the agent as actor, as a locus of moral decisions. Poststructuralism follows Heidegger in holding that it is not an "I" that speaks (or writes) but Language ("Building" 146). It follows that our BA can no longer entertain any notion of the individual as an agent. Any sense we may have of acting or choosing not to act, any intuitions we have about choosing at all based on notions of relative goods, must be dismissed as illusion, ideological self-deception. We give ourselves up entirely to, as Emmanuel Levinas put it, the "impersonal It" (64–65). Such is the outcome of the "constructed" view of the self. It seems reasonable, then, to ask the question Lentricchia asks, "What price the deconstruction of the Cartesian subject?" (116).

Burke shows us that the price need not be so unacceptably high. We can dispense with the Cartesian subject without holding that the individual or the agent is an illusion or epiphenomenon. The individual does not have to be conceived in terms of individualism. Nor does the agent have to be self-transparent in order to act: "The mind that thinks it knows what it is doing, does not" (Lentricchia 115), but this only means that we are finite and fallible, incapable of complete acts, unable to claim a total origin (or originality). Poststructuralism proposes to "solve" the problem of identity by doing away with identity; following Burke, we need only say that the problem cannot be resolved or dissolved but only lived as the drama of moral choice. Burke's way does not drive us into a corner; our BA can refer to individuals and agents and defend a limited notion of uniqueness and choice. Moral responsibility need not be swallowed up by the impersonal It.

In sum, then, we can say that Burke's understanding of the subject is indisputably postPhilosophical. It also responds to the poststructural critique of identity in a way that carries us a step or two beyond the critique itself. Most importantly, Burke's self is no passive victim of transpersonal forces. "Every inheritance," Burke says, "must be earned anew," the only alternative being "alienation and demoralization" (*ATH* 246). Part of this earning is the kind of act Derrida called deconstruction or desedimentation. But to do this alone is worth no more than half a wage. We must also reconstruct, pulling out of the inheritance what is still usable. Otherwise we are still in danger of alienation and demoralization, left with no "comes after" but only a dismantled "was."

On Reason and Logic

Hegel's equating of reality with dialectical reason is the strongest of the strong conceptions of reason associated with Philosophical modernism. But as McCarthy points out, Kant's conception of reason is the more frequent target of end-of-philosophy advocates:

> To the necessity that characterizes reason in the Kantian view, they oppose the contingency and conventionality of the rules, criteria, and products of what counts as rational speech and action at any given time and place. To its universality they oppose the irreducible plurality of incommensurable language games and forms of life . . . to the a priori the empirical, to certainty fallibility . . . to unity, heterogeneity, to totality the fragmentary, to self-evident givenness ("presence") universal mediation by differential systems of signs. (3–4)

Whereas poststructuralism leaves little else but an impersonal Language where persons (individuals and agents) once were, deconstructing Reason leaves something standing—a "weak" or modest reason, entirely relative to history and the context of use. Indebted to Nietzsche, its critique of Reason is actually milder. If Hegel pushes Reason about as far as it can be pushed, to finding even the cunning of its operation in the apparent follies, accidents, and absurdities of history, Nietzsche finds only a terrible and dizzying unreason in the real, a fate wholly indifferent to human desires, for which *amor fati* is his prescription (*Ecce Homo* II, 10).

We may situate the argument about reason thus: We have the two last metaphysicians of Reason, Hegel and Nietzsche. One finds reason in history's movement of Spirit toward complete self-realization; the other finds unreason in the eternal return of the same, a Sisyphus-like world of meaningless effort, in which the spirit triumphs only by pushing the rock uphill with joyous determination despite knowing that it must roll down again. In the contemporary intellectual world, mathematical Reason has displaced Hegel's Idealism (God, some physicists say, is a mathematician [Davies 140–60]), while Nietzsche has a host of followers in the humanities and social sciences, for whom reason is at best a Maginot Line arrayed against the forces of the nonrational and irrational.

In contrast, the postmodern critique of Reason attempts to avoid metaphysics altogether. There is no Reason, capital R. A wholly human capacity, reason is as finite and fallible as human being is. It can therefore tell us nothing reliable about the ultimate nature of things. Although individual philosophers claim relatively more or less for reason's value, the modest, post-metaphysical conception of reason dominates contemporary philosophy.

As the organon of Reason or reason, contemporary attitudes toward logic are less interesting. At one end of the spectrum are philosophers for whom the study of logic is synonymous with philosophy itself. For them logical systems can become a fetish, engrossing as such, quite apart from utility. At the other are those who reduce logic to *only* a tool in service of the will to power. Heidegger takes logical language as inseparable from metaphysics, itself inseparable from instrumental reason, the desire to master beings instead of dwelling within Being ("Dialogue" 7). Some feminists see logic as essentially phallocentric. Many culture critics hold that it functions historically on the side of hegemony, as a symbolic form of compulsion employed by authority until resistance mounts sufficiently to require physical force. In between fetish and rejection (or suspicion) are those for whom logic is praiseworthy, good for assessing arguments, or good if kept in its place—providing, say, that logic does not substitute for empirical inquiry (the general position, e.g., of American pragmatism). Others—students of hermeneutics, for example—concede that logic is entangled with power but take both as neither good nor bad in themselves; everything depends on how benevolent a particular authority is and how responsible in using all forms of power.

Keeping this sketch of the range of opinion on R/reason and logic in mind, let's turn now to Burke's complex reflections on both. As a first approximation to his view of reason, I cite the following passage from *Attitudes Toward History*, where Burke is defending a distinction between the irrational and the nonrational:

> Many of our rationalists have made things more difficult and forbidding by confining us to a choice between . . . the "rational" and "irrational." But if a tree puts out leaves in the spring and drops them in the autumn, its act is neither rational nor irrational, but non-rational. And so it is with many human processes, even mental ones, like the "identification" that the non-heroic reader makes with the hero of the book [s/]he is reading. To call such processes "irrational" is to desire their elimination. But we question whether social integration can be accomplished without them. If we consider them simply as "non-rational," we are not induced to seek elaborate techniques for their excision—instead we merely, as rational [people], "watch" them, to guard against cases where they work badly. Where they work well, we can salute them, even coach them. (171)

Burke's irrational/nonrational distinction seems so obvious and innocuous that we may miss exactly what we are assenting to if we let it go by with only a casual "of course." One of his early critics came close to grasping the implications when he called *Attitudes Toward History* "an anatomy of the non-rational factors in social change." But when he goes on to criticize Burke for neglecting "the element of rational choice in human affairs" (Parkes 112, 114), it is clear that the main implication has eluded him. Burke does not neglect reason. It serves for him the very important "watching" function: that is, critical reflection, conscious assessment, without which "rational choice" cannot have much meaning. However, reason is not primary for Burke. Nor, as we shall see, is unreason or the irrational primary. Rather that which has "first place" for Burke is nonreason, within which all reason functions.

To appreciate more fully the scope and significance of the nonrational in Burke's philosophy, we should set *Attitudes Toward History* aside for the moment and turn to the preceding volume, *Permanence and Change*. That book opens with a section entitled "On Interpretation" and features "orientation" as its key term. An orientation is a "general view of reality" (4); as "a bundle of judgments as to how things were, how they are, and how they may be," orientations "form the basis of *expectancy*" (14, Burke's emphasis).

Put in more familiar terms, what Burke calls an orientation is the

near equivalent of ideology or the hermeneutical "horizon of meaning."
All three conceive worlds as human creations; all three see meaning as
projective, which means denying objectivity. Critical of behaviorism's stimulus-response model, Burke claims that "stimuli do not possess an absolute meaning." The prospect of torture, he says, means one thing to "a
comfort-loving skeptic," quite another to someone who believes in heavenly reward for martyrdom. "Any given situation," Burke concludes, "derives its character from the entire framework of interpretation by which
we judge it" (35).

If we ask, How do orientations and frameworks come to exist?
Burke's answer reveals why he insists on a distinction between the irrational and the nonrational and why he elevates the nonrational over the
rational. Orientations depend on "linkage of outstanding with outstanding" (14), on association, so that "a[n] . . . event derives its character for
us from past experiences having to do with like or related events" (7).
Clearly we cannot call such processes rational in any ordinary sense of
the term. As Burke points out, nonhuman animals learn, through linkages creating orientations of their own (5), presumably without benefit
of reason. Nor can we call such processes irrational, if by irrational we
mean something negative, something to eliminate. For without orientations we could not interpret at all; there would be no accumulation of
experience, no relatively stable meanings, no guides for conduct. Such
processes, then, are best considered nonrational; we form associations
spontaneously, typically without deliberation, "growing" orientations
as trees sprout leaves in the spring.

Of course, we do not, as social beings, make our own orientation out
of nothing; rather interpretational frames preexist us and we acquire them
for the most part "ready made" through the "corporate we's" we identify with. Identification, the key concept in Burke's postPhilosophical
view of the subject, is also the central symbolic process in making human orientations. But whether acquired "ready made" or earned through
hard experience, orientations depend on processes that go on almost
entirely beneath the threshold of consciousness and are therefore overwhelmingly nonrational. Burke would agree with hermeneutical philosophers who say that horizons of meaning have us more than we have
them; they make us what we are so pervasively and profoundly—in
Gadamer's phrase, "over and above our wanting and doing" (*Truth*
xxviii)—that rational choice plays a relatively minor role even for mature persons who have developed a high critical capacity. In that formative period of childhood and early adolescence when orientations are
taking shape, before our entry into what Burke calls "the forensic," into
public life (*ATH* 254–55)—before, that is, the onset of the so-called age
of reason—rational choice hardly plays a role at all.

For Burke reason enters the picture as "rationalization," a term he uses nonpejoratively and synonymously with reason itself (*PC* 20). A rationalization is a verbalization, a formulating in propositions of linkages implicit in our interpretations. To use one of Burke's examples: "A good Catholic may feel that priests and guides are alike; a good Marxian may feel that priests and deceivers are alike" (13). No matter how dependent our linkages are on symbols and language, we are not rational in Burke's sense of the term until linkages are stated as claims. Thus, reason is secondary, nonreason primary. Without nonrational linkages formed through identification and experience, reason has nothing to assert and therefore nothing to call into question.

The "secondness" of reason, its dependency on nonreason, does not mean that Burke devalues the rational or takes it as impotent in human affairs. The capacity to formulate enables the capacity for critical reflection, and critical reflection is distinctively human.

> Though all organisms are critics in the sense that they interpret the signs about them, the experimental, speculative technique made available by speech would seem to single out the human species as the only one possessing an equipment for going beyond the criticism of experience to a criticism of criticism. We not only interpret the character of events . . . we may also interpret our interpretations. (*PC* 6)

Or as Burke will put it more memorably in an essay written almost fifty years later, "a dog can bark" in response to the signs around him, but "he cannot bark a tract on barking" ("[Nonsymbolic] Motion" 810). If reason is dependent on nonrational linkages, reason can do something entirely closed to nonreason—comment on itself. There is, then, in reason a "thirdness" of high potential value: reflexiveness, the ability to reason about rationalizations, the use of language to reflect on language itself. This thirdness permits a degree of control and rational choice, enough to watch our identifications, to formulate and reformulate them in response to their consequences.

In Burke's philosophy, nonreason corresponds to Peirce's "firstness" (75–93), while reason supplies both a "secondness"—propositional formulation—and a "thirdness"—propositions about propositions, metadiscourse, interpretations of interpretations. Before we concern ourselves with his view of the tool of reason, logic, we need to ask how Burke understands the irrational and what role it plays with respect to nonreason and reason.

In another key essay from the thirties, "War, Response, and Contradiction," Burke defines the irrational as "*contradictoriness of response*."

So defined, it is "basic to human psychology . . . for sound biological reasons," so basic in his view that a "[hu]man's responses are *normally* of a contradictory nature"—adding "particularly at those depths . . . implicated in the religious, ethical, poetic, or volitional aspects" of human being. So pervasive and ineluctable is the irrational for Burke that he playfully suggests that, particularly in a capitalist society, beset by the contradictions Marx exposed so well, we ought not to criticize a person's thinking when it is contradictory but rather when it is too "poor in fundamental contradictions" (*PLF* 244–45, Burke's emphasis). It would seem that only a very superficial mind could avoid contradiction.

At this point we should note that Burke explicitly recognizes the irrational in its usual meaning, "merely as error" (244), for example, when our propositions contradict one another or when our deductions do not follow from our premises. But he is plainly not interested in this meaning of the irrational. The special meaning he gives it takes in a good deal more than reason gone wrong. Far from being simply the opposite of rational, the irrational in Burke may be said to "underlie" the rational. That is, our motives are normally contradictory even when we manage to express them with "perfect rationality," without detectable contradiction. Quite apart from any intent to deceive, the rational tends to conceal the irrational. It is the "deep" or "hidden" nature of irreason that interests Burke.

In "War, Response, and Contradiction" and elsewhere in his early philosophy Burke explores various sources and kinds of contradiction. We need not survey all of them to get an adequate idea of what he means by the irrational, but looking at a few should flesh out his concept and help us understand why the irrational is so important in his philosophy.

Given his focus on the "religious, ethical, poetic or volitional aspects" of human behavior, Burke emphasizes the contradictions implicit in social life most, especially in political conduct. For example, there is contradiction in the relatively straightforward sense of self-defeating behavior:

> Liberals have long suffered in silence under this curse, since they are half the time advocating reforms when they know that reforms interfere with fundamental change. And even the Communists, who in America are still living by the dictates of capitalism, become involved in a similar contradiction when they began pleading for unemployment insurance which, if adequate, might put off the Revolution forever. (*PLF* 245)

"If I win I lose"—or sometimes (happier times!) in losing, conditions become so bad that I win: So ubiquitous is this kind of contradiction that anyone involved in practical, political activity can cite example after example. In reflective moments, we ponder such contradictions with bemused irony. But most of the time we "hide" them from ourselves and others in the sense of suppression and for a very good reason: If we thought about them too much, paralysis might set in, and practical activity would cease. In any case, such thinking dissipates energy, and so we more or less "agree" tacitly not to discuss it.

The ultimate source of contradiction in the self-defeating sense and in many other senses as well is ideology, the near equivalent, as noted previously, of "orientation" in *Permanence and Change*. Before *Permanence and Change*, in *Counter-Statement*, Burke was emphatic about the contradictions implicit in *all* ideologies, not just in capitalism: "An ideology is not a harmonious structure of beliefs or assumptions: some of its beliefs militate against others . . . An ideology is an aggregate of beliefs sufficiently at odds with one another to justify opposite kinds of conduct" (163). We can begin to glimpse in Burke's definition of ideology something of his sense of the extent and depth of the irrational. Its extent is all-embracing for us, for human being; we exist always within frameworks of interpretation, or orientations, or ideologies, and they are always contradictory. As for depth: For the most part, we do not suppress an awareness of conflicts in our orientations as we suppress our awareness of self-defeating behavior. We cannot suppress what we have never been conscious of, and ideological contradiction is almost entirely nonconscious. It takes a Nietzsche, a Freud, or a Marx to expose even a little of it (but typically without being able to see the contradictions buried in their own interpretative horizons). The irrational runs so deep and so far ahead of us that it is ludicrous to imagine eliminating it. With a little effort and training, we can minimize or eliminate the illogical, but the irrational, like the nonrational, is infinitely beyond control by elimination. Thanks to rational "thirdness," our capacity for critical reflection, we can reveal *some* of the irrational and so "watch" it in much the same way that Burke advocates our watching of the nonrational. But on the whole the irrational has us, not we it.

Before looking at one other source of the irrational as Burke understands it, we should pause to note relationships. Whereas the relation of the rational to the irrational is indirect, via "thirdness," the irrational is the constant companion of the nonrational. Orientations are formed through the nonrational process of association; ideologies are "aggregates of belief" no less dependent on the nonrational linkages of experience and identification. Too loosely knit to be consistent, contradictions and contradictory responses necessarily abound. Ideologies are rather like political platforms, slung together in an ad hoc way to please constituencies variously at odds with one another. They are a rationalist's nightmare. But the messiness of ideologies will disturb us less if we accept Burke's self of many selves, an "internal constituency" of voices that must be placated in much the same way that platforms unite the interest groups of a political party. We will then not expect "sweet reason" and drop the hopeless struggle to banish the irrational.

We also need to recall Burke's anti-Cartesian subject to understand why Burke believes that the irrational has biological as well as ideological sources. Descartes's subject assumed a mind/body dichotomy; Burke's subject assumes the exact opposite, a mind-body merger. Consequently, Burke pulls together two sources of motivation typically dissociated in modernism: the biological and the moral. For example, near the end of "War, Response, and Contradiction," Burke claims that "even so brutal a performance as modern warfare is ethically rooted"—rooted, that is, in notions of the good and bad, in choices, and therefore in consciousness. And "whatever 'consciousness' may be"—note that Burke is not *reducing* consciousness to the predator's kind of object-centered attentiveness—" it is mainly manifested in those processes involved in the seeking and capture of food" (*PLF* 254–55).

At this point contradiction again enters the picture. Hunger satisfied, the successful predator lapses into the animal equivalent of an after dinner's sleep. Contradiction does not reside merely in alternating states—the intense concentration required for hunting, the relaxed satiety after a meal—but rather in the conflict of ends and means. To achieve our goals—"security, peace, relaxation, comfort"—we employ an "equipment . . . [that] is the soul of turbulence and struggle." Hence, we must recognize

> a "militaristic-pacifistic" conflict at the basis of morals. We seek peace ever by the questionable . . . device of fighting for it. In so far as the organism attains the state of quiescence, its militaristic equipment (that is: nervous agility, bodily and mental muscle, imagination, intellect, senses, expectation, "curiosity," etc.) is threatened with decay. And in so far as this militaristic equipment is kept in vigorous operation, it makes impossible precisely the state of relaxation which it is designed to secure. (*PLF* 254–55)

Given current suspicions of biological reductionisms employed consciously or unconsciously to support the "naturalness" of certain ideologies (a suspicion Burke shares), we need to be clear about what he is saying here—and perhaps more importantly, what he is not saying. His view is not reductive. Morality cannot be reduced to the motives of the predator or the motives of the prey. In the paragraph following the one cited, Burke criticizes Nietzsche for the "excesses of the 'blonde beast'" (*PLF* 255–56). Burke is not seeking a region "beyond good and evil."

What he is saying, and what he praises Nietzsche for saying before

him, is that "the morality of combat is no despicable thing." In answer
to those who would construe the morality of combat as merely an ata-
vistic pathology or an ideological distortion of a "naturally" gentle human being, Burke says:

> We cannot stop at noting the savagery of some slayer or the
> greed of some financial monopolist. There is the same fanati-
> cism, tenacity, and even pugnacity underlying the efforts of
> the scientist, artist, explorer, rescuer, inventor, experimenter,
> reformer. Militaristic patterns are fundamental to our "vir-
> tue," even the word itself coming from a word which the
> Latins applied to their warriors. (*PLF* 256)

Burke is not glorifying war or contending that war is inevitable. His view
is not the view of the social Darwinist, or the apologist for capitalist
competition, which a good portion of "War, Response, and Contradiction" criticizes as an ideology that serves only to fan the fires of fanati-
cism and pugnacity to a white-hot intensity. Rather, what he contends is
that our most constructive, peaceful, "virtuous" activities are caught
inextricably in the "militaristic-pacifistic" contradiction. We seek "peace"
through the equipment of "turbulence and struggle." We are, and not
just ancestrally, irrational creatures.

In our very being, as deep as you care to go, Burke is saying, you will
discover the irrational as contradictoriness of response. Why does Burke
so stress the irrational?

His target is that wing of modernism we call the Enlightenment, with
its capital-R Reason, and the scientific rationale and doctrine of progress
that go hand in hand with it. Science and Reason would transcend the irrational or make it unproblematical:

> Ideally it would have all our responses to stimuli obey the ra-
> tional pattern, so that contradictions would arise purely from
> "error," [or] from insufficient knowledge." Science hopes to
> impose this neutrality of approach upon a kind of mental
> and bodily structure which, according to Veblen, is best fit-
> ted for a state of "mild savagery." It would impose mecha-
> nistic ideals upon a non-mechanistic organism. (*PLF* 257)

Clearly Burke belongs to the Romantic counter-statement, which has contributed so much to the conversation after Philosophy by an ongoing
skeptical critique of all dimensions of Enlightenment rationality. Burke
is an organic thinker. For him there is no disembodied Reason. At the
heart of this kind of thinking is the nonrational and irrational. His stress
on the irrational, then, is of a piece with his postPhilosophical project.

For Burke most human performances will be a mix of the nonrational, rational, and irrational; they will be so thoroughly intertwined, so thoroughly interactive, that teasing them apart is almost impossible. I have somewhat falsified his view by separating them analytically and talking about "firsts," "seconds," and "thirds," and notions of what underlies what. Nevertheless, it is obvious that for Burke reason (synonymous with rationalization or verbalization) is wholly dependent on nonreason (on linkages, on the sense of what goes with what) and that nonreason and irreason (as contradictoriness of response) dance together, especially in the aggregates of belief we call ideologies. Clearly, in Burke's understanding of human motivation, the nonrational and irrational play a much greater role than reason does.

One might then surmise that Burke must have little interest in logic at all. For if reason is propositional formulation of what is implicit in nonrational identifications, logic, for all of its many meanings in the history of philosophy, boils down to the proper sequencing of propositions, rules of inference and deduction basically. Except in Hegelian logics, logic is designed, above all, to avoid contradiction, but Burke believes that contradiction is basic to human responses. Logic must be a very superficial business for him, a kind of self-deceiving curiosity, one of the ways we try to persuade ourselves that we have transcended the condition of "mild savagery."

Such a view of logic certainly seems consistent with how Burke understands the relation of reason to nonreason and irreason. But it is not his view of logic.

Burke works through his understanding of logic most thoroughly in *Permanence and Change*. But before this volume, in *Auscultation, Creation, and Revision*, he made his basic attitude toward logic clear when he referred satirically to "a man in the new mood [the antitraditional, revolutionary mood so widespread in the Depression years] who scorned all logic on the grounds that logic was once an 'enslaving device' of the Roman Catholic schoolmen." Amused by what he calls "this simplified kind of 'insight,'" he accounts for it as the product of antithetical "us" versus "them" habits of thought typical of those who undergo violent conversions from a traditional outlook to some revolutionary one. If "the enemy" of liberation uses logic, we shall "liberate" ourselves by embracing the illogical. Noting that the French Dadaists tried in a programmatic way to embrace the nonlogical and illogical "for a season," he concludes that, the novelty having worn off, "few critics, feeling that the bourgeois philosophers often talked good sense, would counsel the conscientious proletarian to adopt non-sense as the wholesome Antithesis" (97–98).

So far as I know, Burke never commented on more recent examples of this simplified kind of "insight," such as feminists who condemn logic not as an enslaving device of Roman Catholic schoolmen but as phallocentric, an enslaving device of men, period. But it is not hard to see what his attitude would have been. As he says in *Permanence and Change*, "we are logical (*logos*: word) when we specifically state the nature of a problem and then go to see within the terms of this specific statement" (84). In other words, we are being logical when we make our interpretations explicit and test them by what they allow us to see, by what follows from the implications of the formulation itself. Logic is implicit in reason, rationalization, verbalization. Such a procedure is not Catholic but catholic, not phallocentric, but human, so that we can only escape from logic by ceasing to be human, by not using words. For very good reasons we may well oppose Scholasticism or sexism, but we will require logic for the good reasons we have to oppose whatever oppressions from the past we wish to cast off.

For Burke logic is part of word power, inseparable from the politics of language and from the will to power generally.

> Piaget has observed that children gradually learn to socialize their beliefs by logical proof as the result of quarreling. At first they state their differences merely as flat contradictions, of the "You did so—I did not" variety; but in time they learn how to offer "reasons" for their assertions. Seen from this angle, *cogency* becomes a mature form of *compulsion*. (PC 81, Burke's emphasis)

Or, as we say sometimes, we find someone's logic "compelling," coercing our consent when we started with a quite different opinion. In contrast to philosophers who take it as a purely analytical or speculative instrument, Burke has no illusions about logic; it belongs, as he goes on to say in the next sentence, to "the militaristic or combative element . . . at the roots of civilization" (81), which in turn, as we have seen, is entangled in consciousness and morality. Logic is anything but pure and detached; it *is* coercive, a mature form of compulsion. But it also takes us beyond the deadlock of childish contradiction; and compared with other "persuaders," such as the use of physical force, it is relatively peaceful, civil and civilizing. Logic is part of the ongoing "attempt to remold" the militaristic "into something qualitatively different" (81) from the nakedly predatory.

If "the morality of combat is no despicable thing," then surely the attenuated combat of logical cogency is no despicable thing. It is not too much to say that Burke celebrates logic. But he is also quite alert to its limitations and temptations.

The chief limitation of logic is obvious and indisputable: it can evaluate the cogency of a sequence of statements but cannot, as logic, either generate or evaluate the content of propositions. In Burke's analysis, reason can only put into words what is implicit in orientations, horizons of meaning, and logic is limited to assessing the relation of premises to conclusions. It cannot "get at" the orientation itself, which supplies the premises in a chain of reasoning. Consequently, "[m]ost accusations of the illogical [amount to] hidden disagreement . . . over . . . premises. . . . [E]ach of the opponents, accusing the other of being illogical, is in reality moving from premises to conclusion with the syllogistic regularity of a schoolman" (*PC* 85). Burke goes on to "recognize the illogical in the sense that verbalizations may be inadequate even within the given speaker's scheme of orientation" (86)—logic can reveal errors of reasoning *within* an orientation—but it cannot overcome or adjudicate differences between or among orientations. Since most disagreements are differences, hidden or not, over premises, not over what follows from a given premise, logic has very limited utility in practical argumentation.

For Burke the limitations of logic imply its subordination to rhetoric. That is, persuasion must do the work that logic cannot do. To the extent that differences of opinion can be resolved, they are almost always resolved by a process of partial *conversion* (86), clearly a rhetorical affair. That is, one of the speakers succeeds in persuading the other or others to alter part of his/her/their framework of interpretation, linkages of outstanding with outstanding. As we say colloquially, we attempt to "win someone over" to our point of view, our ways of characterizing people, events, and situations, at least in this particular case. If we can change the linkages, shared premises will follow as the night the day and then logic can do its work.

If the chief limitation of logic is its inability to access orientations, its chief temptation is metaphysics, the urge to "make the world over" in its image. The temptation, evident since Plato and the Stoics, is to move from logic (*logos*) to Logic (*Logos*). But even *logos* is not as compelling and inevitable as the illusions of chirography can make it appear to be:

> When a writer gives us a sequence of logical propositions framed to show why he got to his conclusions, he is almost reversing the actual processes of his thought. He presents data which supposedly lead to a conclusion—whereas the conclusion had led to the selection and arrangement of the data. . . . From what we want to arrive at, we deduce our ways of getting there. (*PC* 98)

Pointing out that narratives are also to some extent "written backwards," Burke is quick to point out that "there is nothing scandalous in this" (99), providing that we do not naively accept the illusion we ourselves have created—that matters cannot be otherwise, that the conclusion must

be so. The arbitrary in the sense of a chosen conclusion cannot be eliminated from logic.

Not only do we tend to "forget" that we ourselves have made our
chosen conclusion seem more than merely chosen, we also tend to write
logos large, as if "the very universe must be bungling and misguided unless it proceeds in accordance with the conventions of a barrister's plea."
No longer able to believe in *Logos* in the Platonic, Stoic, or Christian conceptions, we cling still, Hume notwithstanding, to "notions of causality
as a succession of pushes from behind," explicable as "a disguised way
of insisting that experience abide by the conventions of a good argument." But no matter how logical we make our language, or how logical
language makes us, there is no justification, save the metaphysical itch
implicit in logic, for extending it as a principle intrinsic to the nature of
things. "I do not see," Burke concludes, "why the universe should accommodate itself to a [hu]man-made medium of communication" (99).

In his early philosophy, then, Burke sees logic as *logos* only, "a mature form of compulsion," inseparable from power, from everyone's will
to power, and thus worthy of respect—more, worthy of praise as a civilizing instrument. At the same time, he warns us about its illusions of
fatality and its potential for metaphysical reductionism. We shall see in
the next chapter that language is far more than logic for Burke. As for
the universe: "[T]here is so strongly a *creative* or *poetic* quality about its
goings-on" (99, Burke's emphasis) that any view aiming to make it wholly
predictable, wholly subject to our intellectual will to power, must be wrong.

There can be no doubt that Burke's view of reason and logic is post-
Philosophical. Far from Hegel's equation of the real with Reason, Burke
maintains that even the reasoning of the rationalizing human is dependent on nonrational processes. Because we can only rationalize that which
is already implicit in an orientation, all the terms McCarthy applies to
the understanding of reason that emerged from the postPhilosophical
critique of Kant applies to Burke's understanding as well: contingent,
conventional, plural, local, fallible, and so forth. Reason must be like
this because orientations are like this.

Logic is only *logos* for Burke, a human instrument. It comes into play
after reason's "secondness" supplies propositions to structure into se-
quences. We can more or less reliably determine how cogent a particular
set of propositions is. But assumptions, premises, and conclusions come
from orientations, which logic as logic must simply take as "givens."
About all logic can do, therefore, is expose the illogical within a rationalization, which normally results not in "changing minds" but rather
in efforts to eliminate inconsistency. Overcoming differences across rationalizations require "conversions," transformations in the very assumptions, premises, and conclusions logic cannot touch. Conversions, whether

in religion, science, or whatever, are persuasive processes—something Burke grasped explicitly and clearly long before Kuhn and, following Kuhn and others, most of postPhilosophy embraced rhetoric. In a reversal of Philosophical values, Burke elevates "mere rhetoric" over logic, a move crucial to his philosophy as a whole.

But if Burke's view of reason and logic is unquestionably postPhilosophical, a genuine question remains: Which postPhilosophical view does his most nearly resemble? One of the stronger postPhilosophical views of reason is Habermas's. In a key essay he argues that "philosophical conversation cannot but gravitate toward argumentation and justificatory dispute," because "there is only one criterion by which opinions can be judged valid, and that is that they are based on agreement reached by argumentation." Hence, despite attacks on the traditional conception of philosophy, Habermas professes to "stubbornly cling to the notion that philosophy is the guardian of rationality" (309, 314).

As I have tried to show in this section, Burke is no rationalist. Nor is he, for all his insistence on how deeply contradictory human responses normally are, an irrationalist either. In *The Philosophy of Literary Form*, Burke seems close to Habermas in his reading of history as an argument, an "unending conversation" (110). But exactly here, in the nearest approach of the two philosophers, the differences emerge most clearly. For Burke philosophy cannot be the guardian of rationality because reason belongs to *logos*, language, to human being. Caught up in conflict, contradiction, and nonrational processes like identification, we are all guardians of reason. It is one of our tools for coping. We need reason not because we are rational but because for the most part we are not.

Nor does Burke's conversation end in agreement. If, as Habermas says, the only criterion for validity is agreement reached by argumentation, then validity is in deep trouble. As Burke says, likening the "conversation" of history to an evening's discourse, "The hour grows late, you must depart. And you do depart, with the discussion still vigorously in progress" (111). Our goal may be to prevail or to reach consensus, but we rarely do, and even when we do, agreement is almost always short lived. That is why the conversation is unending.

Burke's view of reason cannot be joined with Habermas's. In emphasizing the interpenetration of reason and logic with power, in elevating rhetoric over logic, Burke may seem closer to the intellectual forces Habermas resists—what I have called radical postmodernism—than to Habermas himself. Much of radical postmodernism draws inspiration from late Heidegger, whose radicalness is partly defined by an attempt to overcome metaphysics through resort to a kind of poetic language about as far from the conceptual language of Philosophy as philosophy can go. Any attempt to move beyond conceptual discourse is obviously a move beyond reason and logic in the mainstream, traditional meanings examined here. We saw earlier that Burke's basic move is quite different from Heidegger's; whereas the latter tried to move toward what he took to be the origin of thinking, the primal, world-revealing language of poetry, the former is less interested in origins than he is in coping with current intellectual conditions, conditions that require conceptual language, not the abandoning of it. Thus, even as Heidegger was moving toward poetic discourse as an alternative to conceptual discourse, Burke was saying that, the poetic medium having been weakened by social fragmentation, what our time needs is not a poetic philosophy but a philosophy of "poetry." It is Burke's decision in favor of conceptual language that separates him from late Heidegger and from the radical strategy of overcoming Philosophy by abandoning philosophy. Southwell said it well: "Although he [Burke] insists upon the limitations of reason, he is firmly committed to the value and necessity of logical discourse. This marks the gulf between Burke and the later Heidegger" (73).

"Gulf" is not too strong a word—and I would apply it as well to characterize the difference between Burke's approach to reason and Derrida's. A recent critic has explored in considerable detail one of Derrida's central motivations—the desire to avoid at all costs any version of Hegel's dialectical reason (Megill 271–75). Consequently, Derrida takes contradiction in much the same way as traditional logic does—as an indication of incoherence, discursive failure. Derrida "deconstructs" Philosophy in part by revealing contradictions latent in conceptual discourse. Burke is sensitive to latent contradiction as well but has an entirely different approach to it. Contradiction for Burke is as ineluctable as it was for Hegel, but for Burke its sources are more than the instability inherent in concepts: Contradiction for Burke is rooted in biology, ideology, and nonrational processes such as identification. And so Burke's proper response to deconstructive performances would be to say, "Yes, you have found contradictions, even in philosophical discourse, where they are not supposed to be. But did you imagine it could be otherwise? All you have shown is that philosophy is written by human beings."

For Burke contradiction is not necessarily a sign of discursive failure; that is why he only half-ironically suggests that we ought not to praise a work for avoiding contradiction but rather criticize it for being "too poor in fundamental contradictions." The profounder the work, the profounder the contradictions. In thus "welcoming" contradiction, Burke has clearly committed himself to dialectical reason. And this marks the gulf between Burke and Derrida, a gulf at least as wide and deep as the one separating Burke from late Heidegger.

Burke's view of reason and logic is actually closest to early Heidegger—or rather to Gadamer, who developed early Heidegger into philosophical hermeneutics. Although they understand it somewhat differently, Burke and Gadamer share the commitment to dialectical reason. Both take reason as basically critical reflection on human practices. Both think that critical reflection has valuable work to do and that part of this work is self-understanding, self-construction—even if—as both insist—this self is made of otherness, can never achieve full understanding, is more constructed than constructing, and has only a finite and fallible reason to work with.

As close as Burke's is to Gadamer's understanding of reason, certainly close enough to imagine a useful dialogue between Dramatism and philosophical hermeneutics on this issue, Burke's view is also in some respects quite far removed from Gadamer's. Gadamer places a good deal of faith in *logos*; he believes that if we give ourselves over to it, it will lead us toward truth, albeit a limited, historical, revisable truth (*Truth* 361–67). That is why he is so committed to a dialogical hermeneutics. Burke would agree with Habermas that Gadamer's faith in *logos* is too idealistic, that it does not reckon enough with the systematic distortion of communication by inequitable social and economic arrangements. But Burke would go further than Habermas does in his critique of Gadamer and, in so doing, direct his critique at both. Neither Habermas nor Gadamer detect the importance of the nonrational to anything like the degree Burke does. Both think that *logos* can do much more than it can actually do. *Logos* has little power to alter horizons of meaning apart from rhetoric's power to alter identifications, nonrational associations. And as Burke points out in *Permanence and Change*, horizons change mainly because they prove unserviceable (21)—that is, they change based on what we learn from the nonrational "naked facticity" of failure. We are not changed nearly so much by dialogue alone as Gadamer thinks; and argument, *pace* Habermas, cannot often by itself secure even a partial and temporary consensus. Rather horizons take shape within a particular economic and social dispensation; as conditions change, the horizon increasingly fails to provide serviceable cues for action. If we change, we change when the inadequacy of our interpretations becomes too great to ignore—for example, when billions of dollars and fifty thousand casualties finally led us to reevaluate the wisdom of military adventures like Vietnam. Then, in the midst of disaster or at least acute embarrassment, when "things are not working"—then, maybe, we are open to dialogue and argumentation.

On Figurative Language

The attempt to fix argument by analogy as a distinct kind of process, separable from logical argument, seems increasingly futile.

—Kenneth Burke, *Permanence and Change*

In deconstructing the Cartesian subject while reconstructing the concept of the individual outside the assumptions of individualism, Burke's view of the self is relatively complex. So also is his view of reason. Burke "explodes" the rational/irrational dichotomy by insisting on something quite Other, the nonrational, and by reconceiving the rational and the irrational in ways that escape the usual meanings and the good/bad evaluation. A mark of the complexity of Burke's thought on these two themes is that we hesitate between common alternatives in attempting to locate his positions. His view of the subject is certainly not modernist, but neither is it postmodern, especially if by postmodern we mean poststructural. Likewise, Burke is no rationalist, not even in Habermas's relatively "weak" (as compared with Hegel's or Kant's) version of rationalism. But neither is he an irrationalist—and to call him a nonrationalist is certainly a simplification, since Burke clearly believes that the rational and irrational figure prominently in human motivation.

In contrast, Burke's view of the literal/figurative distinction is straightforward and relatively easy to place in the current spectrum of opinion. For Burke all language use, including the philosophical and the scientific, is dependent on tropes. He therefore rejects the literal/figurative distinction as completely as he rejects the Cartesian subject. Consequently, he also rejects what McCarthy calls "philosophy's traditional self-delimitation from non-philosophy" (13), especially from rhetoric.

We associate this position with poststructuralism, especially deconstruction. But Burke's intent is not primarily deconstructive. Rather he takes a position akin to, citing McCarthy again, "hermeneutic philosophers [who] typically argue that interpretive modes, metaphorical elements, narrative structures, and the like can be incorporated into a transformed conception of rational discourse." McCarthy goes on to say that "much of the writing of Gadamer, Ricoeur, MacIntyre, Blumenberg and others have aimed to do just that" (13)—open up, transform rational discourse. I would advance a similar claim for Burke.

In *Permanence and Change* Burke endorses Henri Bergson's understanding of abstraction as *concealed analogy*. Most people would say, for example, that the following statement is literally true: "*Homo erectus, homo neanderthalensis*, and *homo sapiens* are all hominids." The fossil remains, however, consist of so many individuals, each somewhat different from all the others. Far from being "literal," species classifications are altogether dependent on analogy, on detecting similarities. They are not just "there," as concrete and indisputable as the term "hard science" implies. With a term such as "hominid," we move further up the ladder of abstraction, making classifications out of classifications, analogies out of analogies. The problem, of course, is that we tend to "forget" the creative and partly nonconscious process by which "family resemblances" are invented. The analogies are buried in our abstractions, as undetectable as the "carry over" of "dead metaphors." They cease to feel like interpretations. They become "the facts"—wordish sedimentations that quizzical fellows like Nietzsche, Burke, and Derrida can "desediment," peeling back the settled layers of abstraction in search of the informing analogies characteristic of all discourse.

What follows from the recognition that classifications depend on analogy? For Burke, as the epigraph to this section indicates, the first traditional distinction to go is argument by analogy as opposed to so-called logical argument. All arguments depend on analogy. Some are explicitly analogical, others implicitly so, the former being less self-deceiving, less likely to promote the "almost universal tendency to confuse abstractions with facts" (PC 94).

The next thing to go is any hard-and-fast distinction between the intellectual processes of science and poetry, philosophy and rhetoric, or the so-called primitive mind versus the so-called sophisticated mind (PC 97). So far as philosophy is concerned, Burke's position is indistinguishable from current postphilosophers, who argue that

> [o]nce . . . the omnipresence of the rhetorical dimensions of language [are] recognized, philosophical discourse can no longer be misconceived as logical *rather than* literary, literal *rather than* figurative, argumentative *rather than* rhetorical—in short, it can no longer be conceived of as philosophical in any emphatic sense of the term. (McCarthy 13, his emphasis)

This does not mean, of course, that we cannot distinguish, say, Kant's first *Critique* from a sonnet by Shakespeare. It does mean that we cannot call the former a- or nonrhetorical, the latter rhetorical. Nor can we promote the former over the latter on the grounds that Philosophy is somehow inherently or by virtue of method closer to Truth. Kant called rhetoric a cheat, a fraud (193); we can certainly show that his own discourse uses the very devices and tactics he condemned. But Burke is not content merely to expose the rhetoric of anti-rhetoric. Rather, he calls the whole modernist striving for a neutral language of pure denotation the "semantic ideal" and claims that "the best thing to be said in favor of [it] is that it is a fraud; one may believe in it because it is impossible" (PLF 159).

Early in the next chapter, when we examine the "linguistic turn" in philosophy and Burke's place in it, we will also take up his general view of language. At present, however, we are only interested in one part of it: his contention that the literal/figurative distinction is untenable. It is untenable because the abstractions of so-called literal language are concealed analogies. It is also untenable because philosophical and scientific discourses are dependent on "root metaphors," analogies that inform entire movements in philosophy and what Kuhn calls paradigms in science (see Johnson and Lakoff).

Recognition of the dependence of all thought, including philosophical and scientific thought, on "root metaphors" (itself a metaphor) is now so widespread, so commonplace as to need no defense. I cite Burke's view only to confirm my thesis that Burke was our intellectual contemporary in the thirties. I also want to show that he thought through the metaphorics of language, reaching conclusions at least as radical as any thinker can claim today.

Construing science in the inclusive sense as any organized body of speculation—that is, philosophy in an ancient and still more inclusive sense of the word—Burke notes that "the heuristic value of scientific analogies is quite like the surprise of metaphor." Aware of the strong positivist resistance to what he is about to say, he asks, as if advancing a tentative conclusion,

> [A]s the documents of science pile up, are we not coming to see that whole works of scientific research, even entire *schools*, are hardly more than the patient repetition, in all its ramifications, of a fertile metaphor? Thus we have, at different eras in history, considered man as the son of God, as an animal, as a political or economic brick, as a machine, each such metaphor, and a hundred others, serving as the cue for an unending line of data and generalizations. (*PC* 95)

It is not "reality" or the "nature of things" or "the data" that guide scientific research. Were this the case, the documents of science in each area of inquiry would all presumably "tell the same story." Rather than the data compelling conclusions, the conclusions are implicit in our frameworks of interpretation, each with its own "fertile metaphor." "The data"—what objectivity professes to "discover" simply and unproblematically "out there"—result largely from our own interpretive frameworks, which tell us what to look for, what will count as data in the first place. Thus, in effect, Burke is asking the same question Richard Rorty will ask about fifty years later: "Can we see ourselves as never encountering reality *except under a chosen description*—as, in Nelson Goodman's phrase, making worlds rather than finding them?" (57).

What made Burke's position radical in 1935 and makes it, outside of postPhilosophy, still radical now is his rejection of positivism and objectivism. Early in *Permanence and Change* Burke defined reality as "*what things will do to us or for us*" (22, his emphasis)—as, in other words, not a neutral "thereness" but the projection of a "chosen" (actually mostly learned or inherited) description. Our reality is always a mediated reality. Language is the mediator. It is ubiquitous, not a tool we can pick up and lay down but the medium in which we live. As this paragraph is fraught with metaphors (among them "position," "radical," "projection," "tool"), so our medium is always so saturated (metaphor again) with metaphor and concealed analogies that the very idea of a literal language is no more than, at best, an unattainable ideal. We can believe in it because it is impossible.

In fact, however, postPhilosophy does not believe in it. The "semantic ideal," in the English-speaking world at least as old as the seventeenth century, has played itself out just as modernist ideals for Philosophy in general no longer capture our imagination or harness our energies. The question facing us now is where this insight into the topical nature of all language takes us. Certainly it takes us beyond philosophy in any emphatic sense. Nietzsche, who had explored the metaphorics of language before Bergson, already understood that Philosophy was terminally ill. But are we left with only the negative gesture of deconstruction, with demonstrating over and over that the fraud is a fraud? As objectivists allege, are we left with total relativism, in effect saying "You chose your metaphors, I'll choose mine, and who's to say which set of concealed analogies and root metaphors make or reveal worlds best?"

For Burke simply demonstrating that the fraud is a fraud never seemed especially worthwhile. He did it and moved on, seeking, as he put it, to make "linguistic suspicion" synonymous with "linguistic appreciation" (GM 441). Instead of contributing only to the destruction of Philosophy, Burke's attitude resulted in the positive contribution of a rhetoric of scientific and philosophical discourse. Writing in 1976, Samuel IJessling claimed that "with the exception of Kenneth Burke's work there is relatively little written on the fundamental and . . . hidden persuasive structure of philosophical and scientific texts" (73). This is no longer true. In the last ten years especially, a sizable literature has appeared. Major figures in this movement, such as Hayden White and Clifford Geertz, have all acknowledged their debt to Burke, making him, I suppose, the father of rhetorics of "nonrhetorical" discourse. But the more important point is that Burke takes us beyond negative dialectic to a rhetoric of philosophy and a philosophy of rhetoric. These complementary constructions, I submit, is a significant part of what must succeed postmodernism generally and deconstruction in particular. In this, as in many other ways, Burke is not only our contemporary but also still ahead of us.

The charge of relativism lacks the force it used to have, but how Burke responded to it is worth brief notice here. First, he simply points to relativism as an assumption of contemporary thought. "[O]ur era," he says, is typified by "vast documentation of historical and psychological relativity itself." Here Burke is acknowledging a significant aspect of Lyotard's "postmodern condition," a decentered intellectual world of disciplines and subdisciplines lacking a "total picture," beyond even the possibility of complete synthesis. Second, rather than deploring this condition, he agrees with Lyotard and others in taking it as in some ways an advantage: "This relativistic attitude . . . has furthered the tendency to characterize events from a myriad shifting points of view" (PC 102). In other words, our very horizon of interpretation includes a pluralism of interpretative modalities. This is a good thing if we value a certain limited, pragmatic freedom; insofar as we have but one vocabulary for interpreting an event, we have no choice in how we understand it and little choice in action. Freedom depends on the ability to break free of a single way of "reading" the world, just as totalitarianism depends on the power to impose one reading on everyone.

Simply put, Burke does not want to overcome relativism. "Both the poet's metaphors and the scientist's abstractions discuss something in terms of something else. And the course of analogical extension is determined by the particular kind of interest uppermost at the time" (PC 104). Our orientations just *are* relative—to our interests, in turn related to social, political, and economic conditions of our time and place.

But if Burke does not want to overcome relativism, he certainly does want to *organize* it. This marks one of the great differences between Burke's postPhilosophy and Lyotard and Rorty's postphilosophy. If there are many illuminating ways to interpret human motives, Burke will seek an illuminating way to place and relate the various modes of interpretation. He does just this in the metahermeneutic of *A Grammar of Motives*. More basically, Burke exposes and studies root metaphors not just to reveal that metaphors are in fact present when unacknowledged or denied but also to engage in comparative assessment of the metaphors themselves. Burke maintains that "the universe would appear to be something like a cheese; it can be sliced in an infinite number of ways" (PC 103). But it does not follow that anyone's slicing is just as fruitful as anyone else's. Show us, Burke suggests, what your metaphor can do—how much it can account for. We'll put our metaphors to collective testing and critique. And we will find in the process that, relative to a given interest, some metaphors are in fact better than others. Such a persuasive process will not overcome relativism by yielding up Truth. Nor will it typically yield consensus, and when it does, the consensus will very rarely last long. But it can organize relativism by a clustering of opinion around the most promising options.

Beyond Postmodernism

What is most important about Burke's views of the subject, reason, and figurative language is not that they are strikingly contemporary—that they might well have appeared in the last decade rather than six decades ago. Rather what matters is that they carry us beyond most postmodern thinking. He shows us that we can relinquish the Cartesian subject without giving up the individual or the moral agent. We can retain a modest faith in reason while facing up squarely to the deeply irrational and non-rational sources of human motivation. We can also move beyond the negative use of rhetoric to deconstruct Philosophy to a constructive rhetoric of philosophy and philosophy of rhetoric.

In short, we can pass beyond Philosophy by philosophical means, without denying the possibility or value of philosophy itself. Anyone interested in holding on to postmodernism's best insights while moving beyond it to something more than the critique of modernism will find Burke's early philosophy worth the candle.

We turn our attention now from postPhilosophical themes to three highly controversial postPhilosophical "turns"—to language, to society, and to rhetoric. As we look into how Burke made these turns, the broader outlines of his early philosophy should emerge, allowing us to fit the views discussed in this chapter into a more comprehensive understanding of his thought in that most crucial period of his life and work, the 1930s.

3

PostPhilosophical Turns: To Language, Society, and Rhetoric

[T]he "linguistic turn" . . . is no longer an issue. The question now is where that turn leads.

—Thomas McCarthy, *After Philosophy: End or Transformation?*

If one can say that philosophy in our time converges in anything, it converges in the importance of language or of symbol systems in general. The commonsense notion that language is simply "at hand," a transparent and unproblematical medium by which we put our thoughts in words and characterize our experience with things and events, has no philosophical defenders left. Language is no longer something we can look through and therefore past. It has become, rather, the theme of postPhilosophical themes. Why?

There are many more or less plausible answers to this question. Richard Rorty claims that "the ubiquity of language is a matter of language moving into the vacancies left by the failure of all the various candidates for the position of 'natural starting points' of thought, starting points that are prior to and independent of the way some culture speaks or spoke." Candidates such as "clear and distinct ideas, sense data, categories of the pure understanding, [and] structures of prelinguistic consciousness" ("Pragmatism" 34–35) have all failed to get us "behind," "beneath," "above," or "beyond" language.

Burke would only partly agree with Rorty's explanation. Certainly

Burke holds with Rorty and all postPhilosophy that there are no natural starting points for thought prior to and independent of language. Language is not "at hand"; rather we dwell in it. We do not "find" words for our thoughts; rather our thoughts are always already words and symbols. We do not first have an experience with something "out there" and then formulate propositions about it; rather language is always already "out there," enabling human experience in the first place as well as assertions about experience.

However, Burke's explanation for what we would come to call the linguistic turn is quite different from Rorty's and closely akin to Gadamer's. The problem is not so much that Philosophy has failed; Philosophy has always been more or less failing to achieve its goals. The problem, rather, is more broadly cultural and social:

> In great eras of drama, the audiences *know* why characters act as they do. . . . But we even become muddled as to the motives in these earlier dramas . . . This fact in itself should indicate our growing instability; for in highly stable eras . . . the matter of motives is settled. (*PC* 32, his emphasis)

Gadamer pointed out that whereas the practice of hermeneutics is ancient, the rise of hermeneutical philosophy is comparatively recent, not much older than the social upheavals of the Romantic era ("Scope" 21). Hermeneutics became an important philosophical theme as interpretation became a more or less permanent cultural problem.

Similarly, Burke claims that "[m]eaning or symbolism becomes a central concern precisely at that stage when a given system of meanings is falling into decay. In periods of firmly established meanings, one does not *study* them, one *uses* them" (*PC* 162, his emphasis). Potential for "linguistic turns" exists in all strongly transitional or crisis periods. Language is our only means for attributing motives—our only means, therefore, for understanding ourselves and others. When this understanding breaks down, when motivation becomes uncertain or even opaque, we can no longer "look through" language—we have to look at it.

Modernism attempted to compensate for the lack of *sensus communis* by creating scientific (and therefore supposedly universal) terminologies for explaining human motivation. This is how Burke accounts for the rise of what he calls "the science of symbolism" and how he explains his own, quite explicit and self-conscious, linguistic turn in *Permanence and Change*.

For Burke the dynamics of language are inseparable from the dynamics of social change. This is not the case for all philosophy after the linguistic turn. One can become interested in language in itself, as a formal system, without becoming interested in language communities. Cartesian linguistics through Chomsky managed to do this. Philosophers who would reduce philosophy to a science of logic have turned to language or symbols of some kind without showing much interest in the communities that use them or the conditions of collective existence. Apart from sociolinguistics, science tends still to approach language this way, abstracted from communities. No doubt that is why Burke resisted the science of symbolism he knew in the thirties and why he devoted considerable space in *Permanence and Change* to developing an understanding of natural language that eludes scientific reduction to formal systems.

In resisting the reduction of language to formal systems and in tying the linguistic to the social turn in philosophy, Burke breaks not only with Cartesian science and modernist epistemology but also with the atomistic Anglo-American tradition of language philosophy dominant today. In an essay whose title is an important theme in this chapter, "Overcoming Epistemology," Charles Taylor explicates the tradition with which I would associate Burke's understanding of language:

> The new theory of language that arises at the end of the 18th century, most notably in the work of Herder and Humboldt, not only gives a new account of how language is essential to human thought, but also places the capacity to speak not simply in the individual but primarily in the speech community. This totally upsets the outlook of the mainstream epistemological tradition.

Taylor connects this new theory of language with Heidegger's "notion that our understanding of the world is grounded in our dealings with it," which is "equivalent to the thesis that this understanding is not ultimately based on representations at all." But whereas Heidegger contends only that "the condition of our forming disengaged representations of reality is that we be already engaged in coping with our world" (476–78), Burke's thesis is more radical and strikes at the heart of epistemology. We never, under any conditions, form disengaged representations of reality. Language is not a neutral, disengaged, epistemological instrument. Rather, it is a form of action, symbolic action, "the adopting of various strategies for the encompassing of situations" (*PLF* 1).

We shall explore the implications of Burke's thesis and its significance in contemporary thought about language shortly. For now I would stress the common ground Burke shares with the entire Herder-Humboldt tradition: To think about language is to think about language communities. To turn to language is, *ipso facto*, to turn to society and to a postepistemological philosophy.

If virtually all contemporary philosophers have, in one way or another, made the linguistic turn, far fewer have made the social turn and

fewer still the rhetorical turn. A major barrier to both is a lingering formalism. Yet the rhetorical turn is implicit in the social turn, as communication is implicit in community. As Isocrates said long ago, human society
cannot be created or maintained without the power of speech (50). Even
in our fragmented culture, to be a member of any language community
is to share a common persuasion. However, as it is possible to make the
linguistic turn without making the social turn, so it is possible to make
the social turn and miss the implications that should lead to making the
rhetorical turn as well.

The chief barriers are lingering Philosophical hostility to rhetoric
and resistance to skepticism. According to Hans Blumenberg, "[a]s long
as philosophy was inclined to hold out at least the prospect of eternal
truths and definitive certainties, then "consensus" as the ideal of rhetoric, and agreement subject to later revocation as the result attained by
persuasion, had to seem contemptible to it" (436). Whenever we find a
contemporary thinker privileging some kind of discourse as absolutely
better than other kinds—truer, purer, closer to the source, more authentic, more verified, historically proven, revealed by God, and so forth—we
may read it as someone scratching, perhaps while denying, the Philosophical
itch. Some version of the remarkably tenacious Philosophy/rhetoric contrast is buried somewhere in all such thinking.

Blumenberg implies the central issue involved in the rhetorical turn
when he points out that "Philosophy's program succeeds or fails, but it
does not yield any profit in installments. Everything that remains, this
side of definitive evidence, is rhetoric . . . *Rhetoric belongs to a syndrome
of skeptical assumptions*" (435, my emphasis). The issue is how we understand ourselves, what we take our capacities to be. Are we, as Blumenberg
contends, *Mangelwesen*, "creatures of deficiency" (429), finite, fallible,
unable to grasp the Truth even if we believe, say, that the Truth exists in
the mind of God? If so, Philosophy is impossible. If so, most of what we
say or write remains this side of definitive evidence—remains, that is,
rhetoric. If so, Truth must yield to truths, *par provision*, agreements subject to later revocation. This is all we can have because of what we are.

Later we will investigate Burke's version of *Mangelwesen*, characteristic of philosophical anthropology after the decline of Enlightenment
faith in human perfectibility. At present, the key point is this: Kenneth
Burke was able to make the rhetorical turn so early and so completely
because his philosophy belongs to a syndrome of skeptical assumptions.
We see now why his skepticism, emphasized earlier (pp. 30–33), must not
be underestimated or written off as transient, overcome in his later philosophy. If we read it this way, his commitment to rhetoric becomes unintelligible, his philosophy incoherent. If, on the other hand, we take him as a
thinker from the outset at work "after Philosophy," and therefore a skep-

tic; as a skillful rhetorician aware that his own discourse is rhetoric, who therefore claims not the Truth but only truths *par provision*—then his commitment to rhetoric becomes intelligible and his philosophy as coherent as is humanly possible.

We move now to a more detailed study of Burke's linguistic, social, and rhetorical turns. We begin with all three together in their simplest formulation and then examine each separately.

The "Turns" and the Problem of Motive

Positivism either denies the existence of motivation—What can we point to "out there" as the objective manifestation of a motive?—or ignores motivation as an unscientific problem belonging to the "softer" disciplines. When science does take up the problem of motive, it assumes the commonsense view that we just "have" motives and that all that is problematical about them is detecting what they "really are."

Writing in the heyday of logical positivism, Burke chooses "motive" as the key term of his philosophy. From *Permanence and Change* on, the problem of motivation is Burke's primary concern. This choice is significant in itself and not only as a rejection of positivistic reductionism: It is also a rejection of naturalistic reductionism, which treats human motivation in terms of a few basic instincts or urges and/or as conditioned response, "learning" in the truncated behaviorist sense of the term.

Recognizing Burke's rejection of these two closely related reductionisms, Southwell claims that Burke joins with Heidegger in "abjur[ing] causal thinking" (14). This cannot be true because Burke takes the behavioristic account as a salutary warning: Human beings are always in danger of merely salivating on cue, not really choosing, and therefore not really acting at all. Much of human behavior, Burke concedes, *is* explicable as an unthinking, mechanical response to ossified interpretations. Instead of saying Burke rejects causation, it is better to say that he complicates it to the point that it escapes the *reductionism* of stimulus-response models.

Burke's choice of motive as his key term, then, is significant in a negative way; as Wayne Booth observes, how Burke approaches motivation distinguishes him from all the deterministic "motivisms" characteristic of what Booth calls "modern dogma" (*Modern Dogma* 24, 28) and Burke calls "scientism." But his choice has much more significance in a positive way: Greater by far than what he rejects is the range of thought he is able eventually to integrate in Dramatism. Burke's opting for motive in *Permanence and Change* is the first crucial step toward Dramatism.

Just as important as his concentration on motive *per se* is his treatment of it as an interpretation. Except in biblical exegesis, hermeneutics had no significant presence in Anglo-American thought in 1935. Heidegger was hardly known in the English-speaking world. Gadamer's *Truth and Method* did not appear until 1960. The work of Polanyi and Kuhn also came decades after *Permanence and Change*. Of course, Burke had Nietzsche, Bergson, and William James, all of whom in different ways recognized the centrality of interpretation. The insight hardly originated with Burke. Nevertheless it is remarkable that he claimed so early and without reservations what Rorty still must urge against the resistance of positivistic common sense—that "we never encounter reality *except under a chosen description*" (57, Rorty's emphasis).

As we don't simply "have" language, so we don't simply "have" motives. A motive is not some primal, irreducible datum "in here" with which we can match some independently existing description "out there," in a neutral, disengaged space. Rather a motive is always already a "linguistic product." We inhabit an orientation, a *Weltanschauung*, a scheme or schemes of interpretation. We "have" the motives described by whatever rationalization we inhabit—or rather, the motives have us. It makes no sense to ask, therefore, what our motives "really are" apart from some culture or subculture's attributions. Our motives "really are" what some language community says they are. When our culture was Judeo-Christian, for example, we understood our motives in terms such as sin and guilt. Sin and guilt were "real" because, as Burke says in good American pragmatist fashion, anything that effects human behavior (such as confession and rites of purification) is "real."

In its simplest formulation, what I have just described is Burke's "linguistic turn." It boils down to the equation of motive with interpretation, "linguistic products." It does lead where it would seem to lead, to a cultural relativism as old as the ancient Sophists, our first students of comparative anthropology. Motives have to be relative to culture because there can be no account of motives that is not cultural. As one would surmise, Burke is suspicious of what we now call the hermeneutics of suspicion, various forms of "depth" psychology and sociology, which purport to give us a clear-sighted account of human motives to help us overcome the "illusions" of some past culture's interpretations. Burke does not deny insight to the legions that have carried on the work of Nietzsche, Marx, and Freud—in fact, he avails himself of their insights as well as generating, in the tradition of ideology critique, some of his own—but he does deny that any account of human motives can be preemptive, that is, definitive or complete. He directs his suspicion at the *reductionism* of depth hermeneutics, just as he did at the reductionisms of positivism and naturalism, to which they are closely related.

We will see later that Burke's relativism does not end in a leveling of interpretations that values all alike and therefore values none. The assertion that all interpretation is cultural does not entail the proposition that all accounts are of equal value. Nor does he fall back into the Philosophical position that attempts to overcome relativism by claiming foundational Truth. What he does is much more interesting than either of these possibilities and more promising than our current oscillation between, on the one hand, a characterless relativism and, on the other, an indefensible objectivism.

In being linguistic, however, all interpretations are "equal." Any claim to penetrate beyond language to the "thing itself" we can dismiss out of hand. For apart from language or symbol systems of some kind, there can be no understanding of anything. Burke would agree with Gadamer: "Being that can be understood is language" (*Truth* 474).

All interpretations are also alike in being socializations. As motives are always already linguistic, they are always already and irreducibly socialized. That is, we do not first interpret our motives and then, in a distinct, two-step process, attempt to make them negotiable for the group or groups with which we identify ourselves. Rather, any account of our own or somebody else's motives draws on preexisting understandings and expectations shared by our community. Otherwise they couldn't be *communis* ("common," i.e., communicated, understood) at all.

Again, Burke would agree with Gadamer: Interpretations are necessarily applications (*Truth* 307–8). They are always already strategic in a spontaneous, uncalculated way that affirms, usually without much awareness, our solidarity with some collective entity. Without necessarily intending to appeal for acceptance and assent, we nevertheless do so anyway. Of course, that which is already strategic can become calculated, *crafted* in the consciously rhetorical sense to appeal more strongly. But interpretations are always already rhetorical.

In sum, "Any explanation [of a motive] is an attempt at socialization, and socialization is a strategy; hence, . . . the assigning of motives is a matter of *appeal*" (PC 24–25). This, in a nutshell, is Burke's "social turn," also his "rhetorical turn." Clearly, then, my claim is warranted: By 1935 Burke had made all three turns, made them simultaneously, and made them in an integrated way. In doing so, he "leapt forward," well past most of his own generation of philosophers, the cutting edge of which was preoccupied with overcoming Philosophy; past even much current philosophy, which is still for the most part preoccupied with the implications of the linguistic turn and hesitant about accepting the seemingly drastic implications of the social and rhetorical turns. Is all philosophy merely interpretation? Must we understand philosophy as merely a social and cultural product? Is all philosophy merely rhetoric? These questions certainly retain the power to provoke. No consensus exists on the answers. But for Burke, who would delete the "merely" from all three questions, the answer is yes, yes, and yes. Philosophy can no more be beyond culture or beyond rhetoric than it can be beyond language.

Burke on Language: Three Phases

If motive is Burke's key term, language is his most persistent theme. His interest in language antedates *Permanence and Change*, but in that volume language becomes for the first time a subject of intense reflection—takes on, that is, undeniable philosophical dimension. From this point on to certain important essays of the late seventies and early eighties, Burke seldom talks about anything without making connections with language, and many of his essays are about little else but language.

I distinguish three overlapping and interconnected phases in his explorations of language:

1. From Counter-Statement through Attitudes Toward History (1931–1937). Language as rhetoric. Western discourse theory has long recognized rhetoric as one important use of language. For Burke, however, all language is rhetorical, and not just in the now widely accepted sense of being dependent on tropes. Language is persuasive, a process of appeal to one's self and to others. In some discourse the rhetorical motive is patent, in the rest to varying degrees latent, but for Burke rhetoric is not a function of language but rather how all language functions.

Although this view of language is as old as the Sophists, it is now associated with Nietzsche. So we might as well call this first phase Nietzschean. It gives way to phase two's multifunctional view of language. But Burke never retreats from the proposition that all language is rhetorical. In *A Rhetoric of Motives* (1950), Burke claims that "wherever there is 'meaning' there is 'persuasion'" (172).

2. From *The Philosophy of Literary Form* to *Language as Symbolic Action* (1941–1966). *Language as symbolic action*. Burke recognizes two other functions in addition to the rhetorical: a realistic ambition, which he calls the "chart" function, and self-expression, the "dream" function. Together with rhetoric, the function of petition or "prayer," these three functions are characteristic of all discourse.

Symbolic action is Burke's theory of discourse. From Aristotle on, Philosophical discourse theories tend to dissociate discourse functions, allot distinct kinds of discourse to each function, and privilege one function over another. In this way the Philosophy/rhetoric distinction came into being; in modernism the contrast is typically scientific Philosophy/ mere rhetoric. Clearly, a postPhilosophical theory of discourse must make an entirely different set of moves.

Burke does not dissociate the functions. His theory does not lead to domains of discourse with sharp boundaries and consequent obsession with rules, method, rigor, and purity. Instead, he is always transgressing boundaries, as likely to dwell on the charting function of a poem as he is on the dream function of a scientific tract. Such analysis outrages traditional discourse hierarchies, which dissociate, for example, self-expression from science and privilege science as closer to reality or the nature of things. On this count alone, then, Burke's theory of language as symbolic action deserves postPhilosophical assessment.

3. From *The Rhetoric of Religion* to the last essays (1961–1984). *Language as logology.* After his initial treatment of symbolic action in the title essay of *The Philosophy of Literary Form*, Burke became interested in a fourth function of language, which he called "consummation"—that is, thoroughness, or the desire for "perfection," the drive to unfold to the last implication the meanings inherent in a given vocabulary (*LASA* 16–20). Burke explores this motive in a spirit of ironic ambivalence, with a mixture of admiration and suspicion, since consummation both partly drives human achievement and makes human bondage all but ineluctable.

In time his interest in consummation broadened into a concern for all motives inherent in symbol-using. The result was logology, the philosophical study of language as the prime source of human motivation.

Logology is Burke's original contribution to critical theory. In attempting to expose the motives inherent in symbolism, logology shares with ideology critique the goal of raising consciousness. However, logology is not historicist, as ideology critique is. Symbol-driven motives are transhistorical. Nor does logology belong unambiguously to the Enlightenment project of human liberation. Understanding our symbol-driven motives can result in a measure of control over them, but we cannot be "freed" from language and its motives in the sense that we can cease to find a particular ideology appealing. Dysfunctional ideologies gradually retreat into the past; the motives of language are "eternally" recurrent, with us for as long as our species and its symbols survive.

Since it belongs to Burke's later philosophy, we will take up logology in Part Two. Only the first two phases in Burke view of language will concern us here.

Against Method: Language as Action

Burke advances many theses about modernity, but perhaps the most important one is this: That, in ceding ultimate, unqualified authority to scientific method, it could not understand language and therefore was fated to distort human being. Method's first move is toward a neutral, disengaged stance, supposedly by bracketing all preconceptions and all convictions about "oughts," "shoulds," and "musts." In understanding, say, the age of the earth, such a procedure was powerfully liberating. It helped us to discard the traditional dogma of a four-thousand-year-old creation and open our minds to the far more fertile paradigm of billions of years of geological and evolutionary change. For understanding language, however, the first move is exactly the wrong move. For language is not neutral or disengaged but rather heavily and irreducibly invested in the three moral modals. Method cannot cope with language. Its inability to cope is self-evident in its perennial frustration with it. "Let's purify language," method proposes over and over again, or substitute an artificial language for it. Which means: Let's dominate language as we attempt to dominate everything else, make it over in the image of method itself. And whatever remains strange or Other, let's ignore or push out toward the margins, toward some ghetto or reservation of the mind.

Method's second move is to objectify or decontextualize: Isolate. Abstract. Analyze. Again, method can justify itself by pointing to enormous gains in knowledge, everything from the structure of the atom to the structure of DNA. Even language seems to yield to the analytical gaze: Phonology, morphology, syntax, semantics, semiotics—all sciences of language, working with structures made of structures made of structures, which combine in law-like ways, in ways no different in principle, it seems, from how matter, organic or inorganic, organizes itself. And yet, the "higher" we go in the language hierarchy, the less well the structural metaphor works. We have yet to account for the syntax of any natural language, never mind the problem of meaning. The suspicion that there must be something wrong with the metaphor contends with the usual promise, often kept in the past and thus hardly lacking in credibility: Language is only a very complex problem. In time we will understand it using the same Cartesian methods applicable to all natural phenomena.

But the problem with the second move is much the same as it was with the first; just by making it we move away from, not toward, language. To "de-moralize" language, to empty it of prejudgments, is to miss language. Likewise, to take language in itself, isolated from the community that uses it, abstracted from the contexts of utterance or inscription, is to miss language. The problem is not insufficient knowledge; our knowledge is always insufficient. The problem, rather, is that all that method reveals about language only extends a misunderstanding of it. Abstracted from its living context, language is no longer language.

Of all the philosophers to argue against method as an approach to language, Wittgenstein probably comes to mind first. He tried method as the logical positivism of the *Tractatus*, found it wanting, and turned eventually to the contextual study of language as language games. More radically than Wittgenstein, Heidegger also rejected method; language for him is the dwelling place of Being ("Letter" 193)—not, therefore, something that method's forgetfulness of Being can even begin to approach with understanding.

Burke's rejection of method as an approach to language is even more contextualist than Wittgenstein's and as radical in its implications as Heidegger's. But his argument differs crucially from both.

In the first place, Burke does not condemn or dismiss science wholesale. Science fills an important cultural need, which it also helped to create. Modernity can be characterized as the struggle to cope with an increasingly diverse and decentered society. Such a society necessarily becomes more and more muddled about how to interpret itself, less and less certain about and sensitive to the subtler dimensions of meaning so dependent on *sensus communis*, such as connotation, tonality, and gesture. In modern cultures language in the fuller sense of communication—much more than compiling and transmitting information, which has become immeasurably more efficient—increasingly fails us. Terminologies restricted to groups of adepts displace it. Prestige accrues to a language that tries to be as neutral, as purely denotative, as possible.

One gains nothing, except perhaps a venting of professional jealousy, by attacking science for responding so well to the cultural requirements of modernity. The major reason Burke moved from art to a philosophy of art was to seize the advantages of a highly self-conscious conceptual use of language. *Pace* Heidegger, the problem with Philosophy and science is not conceptual language *per se*. The problem rather is what Burke, following Thorstein Veblen, calls a "trained incapacity" (*PC* 7). The very success of science in perfecting a methodology of suspended judgment—paradoxically, "a *neutral* vocabulary in the interests of more effective *action*"—has made science blind or hostile to language, not least its own language. For

> speech . . . is not neutral. Far from aiming at suspended judgment, the spontaneous speech of a people is loaded with judgments. It is intensely moral . . . a system of attitudes, of implicit exhortations. To call [someone] a friend or an enemy is *per se* to suggest a program of action. (*PC*176–77)

Nor is it only in "spontaneous speech"—everyday human converse—that we find a language "loaded with judgments." Science itself is intensely moral, passionately committed to its methods, hardly neutral about what constitutes good science or what attitudes a good scientist ought to have. To call someone a bad scientist is *per se* to suggest a program of action. No matter how much stock we have in systematic skepticism, no matter how successful it is in guiding action, people "do not communicate by a neutral vocabulary. In the profoundest human sense, one communicates by a *weighted* vocabulary in which the weightings are shared by [one's] group as a whole" (*PC* 162, Burke's emphasis).

In rejecting method's aspiration for a neutral language—equivalent to the "semantic ideal" we touched on previously (pp. 61–62), which

Burke considers not just mistaken but fraudulent—he claims language as and for rhetoric. Burke leaves no doubt about his intention: His case for "poetic meaning" (the opposite of method's semantic ideal) "may be taken as a rhetorical defense of rhetoric" (*PLF* 138).

Why does he claim language for rhetoric? A major reason is that the rhetorical tradition has always stressed *committed* discourse, the use of language to achieve definite aims, and Burke's opposition to method is in part based on its systematic exclusion of the concept of purpose. "Scientific method categorically makes the discovery of purpose impossible. The scientist was saying in effect: 'Let's see what we can discover about experience by programmatically eliminating the concept of purpose, and even considering the phenomena of purpose in terms of mechanism.'" Burke goes on to point out that "such romantic philosophers as Fichte and Schelling"—and also Hegel, with his "ambitious attempt to dissolve the ethical-logical dichotomy," and Schopenhauer, with his philosophy of will—reasserted "the priority of the ethical or teleological" (*PC* 171). But these efforts are Philosophical efforts, burdened with a heavy metaphysical freight that no one sees any profit in floating down the river again.

Burke's point is that we don't need metaphysics, some grand theory "that human beings [are] somehow in partnership with a cosmic Purpose" (*PC* 171), to discover purpose. All we need is language. "A world without metaphor"—without language—"would be a world without purpose." That is, our verbalized orientations are formed in part through "analogical extensions" (*PC* 194); were it not for the "carry over" of metaphor, the capacity to talk about a present situation as being "the same"—that is, similar—to past ones, we could conceive no purpose at all or reasons for responding to a situation in one way rather than another. Concepts of purpose—or, for that matter, concepts of anything, all of which depend on analogical extensions—would not exist.

Furthermore, if we agree with Burke that language is "loaded with judgments," that it is "intensely moral," "a system of attitudes, of implicit exhortations"—if we hold that it is rhetoric, not a neutral, transparent epistemological instrument—then we must also agree that it is always action, and purpose is implicit in action. Ethics is also implicit in language as action, because choice is implicit in action.

This last implication is the most important. If we take language as always a rhetorical act, there can be no logical/ethical dichotomy that has to be tolerated, overcome, or dissolved. The dichotomy creates a notorious pseudoproblem: how to bring fact and value back together again. But fact and value are never sundered. They are together in language, in a *logos* that is always already ethical. At its humblest, the togetherness of fact and value is self-evident in the pragmatics of everyday communication: When people say to us, "These are the facts," they mean, "You should think this way" or "Do this," choose one course of action with its associated values rather than another. At its grandest, fact and value come together in universe-building, in our ideologies, orientations, or horizons of meaning. Science claims a value-neutral, or ethics-free, position. Burke denies all such claims to neutrality. "All universe-building is ethical" (*PC* 250). That the universe-building of science is especially so should be clear not only because it has definite ideas about what good science ought to be but also because, allied with technology, it continues to revolutionize our notions of what is valuable and the purposes we ought to entertain.

Burke castigates method for "foster[ing] . . . the notion that one may comprehensively discuss human and social events in a nonmoral vocabulary" and for holding "that perception itself is a nonmoral act" (*PLF* 164). That is, method's truncated understanding of language distorts human being and prevents recognition that its unintended caricature is a caricature. To "de-moralize" language is, in the end, to distort human being. The semantic ideal cheats us of our own being as creatures that *perceive* the world rhetorically, not as a set of objects to observe but as situations for action, as the desirable and the undesirable, the good and the bad. As Burke says, "What the semanticist would put out, [s/]he never let's in" (*PLF* 153), and chief among the exclusions is ethics.

For his part, Burke leaves no doubt about the centrality of ethics in his philosophy:

> Action is fundamentally ethical, since it involves preferences. Poetry is ethical. Occupation and preoccupation are ethical. The ethical shapes our selection of means. It shapes our structures of orientation, while these in turn shape the perceptions of the individuals born within the orientation. Hence it radically effects our cooperative processes. The ethical is thus linked with the communicative (particularly when we consider communication in its broadest sense, not merely as the purveying of information, but also as the sharing of sympathies and purposes, the doing of acts in common). (*PC* 250)

Obviously, ethics for Burke is hardly one of so many divisions of philosophy, carved up like meat in a grocery store and arrayed without distinction, like the course offerings of a philosophy department. Nor is it primarily an abstract subject for academic debate. Rather human *praxis*, all human *praxis*, including academic debates about ethics, is ethical. Should we be doing what we are doing? What should we want? What is the good life? What means are good means for pursuing the good life? These are the vital questions, the practical, ethical, moral questions. If we push them out of mind or cede them to some group of alleged experts—as if we can avoid such questions or, as thinking beings engaged with the world, allow someone else to answer them for us—we have missed, in Burke's estimation, much of what turning to language means. For language "creates" being, including moral being, which is to say, human being.

Burke ties ethics to language even more tightly in his later philosophy, especially in his lengthy meditations on "the negative," which we will discuss in Part Two.

Before we shift our attention to the social turn, I would make a claim for Burke's linking of the linguistic turn to ethics which he was obviously in no position to make: that for the most part postmodernism misses the ethical implications of the linguistic turn as well. Modernism pushes ethics to the margins by attempting to bracket all prejudgments, by making methodical its prejudice against prejudice. At its objectivist extreme, it construes attitudes and moral judgments as "merely subjective," claiming that nothing "out there"—that is, nothing real as positivists understand real—corresponds with an attitude or a moral judgment. In contrast, postmodernism tends not so much to exclude ethics as to make it impossible or illusory or contemptible.

In the last chapter I showed how Burke deconstructs the Cartesian subject while reconstructing the individual outside of individualism as a moral agent capable of partial acts. We are now prepared to understand how important that reconstruction is. For if we follow postmodernism in denying "the wholeness, uniqueness, intentionality, and generative power of individual human beings" (Oravec 176)—if we allow agents, in Heideggerian fashion, to disappear entirely into the "impersonal It" of Language (or culture, or society, or class, or race, or gender, etc.)— then ethics becomes impossible. If we hold that some "It" is speaking or doing when some person speaks or acts, then no choice exists and moral judgment is pointless.

In practice, postmodernists do usually recognize what nearly everyone recognizes—that morality cannot be made to disappear. But moral judgments are typically not taken seriously as claims. Rather they are "read" (i.e., explained away), as only the way some culture speaks or spoke. Instead of taking a moral claim seriously as a claim, Rorty (for example) encourages us to ask, What sort of culture would entertain such a moral judgment? (47–48).

There is much that is right about the question taken in itself. Ethics cannot exist without language. Everything dependent on language is also situated in culture. The question is therefore indispensable to interpretation.

But the spirit of the asking is crucial. When motivated by an aggressive reductionism, it results in dismissing moral claims as illusory ("merely" ideology) or contemptible (e.g., Nietzsche's morality of resentment). When the question is not a prelude to reductionism, it nevertheless tends to insulate, protecting us from the shock of the Other's claim. The tendency is to foreclose on dialogue. Which is to say: postmodernism, in distancing itself from moral claims, reveals its kinship with the modernism it hopes to escape. Both want to move "beyond good and evil," modernism by methodological neutrality, postmodernism by depriving moral claims of force.

Ethics is in far deeper trouble in the context of postmodernism that it was in modernism. The latter at least took morality seriously enough to construct a highly ethical methodology around the self-deceiving elimination of prejudgment. In modernism, ethics always "comes back" as the return of the suppressed. Postmodernism is acutely aware of the impossibility of setting prejudgment aside. But in postmodernism, ethics can be too easily written off. The accusation Burke levels against modernism applies, *mutatis mutandis*, to postmodernism as well. Neither understands that language is irreducibly moral. Consequently, neither understands that human being is irreducibly moral being. Both, therefore, deprive us of even the potential of self-understanding.

Against Method: Situation and the Social Turn

In this section we turn to method's abstract and analyze imperatives. The structuralist approach to language arose in perfect obedience to them. Distinguish *langue* from *parole*, and make *langue* the object of scientific study. Language is thus detached from use, and therefore from context of situation—and because detached from situation, detached also from society and history. As we noted already in linking Burke's understanding of language with Herder's and Humboldt's, it is precisely this move that Burke refuses to make. Language removed from communication and community is not language. Because language for him is always language in use, Burke is not a structuralist. The existing association of later Burke, especially *A Grammar of Motives*, with structuralism (e.g., Lentricchia 68–69) will not withstand close scrutiny.

In *Counter-Statement* Burke was already thinking about language in situational or contextualist terms. But that which was largely implicit in *Counter-Statement* becomes explicit in *Permanence and Change*

> [People] have ever approached ultimate concerns from out the given vocabularies of their day, such vocabularies being not words alone, but the social textures, the local psychoses, the institutional structures, the purposes and practices that lie behind these words. Piaget, in studying the language of children, noted that frequently the meaning of their sentences was entirely lost unless his investigators recorded along with the sentences the circumstances under which they were said. In a more

complex way, the terms by which we communicate are always
thus *circumstantially* founded. (182–83, Burke's emphasis)

Consequently, Burke resists the idealistic temptation inherent in textuality (and therefore in literacy) that leads us to ignore the rich social and
cultural conditions of utterance and inscription to attend to words only.
"We cannot compare mere verbalizations—we must also correlate the
situation behind them" (183).

There are two common views of situation with which Burke's must
not be confused. The older, modernist view is exemplified well in *The
German Ideology*. In this understanding, "social textures, institutional
structures," and so forth, ultimately grounded in modes of production—
that is, the substructure—determine verbalization. First in *Auscultation,
Creation, and Revision* and then in many places thereafter, Burke rejects
this view, now commonly stigmatized by Marxist philosophers themselves as "vulgar Marxism." Any objectivist or deterministic view of situation, however—and modernist science has produced a legion of them—is
vulnerable to Burke's critique. First, there is no such thing as an "objective situation." Situations exist only as constructions, as interpretations.
Second, these constructs based on orientations are hardly fatalistic. Ideologies are too fraught with conflict and contradiction to permit reliable
prediction of behavior. Third, and finally, the relation between material
conditions and discourse is genuinely interactive, dialectical, not caus-
ative. Discourse *responds* to situations as the speaker or writer interprets
them. Situations also "respond" to discourse, in the sense that discourse
constructs, deconstructs, and reconstructs them.

Consistent with his modest view of agenthood and with his stress on
ethical choice, Burke rejects all deterministic interpretations of situation.
But his view is also at odds with a more recent understanding of situation
gaining currency among postmodern theorists. Semiological in origin
and nurtured by hermeneutical philosophy, this view tends to *reduce* situation to interpretation. The phrase Richard Harvey Brown chose as a title
for one of his books encapsulates this approach well: "society as text."

In one way, Burke would have no problem with the notion of taking
society as a text rather than or in addition to a con-text. Since we have
no direct, unmediated access to social textures and institutional structures, they must be "read" quite as much as anything else that we try to
understand. Used as Brown uses it, to undercut the positivism still dominant in much Anglo-American sociology, Burke would salute the society as text analogy.

However, in another way, he would find it problematical. Uphold-
ing the primacy of interpretation has within it, as Habermas's critique of
Gadamer reveals, a drift toward metaphysical idealism. Society as "read"
can too easily slide into society as "nothing but readings." Aware of the

danger and wishing to defend his own concentration on the symbolic in symbolic action, Burke insists that

> [t]here is a basic difference between metaphysical idealism and my concern with "the word." To say that you can't talk about anything except by exemplifying the rules of talk is not identical with saying that our world is "nothing but" the things we say about it. On the contrary, alas! There's many a time when what we call a "food" should have been called a "poison." And if our ancestors had hit upon too many of such misnomers, we'd not be here now. (*PLF* xvi)

We decree what something is by giving it a name, but the something named need hardly conform to our decree. Besides outright error—misnomer—there is also the obvious fact that no reading of anything so complex as society can be adequate or complete. The charting function of language never yields more than "takes" on reality, an approximation from a certain point of view.

In short, Burke's understanding of what Malinowsky called "context of situation" attempts to avoid two reductionisms, both metaphysical: on the one hand, materialistic fatalism; on the other, idealistic subjectivism. He denies the first by holding that there is no situation apart from interpretations; he denies the second by appealing to experience, which is often negative—our assertions and actions in the world are "refuted" by the world, which "resists" our will to power, our decrees of reality, in various ways. For Burke the world is much more than what we say about it. There is always much more "outside" the text than there is "in" it.

From the standpoint of the conversation after Philosophy, what matters most is Burke's steering away from linguistic reductionism. The current temptation is to drain everything into the language tank, and to celebrate the power of language, confronted by no inconvenient Other, to make any world we desire through the alleged "free play" of symbols. Jameson is right to see Language as the fetish of postPhilosophy, and right in perceiving that Burke does not succumb to it (70). As we can only see a foreground against a background, a text can only be seen against a context. If we say that everything is a text, we will soon be confronted with what Burke calls the paradox of purity (*GM* 35–38), the condition in which an identity completely absorbs otherness and therefore dissolves the contrasts by which it defines itself, filling everything and thereby becoming nothing at all. We must have "not language" (even though our only access to it is through language) to have language.

Burke's linguistic turn in *Permanence and Change* leads to the full-blown social turn of *Attitudes Toward History*. Had he moved in the structural direction, toward Language, rather than to communicative acts and thus to community, his social turn might never have happened. Had he not distinguished utterances and texts from situations and contexts, linguistic idealism might have displaced or co-opted the social turn. The significant insights are in *Permanence and Change*. But in *Attitudes Toward History* society assumes a central place in his philosophy it did not have before, and remains central thereafter.

Writing as if he were aware of postmodern linguistic idealism, Burke points out that

> whatever "free play" there may be in esthetic enterprise, it is held down by the gravitational pull of historical necessities; the poetic forms [e.g., epic, tragedy, comedy] are symbolic structures designed to equip us for confronting given historical or personal situations. (57)

As a philosopher who believes that human beings are capable of limited innovation, Burke affirms the notion of "free play" so characteristic of recent antirealist philosophies. Indeed, in *Permanence and Change*, especially in his comments on what he calls "perspective by incongruity," or "organized bad taste" (111–24), he locates whatever freedom human beings have in the capacity to use the "wrong"—that is, different—names for long-established ways of characterizing things. We can and do decree realities different from our inheritance—and clearly a new way of characterizing events and situations, if it gains sufficient currency, can alter human behavior on a large scale.

If it gains sufficient currency. "Free play"—Burke puts it in quotes to emphasize this point—is actually only free within a very finite range. The greatest of historical necessities is rhetorical: Our "free play" must sooner or later win adherents if any new way of naming is to have consequences. Should an idea gain currency, it still must be adjusted to prevailing conditions and institutions and implemented in some organized way, all collective matters that Burke handles under the rubric, "bureaucratization of the imaginative" (225–29).

In his reading of *Attitudes Toward History*, Lentricchia takes Burke's case for the primacy of the social and collective as a "'fall' into unfreedom" (59). He thereby misses Burke's point entirely. His point is that "'Freedom' is a truncated concept, an unintended *caricature* of human relations. . . . [T]he liberal who rates social organisms by its test alone is vowed to disillusionment. He will find that his ideals are too good for this world" (56). Postmodern linguistic idealism, especially in the United States, has yet to understand fully the emptiness of language as free play. The exercise of freedom only has body and force in collective textures, from which, in any case, it cannot escape. European thought grasps this point better than we do—for example, in Heidegger's insistence that be-ing-in-the-world (*Dasein*) is always being-with-others (*Mitdasein*). The danger here is passive acquiescence in the face of "the marathon charac-ter of historical repression," as Lentricchia put it (79). But the danger of an uncritical freedom is just as great—cynical disillusionment, a disen-gaging from social responsibilities in favor of aesthetic utopias of "free play" that need never struggle to make negotiable "ideals too good for this world."

Living in a country most captivated by the ideology of bourgeois individualism and therefore most blind to and aggressively impatient with collective restraints—as Burke points out, Dewey-style liberals talk much about individual rights while often passing over in silence its nec-essary counterpart, collective obligations (56)—Burke strives in almost every page of *Attitudes Toward History* to reveal the unacknowledged presence of the social, the historical, the traditional in everything we do and say. Implicitly his "free act" is subversive in the root sense of the word, as he plows up the fallow field of bourgeois dissociations—the individual versus society, art versus practical affairs, "pure" science ver-sus social applications, the private versus the public, and so forth. All such distinctions get turned under, as Burke shows how each member of these pairs is entangled in the other. Clearly he hopes to advance the cause of socialism by renaming our existence in more social terms.

As his earlier turn to philosophy was in *Permanence and Change*, so also is his social turn in *Attitudes Toward History*—quite deliberately chosen and defended. For example, in Part Three, "Analysis of Symbolic Structure," Burke describes the symbol in terms akin to Ricoeur's "sur-plus of meaning" (*Interpretation Theory* 45–46). As a synthesis of many ingredients, both conscious and unconscious, "summing up a myriad of social and personal factors at once," symbolic analysis "necessarily ra-diates in all directions at once" (199). How, then, should critics decide what to attend to?

> Facing a myriad [of] possible distinctions, we should focus on those that we consider important for social reasons. Roughly, in the present state of the world we should group these about the "revolutionary" emphasis, involved in the treatment of art with primary reference to symbols of authority, their ac-ceptance and rejection. (200)

Always wary of reductionisms, Burke is here advocating "*primary* refer-ence" to social concerns. Not only is art itself irreducibly social, but criti-cism ought to be as well—*consciously* concerned with ideology and power, both in what is criticized and in the critic doing the criticism.

Burke's emphasis on the collective has itself historical or social justification—"in the present state of the world" this emphasis is appropriate. Given a different situation, perhaps we must make different choices. The social turn can hardly be carried any further than to derive the turn itself from social considerations. And if it leaves us wondering what to do with the social turn itself now that the revolutionary emphasis seems far less apropos, so much the better as Burke sees things. Acts cannot be detached from situations. It was a concern for situation that led Burke to the social turn in the first place.

Instead of Epistemology: Rhetorical Pragmaticism

> How many people today are rotting in either useless toil or in dismal worklessness because of certain technological successes? We do not here aim to discredit the accomplishments of science, which are mainly converted into menaces by the inadequacies of present political institutions. We desire simply to indicate that *the region where testing is of vital importance*, where the tests of success are in turn to be tested, is the region . . . of cultural, moral, political emphases, of ambition, concepts of the good life, notions of ultimate human purpose.
>
> —Kenneth Burke, *Permanence and Change*

Early in this chapter, I said that Burke's rhetorical turn was more significant than either of the other two turns in understanding his early thought. As we approach the end of this chapter, we might try to see just how much of Burke's early philosophy converges in rhetoric.

It was Burke's equating of language with rhetoric that led him to reject modernism's project to neutralize, purify, or replace natural language. It was his understanding of language as rhetoric that allowed him to see so clearly the centrality of ethics in all human affairs, and therefore to call into fundamental question the adequacy of any nonethical vocabulary or beyond-the-ethical stance for understanding human being and human activity. Even Burke's emphasis on language as a response to situations has a rhetorical origin. Rhetoric takes discourse as always situated, and has since the Sophists and Plato made *kairos* (timeliness and proportion, or fitness) a central concept in rhetorical theory (Kinneavy 80). We can derive both Burke's linguistic and social turns from the rhetorical turn, whose tradition reaches back twenty-five hundred years and which has always seen language as the distinctly human power of civil action and human being as meaningful only in social existence.

Looking back to the last chapter, we can now more fully appreciate that rhetoric is the common denominator of his positions on the three postPhilosophical issues discussed there. The disengaged Cartesian subject is exactly what the rhetor is not—Burke deconstructs the subject. But he is unwilling to part with the individual as moral agent because that would mean parting with the rhetor. If language amounts to strategies for encompassing situations, there must be a strategist.

Rhetoric has always recognized the importance of *logos* in the sense of the appeal to reason. Burke defends a modest but vital reason against modernist and what would become postmodernist irrationalism. But reason and logic are not ultimate for Burke. Both belong to persuasive strategies, both are enmeshed inextricably in power and desire. Logic is subordinate to rhetoric because persuasion forms and transforms orientations, whereas reason and logic have mainly to do with justifying and refining existing ones.

Finally, Burke undermines the literal/figurative distinction because its de-struction removes a major barrier to full recognition of language as rhetoric. Language is not rhetoric if there is some kind of privileged, literal language that can make good the traditional claim to be Philosophy rather than rhetoric.

If we return to our setting out point, to *Counter-Statement*, where Burke advocates the virtues of a disintegrating art, whose skeptical task amounts to making uncertainties out of certainties, we should not be surprised to find in the same volume a summarizing essay called "Lexicon Rhetoricae" and in another the following defense of rhetoric:

> The reader of modern prose is ever on guard against "rhetoric," yet the word . . . refers but to "the use of language in such a way as to produce a desired impression upon the hearer or reader." . . . [T]hus the resistance to rhetoric *qua* rhetoric must be due to a faulty diagnosis. (210)

Burke goes on to explain that in rejecting the rhetorical conventions of some past age, people sometimes sloganize their rejection as "no rhetoric," thereby deceiving themselves about the rhetorical nature of all discourse, including their own. But the larger point I wish to make again is that skepticism and rhetoric go together: "Rhetoric belongs to a syndrome of skeptical assumptions." Furthermore, rhetoric must return as a central theme in postPhilosophy not just because all discourse is topical but, more importantly, because rhetoric is what we are left with after the end of the quest for Philosophical foundations and certainties. Our guiding axiom must then become "the principle of insufficient reason," which, as Blumenberg says, is "the axiom of all rhetoric" (435, 447).

My summarizing term for Burke's early philosophy is *rhetorical pragmatism*. I shall attempt to explain and justify "pragmatism" in a moment. But first let's consider the significance of what Burke does with rhetoric in the context of more recent philosophical efforts, and then the limitations of rhetoric as an approach to his philosophy as a whole.

The contemporary revival of rhetoric is broadly based, involving virtually all the humanities and social sciences. Part of this movement are philosophical defenses of rhetoric, which have generally pursued one of two overlapping strategies. On the one hand, historians have taken rhetoric's part in its long-standing conflict with Philosophy. Brian Vickers's *In Defence of Rhetoric* is a good example. On the other hand, theorists, not content with only refuting Philosophical charges against rhetoric, have gone on to make cases for rhetoric *as philosophy*, thus mounting in one way or another a frontal attack on the traditional Philosophy/rhetoric distinction. Ernesto Grassi's *Rhetoric as Philosophy* is a good example of this second strategy.

To the extent that negative attitudes toward rhetoric traceable to Philosophy still survive, the first strategy has value, but decreasing relevance as Philosophy itself loses adherents. Because it answers the question, What does rhetoric offer as an alternative to Philosophy? the second strategy has greater potential. In Grassi's case, for instance, we have a yoking together of Heidegger's postPhilosophy with the Latin rhetorical heritage, which from Cicero on has always found in rhetoric something more than a *techne*, an art of persuasion. Grassi's synthesis is powerful and stimulating, one of the few treatments of rhetoric that can match Burke's *A Rhetoric of Motives* for scope and profundity (see McPhail).

But there is a step beyond the second strategy: to create a contemporary philosophy through-and-through rhetorical. Instead of making a case for rhetoric as philosophy, we can make a philosophy out of rhetoric, from concepts like *kairos* and axioms such as the principle of insufficient reason. Burke can help us envision this step because he had already taken it by the end of the 1930s. He defends rhetoric from Philosophy, but his early thought is not a defense of rhetoric in Vickers's sense; likewise, he makes his own case for rhetoric as philosophy, but his early work is not limited to such an argument. Rather, Burke creates a *rhetorical philosophy*, a body of thought that is more than rhetoric while being, as I tried to show above, in all significant respects derivable from rhetoric.

What Burke does with rhetoric is not necessarily more significant than what Grassi does. Nor is Burke's rhetorical philosophy definitive. The point is that once we take rhetoric as philosophy, much remains to be done, and Burke's early philosophy is one way of moving the argument forward. As usual, he is "out there" ahead of us, but no doubt we will have to do something different to create a rhetorical philosophy suited to intellectual conditions in many respects different from the 1930s.

We will now consider the limitations of a rhetorical approach to Burke's philosophy as a whole. I think it helps in revealing the coherence of Burke's thought to place his turns to language and society in the context of a rhetorical philosophy. But I also think it would be reductive to see the turns only in this context. In the later philosophy his interest in language develops well beyond the needs of rhetorical philosophy, to become a focus of interest in itself. He also develops contemporary versions of the three other ancient verbal arts—dialectic, hermeneutic, poetic—to the point where they at least rival rhetoric in his work. However useful rhetorical pragmatism may be as a summarizing term for Burke's early philosophy, it would have to be stretched far beyond the breaking point to accommodate the later.

Much the same reservation applies to the social turn as construed solely in rhetorical terms. Already in *Attitudes Toward History* Burke's inquiries into social dynamics quite exceed the needs of discourse as symbolic action, as rhetoric. In the later philosophy Burke becomes interested in social organization *per se*, especially in the context of a *praxis* dedicated to "purifying war"—that is, achieving "peace" by limiting conflict to verbal eristics—and to ecology, developing sufficient control over our symbol-driven ambitions so that our separation from nature and our will to power over nature does not destroy the biosphere on which our own existence is dependent. However much rhetoric can contribute to making these concerns articulate and prominent in the collective awareness, they are clearly beyond its ken. Rhetoric is necessary, but not sufficient. In short, then: Burke's philosophy is always rhetorical and aware of itself as rhetoric; but it is also more than rhetoric.

Pragmatism and Knowledge as Action

I distinguish three main senses in which the term "pragmatic" can be applied to Burke's philosophy:

1. His primary concern is with praxis in the broad sense of this concept, which includes, but is not limited to, patently political activity. "Pragmatic" in this sense is equivalent to "practical": Burke wants his philosophy to be useful, applicable in the world for constructive change.

2. "Pragmatic" also applies in the meaning emphasized in this chapter: the "pragmatics of natural language," the "politics, rhetoric, and poetics of language in use." Burke's linguistic pragmatism links him with such philosophers as Wittgenstein, Heidegger, Foucault, Habermas, Ricoeur, Blumenberg, and MacIntyre, all of whom share a pragmatic approach to language (McCarthy 6). For Burke, however, pragmatics is not just an approach to language. Language only exists contextually. To abstract language from situation, to analyze language in itself, is to miss language, which eludes method's ways of understanding and control. Burke's interest is in the motives for discourse and, especially in his later

philosophy, the motives inherent in symbol-using. "Pragmatic" in this second meaning, then, is equivalent to "motivational."

3. "Pragmatic" also designates a certain stance in assessing propositions or entire philosophies. Traditionally, assessment has amounted to a focus on formal validity, correspondence with reality, or both—in other words, with logic, questions of knowledge, and truth. In contrast, pragmatists focus on assessment in the sense of outcomes in the world. That is, if we accept a proposition as provisionally true and act based on this belief, what happens? Do we get the results expected or desired, or not? Hence, the pragmatic test is the test of "what works"—or as James put it, with deliberate provocation, a philosophy's "cash value" (311). If a philosophy cannot be lived, if it cannot be applied and tested in some way, then a pragmatist would consider it inconsequential, not worthy of attention. Since pragmatists either reject the epistemological theory of truth as correspondence or ignore it in favor of the test of what works, pragmatism is equivalent to an anti- or non-epistemological position.

It is this third meaning of pragmatism that will concern us here as I attempt to explain what I mean by calling Burke's early philosophy "rhetorical pragmatism." Epistemology assumes the existence of things and events apart from consciousness or language. Invoking Santayana's "animal faith" in the reality of a world "out there," Burke makes the same assumption. But the theory of truth as correspondence also requires positivistic faith in an unproblematical ability to compare propositions with nonlinguistic phenomena, the information supplied about the world external to mind via the senses. It is this faith that Burke cannot share. As we have seen, Burke holds that perception itself is conditioned by language and by what language makes possible, by our orientations, interests, and ethical beliefs and commitments. The important word here is "conditioned," *not* "determined." We do not encounter the world in a blankness of expectation. Rather we approach it with marked, if mostly nonconscious, anticipation of what we will see based on past experience. Often we see only what we are predisposed to see—or if we detect something anomalous, we block it out. But we can because we sometimes do detect nonfit between what we say about phenomena and our total experience with it. Were this not the case—that is, if expectations determined perception—the negativity of experience would be impossible, and provisional truth would be meaningless.

Burke is no idealist. There is much more to existence than mind. Nor, in Burke's view, can phenomena be reduced to linguistic constructions. Language is not all there is. Furthermore, although very critical of positivistic reductionism, Burke does not join in the current fashion of rejecting positivism completely.

For Burke many propositions—indeed, many subject matters—*ought* to be approached positivistically. In his later philosophy, the key distinction is between nonsymbolic motion—nature minus human being—and symbolic action ("[Nonsymbolic] Motion" passim). In his early philosophy, the roughly corresponding distinction is between the *drama* of human affairs and the *scene* of this drama, the former belonging to social science, the latter to the physical sciences. According to Burke, the physical sciences are and ought to be "a calculus of events," for which a positivistic attitude is appropriate (*PLF* 114–16). As the relative success of the physical sciences in predicting and controlling events suggests, here we can test—though hardly unproblematically—what we say (our theories) against carefully controlled experimentation and observation. But "the error of the social sciences has usually resided in the attempt to appropriate the scenic calculus for a charting of the act" (*PLF* 114). Social science, in other words, usually applies a calculus of events to a subject matter that should be approached as a calculus of *acts*. It treats people, who have motives and purposes, as if they were things, which can but move and be moved. Systematic distortion of its subject matter is the inevitable result, together with a deeply antisocial and sometimes sinister intent to manage and control people rather than interact with them. Burke proposes to substitute "dramatic criticism" for the scenic calculus appropriated by the social sciences, observing wryly that there is "more to be learned [about the human drama] from a study of tropes than from a study of tropisms" (*PLF* 114).

Burke's philosophy opposes method primarily in its claim to unlimited competence—insofar, that is, as it proposes to study human being via the "planned incongruity" of applying "an idiom of mechanistic determinism" to something that cannot be reduced to lifeless matter (*PLF* 115). Everything under the title "against method" in this chapter should be read in the light of his opposition to the elimination of action and all its associated notions from the human sciences. His opposition to epistemology may be traced to the same source. Epistemology divorces knowledge from the act. As method, simply by making the moves it makes, fails to understand language, and therefore human being, so epistemology, in attempting a mechanical matching of words and things, misses the nature of propositions: They are assertions, which is to say, actions. A theory of knowledge must deal with propositions as actions-in-the world, and therefore be dramatic, not a calculus of events but a calculus of acts.

Knowledge begins with "poetry." That is, it begins with the "creative, assertive, synthetic act" (*PC* 257) that does, as Rorty and others claim, make a world. Languageless animals "have" an environment, but they do not make worlds. Human beings typically do. The "creative, assertive, synthetic act" is equivalent to the "rhetorical" in rhetorical pragmatism. Rhetoric is the means by which worlds are made.

But reality is always more than our acts can synthesize. We know this because reality resists our will to power. Rather like a tragic protagonist, whose actions set into motion consequences beyond anticipation, so our assertions in the world encounter what Burke calls "recalcitrance" (PC 255). This resistance has many modalities, of course, but all amount to versions of the negativity of experience: the argument that fails to convince, the experiment whose results are at variance with other experiments, the "unsinkable" ocean liner that hits an iceberg in mid-ocean and sinks, the enlightened policy subverted by ignorance, jealousy, greed, and ingratitude, and so on and so forth. When learning occurs, we revise our interpretations, act anew, and again "organize" the resistance by which we can learn still more. The process is clearly dramatic.

It is also pragmatic. Truth is not correspondence or adequacy to the real, which experience keeps telling us we do not have anyway. Truth rather is "what works"—for now, at any rate, until some better creative act comes along, or until recalcitrance to our current assertions becomes too great to ignore.

Knowledge, Burke is saying, amounts to a perilous and uncertain adventure, never secure or securable. His dramatic theory, therefore, is anti-epistemological, since the aim of epistemology is to secure knowledge. Besides being anti-epistemological, it has other features worth noting here:

1. It can account for scientific knowledge, which is partly evolutionary (revisions within a paradigm) and partly revolutionary (the succeeding of one creative act by another), but never complete or secure.

2. It can reveal why the emphasis on making worlds is only half a dialectic. In making worlds we also "find" them—discover the inadequacy of our own interpretations. We make reality eloquent, enlist it as a partner in the dialogue of knowing.

3. It shows why truth must be preponderantly truth *par provision*—rhetoric, not Philosophy. (Pragmatism, like rhetoric, belongs to a syndrome of skeptical assumptions.)

4. It encourages us to assess truth in the broadest notion of what works—not merely the empirically verifiable, or even what "pays off" within a narrowly capitalist rationale, but the socially beneficial. What matters most are "cultural, moral, [and] political emphases . . . concepts of the good life" (PC 102), about which science and method can tell us nothing. Burke's is a *rhetorical*

pragmatism, a pragmatism of the social turn. The pragmatism of classical American philosophy is, from Burke's
point of view, too scientistic and too uncritical of bourgeois concepts of the individual and of freedom.

5. It opens a way that is neither modernist (caught up
in objective truth) nor postmodernist (given over to
whimsy and the abyss). In other words, rhetorical
pragmatism offers good reasons for a continuing
conversation that neither modernism not postmodernism can provide. There is work to be done, constructions and reconstructions, though the foundations
are as shaky as the ground in California.

Making and finding worlds.

4

Being Without Metaphysics

In order to think and infer it is necessary to assume beings.
Knowledge and becoming exclude one another.

—Friedrich Nietzsche, *Will to Power*

There cannot be a more vexed and confusing question in contemporary
philosophy than the question of Being. For the most part, professional academic philosophy does not even pose the question: It is anachronistic; it
is unanswerable; no answer to the question can possibly matter—all of
these are reasons I have heard for letting the question slide. But if the
question of Being is a question best left unasked, why has so much philosophy from Nietzsche to Derrida sought to destroy the category itself?
Why did Heidegger devote a long career to this one question? Why do a
significant minority of current philosophers—for example, Iris Murdoch,
Alasdair MacIntyre—consider the question vital to their own concerns?

While specific philosophies that engage the question are many, too
many to review here, the basic stances toward Being are these:

- Concern for Being is over; it belongs to the history of
  philosophy. The stance of indifference.

- Being has such a hold still on contemporary minds
  and is so politically reactionary that it must be
  deconstructed. The stance of suspicion or hostility.

- Being cannot be deconstructed; it is very much alive,
  an unavoidable question, at least in some areas of
  philosophical concern. The stance of openness to
  Being or resistance to nihilism.

Not surprisingly, we find a similar dissensus about Kenneth Burke and Being in the recent criticism. In every one of Burke's critical-philosophical books, he engages in some way the question of Being (or, an old synonym for Being, substance). Yet the vast majority of his critics say nothing about Burke and Being. Lentricchia takes the subject up but, because Burke's concern with Being threatens any Marxist reading of him, dismisses it as an "essentializing impulse" (59–60). Gunn defends Burke from Lentricchia's charge but in doing so misses what Lentricchia could not ignore—that Being does concern Burke. Gunn wants to dissociate Burke not only from "essentialism" (i.e., Platonism) but also from any serious engagement with Being at all (77)—presumably because Being threatens Gunn's pragmatist reading of Burke quite as much as it threatens Lentricchia's Marxist reading. Finally, Southwell advances a thesis unacceptable to both Lentricchia and Gunn: In Burke there is a minimalist version of what Southwell calls "the necessary metaphysics" (73–76). Southwell requires this of Burke as part of his attack on Derrida and de Man—on deconstruction generally—for denying "every possible 'being' of any kind" on the grounds that all being is "the illusion of 'presence'" (77).

It may seem that my interpretation so far ought to result in a position similar to either Lentricchia's or Gunn's. I have called attention to Burke's skepticism, hardly a stance that one normally associates with philosophies of Being. In the last chapter I proposed "rhetorical pragmatism" as a summarizing term for his early philosophy. "Rhetoric" and "pragmatism" both suggest a philosophy of becoming, the former because of its emphasis on adjustment to constantly altering situations, the latter in the restlessness of the "what works" test over any settled, abstract, and finalized Truth. Finally, I have argued and will continue to argue that Burke's thought is postPhilosophical. Since ontology is tied to both metaphysics and epistemology, it would seem wholly out of place in postPhilosophy.

As what I call "*praxis* Being," Burke's Being is quite foundationless, requiring no metaphysics and avoiding ontology in the traditional meaning of the word. We will see that Burke is able to affirm Being in a way that the Nietzschean tradition cannot. Though entangled in it beyond extrication, Being for Burke is not *reducible* to the will to power, the imposition of stability, order, and coherence on a fundamentally chaotic world. Nor is Being the illusion of presence, primarily because presence for Burke is not something that can be equated intelligibly with illusion. At the same time, while resisting the destruction of Being that is part of Nietzsche's legacy, Burke also avoids the crypto-religious and arcane struggles with it that afflicted late Heidegger. Being is for Burke a genuine mystery; but he is suspicious—deconstructive—of efforts to mystify it. It is clear from a passage in the later philosophy (*LASA* 454–55) that he takes Heidegger as one of the more ingenious mystifiers.

As I see things, then, Lentricchia, Gunn, and Southwell are all mistaken. Gunn is the furthest off course in denying Burke's concern with Being altogether. But Lentricchia is not much closer to understanding this important dimension in Burke's thought. Burke is no Platonist. But he is deeply concerned with essence in the sense mentioned in the last chapter—that is, the "decreeing of essence" in discourse, or symbolic action (*PLF* 4–6). Understood as Burke understands it, essence has nothing to do with essentialism.

Southwell is the closest of the three to grasping Burke's approach to Being. Burke agrees with Southwell that metaphysics is ineluctable (*GM* xxiii). Our orientations or horizons of meaning always imply a metaphysics. Being is a postulate of all thinking according to Nietzsche, of all language use according to Burke. In this sense, metaphysics and Being are necessary.

However, it is one thing to say that any claim to no metaphysics is self-deceiving, quite another to claim Truth for a metaphysics. Burke exposes the metaphysical implications of many kinds of thought, including his own. For example, to look ahead to the later philosophy: In *A Grammar* Burke confronts the metaphysical implications of his featuring of the term "act" in Dramatism. What would be the "ultimate act," the Act of acts? In Jewish-Christian-Islamic culture, obviously, it would be God's Act of Creation as depicted in Genesis. And so Burke calls Creation the "representative anecdote" of Dramatism, a story we can study to learn about the dialectical resources, embarrassments, and quandaries of a philosophy of action (*GM* 59–61). But he never says: God actually exists and actually made the world out of nothing or ordered it out of formless chaos. He does not say: Our acts are grounded in God's act, or we can act because God can act and we are made in God's image. In short, he never affirms a metaphysics. If he had, he would not be a skeptic. If he had, his thought would belong to Philosophy, not postPhilosophy.

Southwell's effort to extract a metaphysics out of Burke is unconvincing. Burke represents a doubly skeptical attitude toward metaphysics. On the one hand, he doubts that it can be overcome or simply put aside. We can change the subject, but it will keep coming back. On the other hand, he finds no grounds for affirming an assured grounding. As all *genuine* skeptics must do (deniers of Being and beings are sometimes called skeptics, but they are, of course, nihilists), he simply leaves the metaphysical question open. His affirmations, his constructions and reconstructions, are all, so to speak, suspended in mid-air or "grounded" in ways that are ultimately groundless themselves. In this sense he offers Being without metaphysics.

Above all, what we must not forget in trying to understand Burke on Being is that he takes everything significant that anyone says and writes as rhetoric, as strategies for encompassing situations. This means that all notions of Being are tools for coping with ourselves, with others, with life. Burke does not purport to reflect on Being-in-itself. What interests him is not Being as such, but the value of concepts of Being as part of an art of living. Consequently, I have divided this chapter into three strategies in which Being and beings figure in Burke's early philosophy.

Strategy I: Being as Enigma

At the very end of *Permanence and Change*, after 271 pages devoted to a critique of modernity, capitalism, imperialism, and idolatry of the machine, Burke advocates peaceful resistance through—by now we should expect it—rhetoric, "education, propaganda, or suasion." He specifically counsels us against violence, except to defend ourselves from the violence of those "who attack . . . [the] peaceful work . . . [of] propound[ing] . . . new meanings" (272). But since ideological change is often frustratingly slow, and peaceful means require respect for the opinions of others and continual adjustment of our discourse to sensibilities not our own, what we require most of all to endure in resistance is patience. But how do we cultivate this virtue?

The answer for Burke is Being. "We may find it wise on occasion," Burke suggests, "to adopt incongruous perspectives for the dwarfing of our impatience":

> We in cities rightly grow shrewd at appraising [hu]man-made institutions—but beyond these tiny concentration points of rhetoric and traffic, there lies the eternally unsolvable Enigma, the preposterous fact that both existence and nothingness are equally unthinkable . . . [A]lways the Eternal Enigma is there, right on the edges of our metropolitan bickerings, stretching outward to interstellar infinity and inward to the depths of the mind. And in this staggering disproportion between [the] [hu]man and no[t]-[hu]man, there is no place for purely human boasts of grandeur, or for forgetting that [people] build their cultures by huddling together, nervously loquacious, at the edge of an abyss. (272)

In this example of what Burke calls "perspective by incongruity" (*PC* 69), we are far away from Heidegger's Being and his notion of the human potential for "sheltering," for being "shepherds of being" ("Turning" 40–42). There is nothing in Burke's Enigma or the thought of benefit from "an occasional shiver of cold metaphysical dread" (272) that reminds us of what Derrida calls "the metaphorics of proximity" of Being characteristic of Heidegger ("Ends" 146).

The first point to note about Being as the Eternal Enigma is that it is of use *only occasionally*. It is not the single thought for an entire philosophical career. To make it so is to turn one's back on *praxis*, to rhetorical action in behalf of a better life. For Burke the point of philosophy is practical effort in the world, and Being as Enigma is needful only as a perspective that prevents loss of perspective, that helps us to cope with the frustrations of a recalcitrant world and the irritations of trying to appeal to the uncomprehending or to persons of ill will.

The second point to note is that Burke's glum consolation is not Philosophical. His skepticism could not be any more explicit or complete. Being is an impenetrable enigma; "existence and nothingness are equally unthinkable." Wisdom resides not in passing beyond the metaphysical question but in silence before it—or in confessing the total blankness of our ignorance. Few have expressed our human limitations more powerfully and memorably than Burke does here.

My third point is that Being as enigma is the overwhelmingly Other, dreadfully because dwarfingly more-than-human. Because Being somehow *is*, "out there" and "in here," always recallable from "the edges of our metropolitan bickerings," it wordlessly poses its unanswerable question about itself as a constant reminder of our radical finiteness. It performs, therefore, part of the God-function of theism—a forestalling of *hubris*—but Being is no more God in Burke than it is in Heidegger.

Finally, while existing independently of human projects, Being as Enigma has nothing of the initiative it has in late Heidegger. It does not act. It just moves according to its own dynamics. Save the unthinkable, it sends nothing in particular. So far as human activity is concerned, it hardly matters at all, just as the existence of volcanoes on a moon of Jupiter or black holes is quite irrelevant to a better life through social *praxis*. It comes into play only as a strategy for coping with a life dedicated to practical action, and therefore in need of that which Lear, no longer having a king's power to command and therefore resorting to persuasion for the first time in his life, prayed for—patience, a rhetorical virtue.

Strategy II: Being as the Answerable Other and the "Unanswerable Opponent"

In contrast to the first strategy, Being as the answerable other and the unanswerable opponent plays a key role in all *praxis* and responds in and to human activity in a way the impassive Otherness of the first strategy cannot. In explicating it, we will engage an important aim of Burke's *praxis*—advocacy of democratic socialism—in the context of an art that matters as much to Burke as rhetoric, dialectic. This section therefore anticipates the essays on *praxis* and dialectic-dialogics in Part Two.

Of the American pragmatists, Burke is friendliest to William James and George Herbert Mead. In an essay on the latter, Burke writes approvingly of the emphasis in *Mind, Self, and Society* on the role of language. "The individual's responses [as conditioned by his/her environment] are matured by such processes of complication and revision as arise from cooperative and communicative factors" (*PLF* 380). In other words, Burke finds in Mead an action-centered view of knowledge similar to his own, including recognition of the all-important dynamic of assertion-against-resistance, discussed in the last chapter as "recalcitrance."

Characteristically, Burke pushes Mead's thinking in a political direction. Assertion-against-resistance is dialectic, and Burke wants to tie dialectic to democracy in an "integral relationship":

> [D]ialectics deals with the converse, the conversational, while democracy is the ideal of expression in the market place, the dramatics of the forum. *The truth of the debate arises from the combat of the debaters*, which would transform the competitive into the cooperative. (*PLF* 380, my emphasis)

Civilized by the word, dialectic is the "morality of combat" we have previously found Burke praising in Nietzsche—"no despicable thing" (*PLF* 256) at all providing that the conversation is open to a genuine diversity of voices in a society whose dialectical forums are not subverted or co-opted in advance by a power elite.

Burke is sufficiently Marxist enough to appreciate what Habermas would later call "systematically distorted communication" (*Theory* 12). But, charitable as usual, he only notes that Mead's philosophy belongs to "the promissory mood that went with the happier days of progressive evolution" (*PLF* 381), prior to the Depression and the rise of Fascism. Put another way, he is acutely aware that the open conversation is always more of a utopian goal than a reality. Nevertheless, utopian goals are indispensable to an energetic *praxis*, and in another essay written about the same time as the one I have been citing from, he leaves no doubt where he stands: "Full opportunity for the enacting of the dialectical process *should be absolutely affirmed and indoctrinated*"; a paragraph later, he insists again that "the dialectical process *absolutely must* be unimpeded" (*PLF* 444, Burke's emphasis).

Absolutes are very rare in Burke. Almost always he has reservations about anything he endorses or discommends. But dialectic for him is an *unqualified good*. Why?

The reason is that dialectical processes and forums bring Being as the *answerable* Other into play. "I take democracy," Burke explains, "to

be a device for institutionalizing the dialectic process . . . in which the protagonist of a thesis has maximum opportunity to modify his[/her] thesis,
and so mature it, in the light of the antagonist's rejoinders" (*PLF* 444).
But it is not only human being that our assertions and projects organize
into the resisting other. Commenting on Mead's "metaphor of the conversation," Burke says:

> "The parry is an interpretation of the thrust," as one even
> "converses" with objects, cooperating with them to his[\her]
> benefit only insofar as [s/]he allows them to have their say,
> takes their role by telling him[/her]self what their modes of
> assertion are, and corrects his[/her] own assertions on the ba-
> sis of their claims. (*PLF* 380)

Gadamer holds that "a text can begin to speak" (*Hermeneutics* 57), that
what is "objectively" only an artifact of paper and ink can challenge our
horizons of meaning by asserting its own. Mead and Burke claim more.
The wordless things comprising most of Being can begin to speak—do
in fact speak through us if we are prepared to listen to their modes of
assertion. As Burke put it in a poem of this period, appropriately called
"Dialectician's Prayer," and dedicated to *Logos*, conceived as a wholly
human capacity to speak for the speechless:

> may we help Thine objects
> To say their say—
> Not suppressing by dictatorial lie,
> Nor giving false reports
> That misrepresent their saying.
> If the soil is carried off by flood,
> May we help the soil to say so.
>
> (*CP* 40)

The Dust Bowl of the thirties was "eloquent" about the farming
practices of the day. We had only to give it words and a hearing. Anything we can speak for belongs to Bakhtin's "architectonics of answerability" (Clark and Holquist 64–65). Being can begin to speak as the
answerable Other.

But it can also confront us, "refute" us, as the unanswerable opponent. Burke's unqualified support for democracy implies an equally unqualified rejection of totalitarianism:

> Dictatorships, in silencing the opposition, remove the inter-
> mediary between error and reality. Silence the *human* oppo-
> nent, and you are brought flat against the *unanswerable* oppo-
> nent, the nature of brute reality itself. In so far as your meanings

are incorrect, and you spawn them and maintain them by
organizational efficiency without the opportunity of correction, you are hurled without protection against the unanswerable opponent, the opponent that, not speaking, cannot be
quashed by the quietus. The "unanswerable opponent" is the
actual state of affairs that is of one sort while the authority
would decree it other. (*PLF* 444–45)

I am reminded of Hitler in his bunker directing forces that no longer
existed, only among the last and least of the systematic distortions of reality attending twelve years of the quietus and the one voice. The greatest
disaster ever to befall the human race—World War II and its aftermath—
had its source in the Fuehrer-principle, which Burke, in this and other essays of the late thirties, especially the one on *Mein Kampf* (*PLF* 191–220),
sought to expose as the malignancy it was already and would yet become
beyond all imagining. It is in this context we should see Burke opposing
dictatorship "absolutely and undeviatingly" (*PLF* 444). He had learned
the lessons of his time long before the unanswerable opponent had had
its full say.

In the last chapter we were able to glimpse how much of Burke's
thought converges in rhetoric. Perhaps here we can see a little of the logic
of convergence in dialectic, according to Aristotle, rhetoric's "counter-
dance" or *antistrophe*. The common ground they share is Burke's dramatic anti-epistemology, and their mutual entanglement in each other
and in Being as the answerable other and the unanswerable opponent.

Basically, the logic is as follows. First, as noted before, there is "animal faith" (*GM* 217) in a Being vastly more than language—no casual
allegiance for Burke, but active in all of his thought. He assumes not
only the existence but also the potential "responsiveness" of Being, whose
answerability comes into play as a consequence of the human power of
speech and in the context of human assertions and projects.

But, second, both Being in general and beings in particular are not
directly or finally knowable. Always prestructured by our neurological
constitution, by our culture, history, education, and interests, and by
our peculiar, individual experiences in living, we can have only perspectives on Being and beings, or what Gadamer calls a horizon of prejudices
or prejudgments. We are creatures who are endowed with the capacity
for a point of view—and there is no seeing, no place to stand that isn't a
point of view, no matter how much collective sanction it may enjoy.

Epistemology, then, as Philosophy understands it—standpointless
correspondence of word and thing—is impossible. Nevertheless, third,
as uncertain and unsecurable as our horizons are, we must assert ourselves in utterance and deed. So far as the epistemic (but not epistemological) drama of knowledge is concerned, rhetoric is "first," the *strophe*

by which things come into being and are—our claims to truth, our decrees of Being and beings, in turn the basis of our acts.

Fourth, simply by asserting ourselves, we engage Being and beings, set into motion the antistrophe of dialectic, which includes conflict with other points of view and with the modes of "assertion" our own activity provokes from a "given" that is never the wholly malleable stuff technical reason must assume that it is. Being is profoundly and "deviously" recalcitrant; even when it seems to retreat meekly before our will, it typically eludes it in some way. For example, we "subdued" the plains of the American Midwest, killing or displacing the native American population, destroying the buffalo, and turning this vast region of grassland into a huge granary capable, so we once boasted, of feeding the world. But first we had the Dust Bowl and now a polluted and dangerously reduced water table that threatens the productivity of the entire area. And (of course!) economic, political, and social recalcitrance, also part of the "givenness" of Being, prevented the region from ending hunger even in the United States, much less globally.

Thus far, the logic that ends in the absolute value of dialectics is "compelling" almost in the sense of indisputable. Being just is vastly more than language and typically more or other than what we say it is. Our knowledge is always insufficient, sometimes tragically so. If only to survive, we have to act. And in acting we have to suffer the consequences, short and long term. This is the dialectic of Burke's *Dasein*, human-*action*-in-the-world that constantly exposes the folly, arrogance, and hollowness of a heedless will to power, especially in the modernist form of methodical mastery.

But with the fifth step in Burke's reasoning we confront a choice that might deliver us from some of the brutality of Fate. Burke pleads for full scope to the dialectical process precisely because the process itself is hardly ineluctable but rather a very fragile accomplishment. The problem is not the superficial puzzle of how a speechless other can speak; the problem rather is whether we are prepared to listen, whether we are open enough to allow our horizons to be corrected and matured by otherness. If not, we are indeed fated beings, destined to confront the unanswerable opponent. If, however, we receive the answerable other in competitive cooperation, we can sometimes "see better" and perhaps avoid at least the most drastic consequences of our selective blindness. Burke supports democracy because, however imperfectly, it institutionalizes the hearing of many voices. He advocates the metaphor of the conversation not because he thinks that human societies really are open conversations but rather because he thinks they aren't, and because mere hearing must become a genuine listening.

Strategy III: "Through Symbolism to a Philosophy of Being"

That all recurs is the most extreme approach of a world of becoming to one of being.

—Friedrich Nietzsche, *Will to Power*

Taking in as it does both nature and second nature, the inorganic, organic, and social dimensions of existence, Burke's Being is always much more than the situations action would encompass and the strategies used to pursue our ends. If it is not fully autonomous—our actions do alter Being—yet it remains stubbornly Other, not something our projects can confidently appropriate. And yet Being for Burke is also *always strategic.* As a concept, or what Burke would call a term in our vocabularies, Being "belongs" to language, and language is always already rhetorical, or strategic. What can Being contribute to a better life? is Burke's question.

Being amid becoming is my summarizing phrase for the third and most important of Burke's Being strategies: His effort *to retrieve a philosophy of Being from Becoming itself.*

The key text for this third strategy is the concluding section of Part II of *Permanence and Change,* "Towards a Philosophy of Being." First, Burke insists on the commonplaceness of his own version of Nietzsche's idea that "all recurs." "[I]nsofar as the neurological structure [of the human body] remains a constant, there will be a corresponding constancy in the devices by which sociality is maintained" (162). After Darwin, to find constancy in the biological domain may seem paradoxical. But Burke is only claiming that the human body recurs—*approximately.* The neurological equipment of the species that evolved into *homo sapiens* did alter, and the equipment of the species we call *homo sapiens* is altering. However, biological evolution is so slow relative to historical change as to be, in practical terms, "the same." Since what he is after is a *practical* philosophy of Being, this "sameness" is good enough.

Unlike the older *theoria* of Being (contemplation of the eternal), Burke's *praxis* Being is not driven to deny the reality or significance of change. In the sentence immediately following the one cited above, Burke says that "changes in the environmental structure will, of course, call forth changes in the particularities of rationalization." By "environmental structure" Burke has in mind "situation" as he understands it. Since the latter is historical and includes history, Burke is affirming the value of historical study. But he resists historicism, primarily because it fails to recognize that

[s]ituations do overlap [from one time to another], if only be-

> cause [people] now have the same neural and muscular struc-
> ture as [people] who have left their records from past ages.
> . . . Furthermore, even the concrete details of social texture
> have a great measure of overlap. And . . . the function of ab-
> straction rooted in the nature of language, also provides us
> with . . . [generalizations] by which situations greatly differ-
> ent in their particularities may be felt to belong to the same
> class. (*PLF* 2)

The human body and the natural world as a whole is not all that "recurs
approximately." Societies separated from us in place and time overlap
enough with ours to allow a degree of understanding—mainly because
language permits classification, allowing us to disclose "sameness" amid
difference.

Burke's point is that we do have a choice—not between being and
becoming, because language reveals both—but rather between two quite
different emphases:

> If we choose to emphasize the shifting particularities, we ap-
> proach human problems *historically*, as in the philosophies
> of becoming which seemed to have reached their flowering
> in Nineteenth Century thought (Goethe, Hegel, Marx, Dar-
> win, Nietzsche, and the vast horde of lesser evolutionary or
> revolutionary thinkers). If we choose to emphasize the un-
> derlying similarities, we return through symbolism to a phi-
> losophy of *being*, the Spinozistic concern with man *sub specie
> aeternitatis*. (163, Burke's emphasis)

I interpret Burke's claim as follows. Contemporary thought tends to assume that the great Philosophers of Becoming have closed the door forever on Being—that all we can do is reflect on what the destruction of
Being compels us to relinquish or, following Heidegger, "save Being"
by making it entirely a function of time. Burke denies that Becoming can
displace Being, or that we can only ignore, destroy, or assimilate it to history or process. However, any return to a philosophy of Being must be *via
symbolism*, not through some transcendent metaphysics.

As we have seen, Burke agrees with Nietzsche: Language "creates"
Being. If we take away language, then "picked out" entities (beings) disappear as does any concept of existence as a whole (Being). In *A Grammar of Motives* Burke uses a geological metaphor (xix): Extralinguistic
existence is like the molten layer of the earth's crust—everything merged
together, existence without distinction. Language's power to single out
and conceive resembles the "new earth" that rises from the molten center and for a time becomes the entities of our world. But the current ways

of designating and conceiving return, like the solid portion of the crust floating on the liquid interior, to the molten center again and are "remade," replaced by new solidifications. The process is dynamic, its particular, concrete results unpredictable; but the pattern repeats itself and human beings always live among Being and beings. In short, Burke finds in language Being amid Becoming, "sameness" and difference, the "recurrent" and the new.

To advocates of pure process, Burke and practical philosophy generally respond as follows. We must cope with the prevailing solidifications: *Nature as we now understand it. Human bodies in their present configurations. Society, culture, economic and political systems as constituted in our time and place.* That "this too must pass" and is passing is true but irrelevant. We must cope with the world of our era, with that which we make and find in our lifetime. This is a rhetorician's and a skeptic's Being without metaphysics.

Poststructuralists will ask: If we say language "creates" Being and beings, mustn't we also affirm that Being and beings are an illusion of presence, the presence that language itself necessarily creates? There are a number of ways Burkean philosophy could respond. It would be suspicious of the term "illusion." To call something an illusion is to claim clear-sightedness against which something can be called an illusion. If we say that Being and identity is an illusion, we are actually affirming that Becoming and difference is the Truth. Far from suspending metaphysics, "the illusion of presence" view actually affirms one. Because of the current dominance of metaphors of process and progress, Burke locates *praxis* Being within the assumptions of Becoming—a good rhetorician will always appeal to the audience's predispositions—but this does not mean he lays claim to Truth. He sees no compelling argument for calling Being and identity an illusion and Becoming and difference "the real" or "the Truth" (or vice versa). His skepticism, then, enables the choice in emphasis he maintains that we have between historical and ahistorical frames of interpretation.

Insofar as Nietzsche and Derrida take this choice away and can offer no compelling reasons for doing so, their foreclosing on Being amounts to an arbitrary preference that diminishes our dialectical resources unnecessarily. Since Being can only be thought or spoken of in the context of Becoming and vice versa (how could we invoke the one without at least implying the other?), since identity requires difference and difference identity (otherwise, how could we distinguish anything from anything else or assert relationships?), why opt for a one-sided dialectic of Becoming and difference only? This is the question Burke's dialectical philosophy would pose of Derrida's anti-dialectical philosophy.

Besides being suspicious of the Philosophical implications of the term "illusion," Burke would reject the linguistic idealism detectable in the view of Being as an illusion of presence. That we have no unmediated access to Being and beings is not equivalent to saying that the Truth of Being is Mind or Spirit—idealism, old style—or only interpretations, linguistic constructions—idealism, new style. Although we cannot know Being and beings as such, in themselves, we do know that they are always more than we say that they are—we know this, like blind Gloucester in *Lear*, "feelingly," by the recalcitrance they manifest to our interpretations and actions. The negativity of experience is enough to affirm that there is plenty outside the text, that extralinguistic reality has an integrity and force of its own.

As we have seen, Burke stresses our obligation to speak for the speechless. In sharp contrast to Derrida's deconstruction of Being as an illusion of presence, Burke's intent is to make more of the "absence" of Being and beings present. His metaphor of the conversation stands opposed to Derrida's "archewriting" metaphor. Is it, then, phonocentric, a mistaking of the presence of the voice for the presence of Being?

I have argued elsewhere ("Orality" 123–27) and will argue again in the essay on dialectic in Part Two that Burke's understanding of language *integrates* oral and literate noetics and values. He is not, therefore, phonocentric; he does not elevate speech over writing. Furthermore, Burke clearly recognizes in what he calls "naive verbal realism" (*LASA* 5) a temptation in language akin to the illusion of presence. The tendency of most people most of the time is to think that "our" ways of characterizing reality are True—or, at least, truer than some other culture's ways. We now call this ethnocentricity. But naive verbal realism does not have any special affinity for speech. On the contrary, chirography tends to reify and fix meanings more than the always fading utterance does.

Burke's rhetorical philosophy seeks neither the comfort of epistemological certitude nor the alleged "unconstrained joy" of "free play" that supposedly results from overcoming the "illusion" of Being's presence. As we have seen, certitude is rhetoric's Other. But the implications of "free play" are no more favorable to rhetoric. As Chaim Perelman pointed out, the very task of rhetoric is to create presence (*Treatise* 115–20), to make the speaker or writer's view of things more salient, more convincing and illuminating, than its competitors. "Free play" is hardly the way of rhetoric, whose task it is to create or strengthen commitment to a point of view or a course of action.

Furthermore, if we are free to make any world we please, unconstrained by recalcitrance in all its modalities, what would be the point of conversation as dialogue, as competitive collaboration? Dialectic, rhetoric's counterpart, also suffers when language is idealized as "free play."

In sum, we cannot call Being an illusion of presence unless we are prepared to call Becoming the Truth and thus fall back into metaphysics. We cannot call Being an illusion of presence without succumbing to linguistic idealism, which means that we have no way to recognize, much less cope with, the negativity of experience. Finally, when we consider that the very task of rhetoric is to create presence, we may wonder what practical sense there is in maintaining that Being is an illusion of presence. In practical terms, presence is no illusion. How we say things are, our decrees of reality, become the grounds for our action in the world, and are thus real by any pragmatic measure.

The Metaphor of a Norm and the Critique of Becoming

Burke's concern with metaphysics is negative, but in a way quite different from Derrida's. Derrida equates metaphysics with philosophies of Being and professes to find the illusion of presence even in Being philosophies as processual as Heidegger's. Burke does not equate metaphysics with a philosophy of Being. Nihilism is a metaphysics. It denies Being. What characterizes metaphysics is not a Philosophy of Being but rather a metanarrative about Truth. Any metanarrative about Truth is a metaphysics.

As a skeptic, Burke does not single out one of the metanarratives as especially in need of deconstruction. His concern with Truth extends only so far as to deny that our current preoccupation with metaphors of becoming, process, and progress can be equated with Truth. He accepts the current dominance of Becoming and offers a *praxis* Being that does not require us to abandon temporal modes of thought at all. *The Being of Becoming is approximate recurrence of "the same"*—if we can accept this, we can accept Burke's Being.

Burke sees no profit in debating the Truth of Becoming. But he is very interested in the consequences of taking Becoming as the Truth. A Philosophy of Becoming has unlivable consequences, not the least of which is the destruction of *praxis* itself.

We are so accustomed to theoretical critiques of Being that we may find Burke's practical critique of Becoming somewhat disorienting. Perhaps this is why his critique of Becoming in *Permanence and Change* has received little previous commentary. It goes unnoticed for the most part because it is unexpected and difficult to assimilate. But the critique of Becoming is only the suppressed Other of modernism and postmodernism's antipathy to Being. The more Becoming displaces its rival, the more it exposes itself to critique, and we are now hearing this voice more and more, especially among contemporary ethical philosophers. In this, as in so many ways, Burke's critique is contemporary with the currently increasing resistance to purely process philosophies.

As noted before, precisely because we cannot know the Truth, Burke argues that we are free to construe the world both historically and ahistorically. We will anyway, he contends. However, what we emphasize does matter. If we emphasize, as the young Marx did, "species being" ("On James Mill" 115–16),

> [we] replace the metaphor of progress (and its bitter corollary, decadence) with the metaphor of a *norm*, the notion that at bottom the aims and genius of [hu]man[ity] have remained fundamentally the same, that temporal events may cause [us] to stray far from [our] sources but that [we] repeatedly struggle to restore, under new particularities, the same basic patterns of the "good life." (PC 163, Burke's emphasis)

Among thoughtful people now, progress is generally understood as a question-begging term. Progress in what sense? and For whom? we want to ask. We no longer automatically link "progress" with "the good." But schooled as we are (and as Burke was) in anthropological relativity and on guard against the Enlightenment's "universal human being," we are likely to resist even the *metaphor* of a norm with at least equal strength. Given the extraordinary diversity of ways of life, how can we say what is normal for human being? Who would dare offer now—as Aristotle in his *Rhetoric* did offer (24–29)—an outline of the "good life"?

In other words, we may well agree with Burke that "the whole idea of progress . . . seems to have cloaked one long hysterical attempt to escape from a grossly mismanaged present" (163), but we are likely to be diffident if someone asks us to specify the standards or criteria we have used in making our judgment. We tend to deny the validity of the very norms we use, especially in moral or ethical judgments. We think they must be arbitrary, insupportable. And so we feel secure only by claiming ethical neutrality or by saying "it's only my opinion," as if an ethics could actually be a private or individual construction. But judgments involve norms, and norms cannot be norms and be neutral or just an individual's opinion. And once we admit the existence of norms we must also admit the existence of Being. As Burke says, "An ethics involves one ultimately in a philosophy of *being*" (PC 271, his emphasis).

We know enough by now about the general argument in *Permanence and Change* to follow the logic by which he would lead us to a philosophy of Being. Language is loaded with moral judgments. We are moral beings even at the level of sensory perception. All human activity is ethical. The worlds we make and find are ethical worlds, where judgments of good and bad have everything to do with choice and action. If we reject the neutral, objective ideal of language, we must embrace ethics. We have no choice. And if we embrace ethics, we cannot avoid norms and concepts of the "good life." Since "any schema of the 'good life' tends to be anhistoric in quite the same way that an account of digestion or metabolism would be" (271), ethics leads to a philosophy of Being.

We can see Burke's point by recognizing that some ethical claims are quite transhistorical, even if, as is always the case, they have a history. To claim, for example, that "Hitler's Final Solution was wrong" does not mean wrong in the 1930s and 1940s but perhaps right at some date in the future or right at some moment in the past. It means wrong, period, any place, any time. It means that genocide must never figure in any defensible concept of the "good life." It is, in short, a transtemporal claim about the good.

But even if we find this reasoning compelling, the very term "norm" is still no less disturbing in its implications. For norms imply abnorms, and if norms allow us to categorically condemn Hitler's motives, they also suggest the potential for intolerance and restrictions on our own freedom. And so we quite rightly want to know exactly what Burke means by referring to norm as a metaphor and by putting the "good life" in quotes. Does Burke really believe in norms? If so, what are they? From what do they derive? Does Burke really believe in the good life? If so, in what does it consist?

As a context for answering these questions, we need to examine at least part of Burke's critique of Becoming. "[S]ince the days of Hobbes, with his *homo homini lupus* formula," Burke complains, "many thinkers [have] . . . situate[d] the essence of human relationships in the sphere of the brutal." Burke does not mention Nietzsche, but the sentence just quoted and the first sentence that follows certainly apply to him:

> Philosophies of *becoming* made life look like a perennial battlefield. Such an attitude fitted the ideals of positivistic science, in laying stress upon the notion that [humans] must patch up the discordancies between [themselves] and [their] environment by reshaping the environment. [They] must not *surrender* to the environment . . . [they] must *change* it. (172, Burke's emphasis)

Burke goes on to connect Philosophies of Becoming with "empire-building . . . capitalism . . . the belief that the 'good life' resides in the acquisition of commodities . . . and progress" (173), along with many other concepts and motives characteristic of both modernity and postmodernity. His point, of course, is not that we can deposit everything we like or dislike about modernity and postmodernity at the feet of the metaphysics of Becoming. Philosophies of Becoming antedate both. In any case, he is not postulating causal relationships. His point, rather, is twofold: that Becoming is part of a "package deal" of philosophical, cultural, economic, political, and educational emphases that threaten the natural environment as well as individual and collective human survival while badly deforming our image of the "good life"; and that Becoming *per se* can offer no critique for resisting or deflecting the general course of events.

Burke is mainly critical of modernity because it fosters extreme and distorted notions of human being. Here Burke does refer to Nietzsche's blond beast as "the most picturesque example." But Nietzsche's power fantasy is only one instance, and not nearly so generally influential as social Darwinism.

> Darwin . . . specifically recognized that the struggle for life gives rise to cooperative attitudes, that tenderness, charity, good humor are as truly factors in the survival of man as was any primitive ability to track and slay animals in the jungle. But this aspect of his doctrine was generally ignored—and the struggle for life was usually interpreted in a bluntly militaristic sense. (174)

Even when modernist views do manage to achieve a degree of "ecology," an interaction or balance of conflicting motives, they are often interpreted—reduced—to one-sided, brutal essences, unintentional caricatures of human being. Burke blames "the growing intensity of economic conflict itself"—capitalism's own rationale of the "survival of the fittest," which certainly played a major role in Darwin's metaphorics, for skewing human understanding of itself toward the bluntly militaristic. But however we explain it, modernism tends to decree human essences that leave us with no choices (just complicated rats in complicated Skinner boxes) or with "harsh antitheses, impossible choices, like the choice between *conquest* and *surrender*" (174, Burke's emphasis).

Clearly, if we are to be critical of such reductionisms of human being, we require the metaphor of a norm. But Philosophies of Becoming deny norms because they deny Being and beings. The characteristic poststructural stance that all essences are illusions of presence is worse than no help at all. In practical terms, undecidability is not an option; the empty place will be filled by *some* decree of essence. In another essay of the thirties, "The Calling of the Tune," Burke warns against a temptation to which postmodernists are prone (as indeed we all are insofar as the Enlightenment is still calling the tune): "Begin by rejecting all authority, and you end by accepting any" (*PLF* 233). You end this way because, in rejecting authority as a principle, you devote no thought to the norms or criteria of a satisfactory authority. Likewise, begin by rejecting all essences, and you end by accepting any. But probably not just any: Given the wholesale rejection of traditional humanism and proclamations about the End of Wo/Man, given the tendency to make sophistication indistinguishable from cynicism, and you will select an essence as far away from "rational animal" as you can get. Nietzsche's blond beast, perhaps, or Skinner's complicated rat—both, and a host of others, will do. Far from resisting reductionism, the "no essence" position collaborates with it. The cynical and the brutal are near relations.

Contrary, then, to the common association of Being with reaction and Becoming with forward-looking social change, Burke insists that his

> philosophy of being . . . must not be taken as synonymous with a philosophy of passivity, or acquiescence. . . . Our anhistoric position does not in the least imply surrender to historical textures through failure to consider their importance. On the contrary, we believe that in many respects it is the *historical* point of view which leads to such surrender on the grounds that one must adjust . . . to temporal conditions as [s/]he finds them (. . . for instance, [accepting] more and more mechanization simply because the trend of history points in this direction). (271, Burke's emphasis)

Burke's *praxis* Being does not turn away from history because it is, as I have shown, a notion of Being *amid Becoming*, which affirms the reality and significance of historical textures. No rhetorical philosophy can ignore the reality and significance of change—regard for *kairos* alone assures that. However, *praxis* without norms, without Being, is impossible. In the absence of a utopian vision of how things ought to be or an ahistorical notion of the good life, we just "go with the flow," allowing ourselves to be carried wherever the Heraclitean river happens to take us.

Burke's critique of Becoming amounts, in short, to two accusations: that it "makes life look like a perennial battlefield," brutalizing human being by overstressing the competitive or combative and leaving us with no choices or bad choices like that between conquer or surrender; and that it deprives us of the means of resisting its drastically one-sided and reductive understanding of human purposes. It is in this context, then, that Burke advances his "metaphor of a norm" and his notion of human being as a struggle to sustain or recover the "good life" amid constantly altering historical conditions.

So what does Burke mean by his metaphor of a norm? In the first place, it *is* a metaphor for Burke, not to be taken literally as naive advocates of progress take progress literally. Literally, one must assume that there are few norms characteristic of all humans everywhere and at all times. Alas, even Hitler's project of liquidating the Jews still appeals, and not just to Arab extremists. But if we cannot "prove" the existence of norms, say, by doing a statistical study of all known human societies, we can recognize their existence and significance simply by reflecting on our own judgments of people and events. Norms are implicit in our moral engagement with the world.

Burke insists that we take these norms seriously. They are not merely subjective. We share many of our most important norms with others. They are not merely emotive, a matter of irrational feeling. Many of our norms are quite rational: A desire for peace, for example, is as rational as not wishing to be killed or maimed on a battlefield. Nor are our norms necessarily arbitrary, a matter of whim or personal preference. AIDS, for example, is teaching us once again that the norms surrounding sexual restraint and responsibility are not arbitrary, Puritanical impositions on human freedom.

Burke's proposal to "return through symbolism to a philosophy of being" amounts in part to making ethics central in post-Nietzschean philosophy. On the one hand, Burke denies that human being can reach "beyond good and evil," or that we would like the results if we could. Clearly this claim is important as we try to cope with the disastrous results of a world that has tried to be post-ethical, whose norms purport to be "value neutral"—that is, "faultless" technical manipulation, "efficiency," acquisition, power, profit. If we are to respond meaningfully to the ethical vacuity of business, politics, and education in the postmodern world, we must begin by insisting that human engagement with the world is always, whatever else it may be, moral engagement.

However, on the other hand, Burke also denies that we can return to some pre-Nietzschean ethical outlook. MacIntyre's attempt in *After Virtue* to resurrect classical ethics (109–20, passim), for example, would have only limited appeal to Burke—we can't resurrect classical ethics because our situation only overlaps in small measure with classical conditions of living, and even if we could, we wouldn't like the results. Cultural diversity alone and the political necessity of tolerating difference separates us from Athens.

Norms have to be metaphors, and they have to be open to discussion. The existence of some ethical absolutes does not mean that ethics is typically or should be typically closed to negotiation. Even in the case of Final Solutions, we want opportunities for discussion to dissuade those entertaining such motives. Otherwise we have only two choices: abandoning our convictions or physical force. Burke's linkage of democracy with dialectic and his cultivating of Being as the answerable other are inseparable from his ethics. They share the metaphor of the conversation, and Burke's ethics is an ethics of the conversation.

It is the claim to THE foundation, the "unshakable ground" of morality, that leads, as the night the day, to the quietus. Burke's rhetorical pragmatism can never tolerate this. Our claims to truth, including most ethical truths, must be truths *par provision*. And yet any ethical claim invokes or implies a context of some kind within which judgment or admonition makes sense. There must be a "ground" in the sense that a figure has a ground, an "against which" or "within which" we judge or admonish. It is primarily these "groundless grounds" of morality that require discussion, for once we agree on the background of whatever it is we are attempting to evaluate, the evaluation is usually implicit in the background of placement, and our course of action more or less implicit in the evaluation. What, then, are the groundless grounds of Burke's ethics? From what does he derive his norms?

The approximate recurrence of the human body is a powerful source of norms for Burke—so much so that he characterized his philosophy in *Permanence and Change* as a metabiology (168) rather than a metaphysics. Providing that we do not confuse metabiology with biologisms such as sociobiology, the designation is useful even for the later philosophy. Human beings are "bodies that learn language" ("Poem" 263) and because they learn language, they inhabit an entire realm of motives *not* reducible to biological needs and drives. But, shifting the stress, we are also *bodies* that learn language. From *Permanence and Change* on, Burke never neglects the body as a source of recurrent motives and as a "ground" against which to assess the "figures" of history, past and current social, economic, and political arrangements.

"In subscribing to a philosophy of being," Burke explains, contrasting the resources of his philosophy with philosophies of pure immanence, "one may hold that certain historically conditioned institutions . . . affront the permanent biological norms" (271). In the contemporary United States, for example, we face the following injustice, one among many that elicit and should elicit negative moral judgments. On the one hand, a sizable group of Americans spend hundreds of millions of dollars annually trying to lose weight, to overcome the results of a superabundance of food consumed to excess in a culture that valorizes excess—conspicuous consumption—in everything. If we could forget the genuine distress of the morbidly obese, the situation would be almost comical—here is a case where conspicuous consumption is all too conspicuous.

On the other hand, there is another sizable group of Americans, many of them children, whose nutritional needs are not even met minimally, who normally go to bed hungry, and whose health in general and ability to learn and contribute to society are seriously compromised. Similar gross inequities exist in every dimension of material provision for basic bodily needs in the United States, and this in a country whose resources are far more than adequate to be enough for all of its citizens. When we shift to a global perspective of contrast between, roughly, the northern and southern hemispheres, the one prosperous beyond its needs, the other a scene of abject poverty and sometimes mass starvation, the ethical case against current economic and political conditions is overwhelming.

Bodily norms are relatively unproblematical as compared with another source of norms for Burke—language. In the later work, his attitude toward language becomes more and more ambivalent, but in *Permanence and Change* language is almost altogether positive, used as the body is used as a standard against which to critique historical textures. "Life, activity, cooperation, communication," Burke decrees, "are identical" (236). Anything, therefore, that threatens one or all of them he condemns. With respect to cooperation and communication, he holds that

> [a] sound system of communication . . . cannot be built upon a structure of economic warfare. . . . The segregational, or dissociative state cannot endure . . . [because a] sound communicative medium arises out of cooperative enterprises. . . . Let the system of cooperation become impaired, and the communicative equipment is correspondingly impaired, while this impairment . . . in turn threatens the structure of rationality itself. (163)

The segregational state—Burke's term for the conditions of late capitalism—pits people against people, which can do nothing else but produce mis/disinformation. Economic warfare, which has had so much to do with the almost continuous warfare since capitalism became the paradigm of human effort, must be eliminated or greatly reduced—otherwise, there is no remedy. If the segregational state has proved tenacious far beyond the prospects it seemed to have had in 1935, the damage it does to cooperation, communication, and rationality has also proved enduring. We may be witnessing the collapse of American society—and, although socialism has made the consequences of economic warfare less drastic there, some of our troubles have parallels in Europe as well.

When it is conceived pragmatically, as communication, language can be a powerful source of norms. But the most important source for Burke is ecology. I cite the following prescient statement from *Attitudes Toward History*

> Among the sciences, there is one little fellow named Ecology, and in time we shall pay him more attention. He teaches us that the *total* economy of the planet cannot be guided by an efficient rationale of exploitation alone, but that the exploiting part must itself eventually suffer if it too greatly disturbs the *balance* of the whole. (150, Burke's emphasis)

In many ways, ecology is an ideal concept for Burke's metaphor of a norm. An ecosystem exemplifies Being amid Becoming. Ecosystems are dynamic, in constant flux. But despite fires, volcanic eruptions, climactic changes, meteor impacts—despite even periods of mass extinction of species—one may speak metaphorically of the system's struggle for equilibrium, for a state of relative Being. The "good life" from an ecological point of view is a life in equilibrium, lived with regard for the "total economy" of existence in some place and time.

It is impossible to overstress the importance of the notion of ecological balance in Burke's philosophy. Ecology furnishes the "Ground" of groundless grounds for an ethics based on a metabiology rather than a metaphysics. When Burke is critical of an idea, an institution, a system, or a practice, he usually finds fault with it for lacking "ecology." The problem with modernist method, for example, is not so much that it fails to understand itself. The problem, rather, is its overemphasis on technological manipulation.

Burke is not urging us, as Heidegger did, to let Being be ("Letter" 228), a prescription for hapless acquiescence to current political and economic systems. Nor is he to be numbered among the so-called deep ecologists of today. We cannot simply abandon technology and return to nature. Rather he is urging us to listen to the claims of Being as the answerable other before Being as the unanswerable opponent "refutes" the very rationale of mastery beyond hope of rejoinder. If the human species is driven in its will to power to control and manipulate, then it must bend technology itself to serve the total economy of the planet. To some extent, we can let Being be, as in setting aside and preserving natural ecosystems. But for the most part, "our" claims must fuse with "its" claims, technological human being with ecology, for even our projects in "letting be" to have a chance of long-term success.

We see from another angle why Burke finds absolute value in dialectic. Dialectic and ecological balance are intertwined, as means and goal. Furthermore, normative metaphors in Burke are dialectical in conception as well as open to discussion, dialectical in function. In 1925 Burke defined norm as "a conflict become fusion" (CS 56). Patently or latently, then, all ethical norms must be dialectical. They involve the conflict of metaphor itself, the "identity in difference" implicit in all analogies, without which we could not compare present situations with past ones, thereby deciding what we ought to do. That is, norms entail the contradiction inherent in the will to power, by which "sameness"—Being—is imposed on Becoming. Put another way, ethical norms often claim or imply ahistorical or transhistorical standards. But they can only be applied to people, actions, and events in time, to history. The "ahistorical" and the historical fuse in *this* ethical judgment *now*.

We see the dialectical tensiveness of norms in Burke's discussion of the "good life" in *Attitudes Toward History*. In summary, Burke advocates:

- A "maximum of physicality." "The neuroses . . . of the over-sedentary leisured are bad poems."

- Countering "an over-emphasis upon 'things of the mind,'" since the elevation of intellectual work "is a secular variant of the early religious duality between 'mind' and 'body,'" which takes the body as "vile," the mind as "pure" and "spiritual."

- Cultivating "the sentiments"—for example, charity— while "distrust[ing] . . . the passions." "Inordinate ambition" especially merits distrust. In losing it, "[we] cease to want all sorts of idiotic baubles that keep millions frantically at work."

- "[P]atient study of the 'Documents of Error.'" Here is the most useful role for "things of the mind." But, Burke warns, "[n]ot with the self-congratulatory notion that everybody was a fool before November 14, 18——, and so forth. Our stupidities are ever born anew."

- "Stress always upon the knowledge of limitations."

- "Distrust hypertrophy of art *on paper*. More of the artistic should be expressed in vital social relationships." (256–59)

Granted, Burke's notion of the "good life" is not everyone's notion, nor does he suggest that it is or should be. He presents his view to make the norms of his own *praxis* more explicit and concrete and therefore open to scrutiny, and as a challenge to others to do the same. They are "talking points," provocations to serious dialogue about the "grounds" by which we assess current rationales of human effort.

Each of the norms are also themselves dialectical or ecological, claims for Being *in response to Becoming*, thus preserving the tension between them. "Maximum of physicality," for instance, can appeal to such transhistorical norms as "a sound mind in a sound body," always desirable even when it is not, because of age, disease, injury, or disability in fact attainable. But clearly the norm itself is offered as a corrective to a capitalist-technological society where too many people can hire others to do all their physical labor or get their machines to do it by pushing a button. In such ways the ecology of the body, its need to exert itself *both* mentally and physically, is disrupted. As Burke put it in "Dialectician's Prayer":

If our ways of living
Violate the needs of nerve and muscle,
May we find speech for nerve and muscle,

To frame objections
Whereat we, listening,
Can remake our habits.

                                                    (CP 40)

The point is *ecological balance*—not inflexible norms to be applied blindly without regard for historical textures. Faced now with the Cult of the Jog, the seeking of Nirvana by literally running away from "the neuroses of the psychologically unemployed, the over-sedentary leisured"— for us perhaps a measure of the walking philosophy, a little peripatetic exposure to "things of the mind," might be a better solution.

But however we try to cope with the imbalances of current existence, we cannot cope at all without the metaphor of a norm, without "grounds" for the "figures" of history. These norms are conflicts become fusion, a merging of permanence and change, identity and difference. It follows that ignoring Being or denying Being is fruitless. If, in a postPhilosophical age, we require a Being without metaphysics, a Being that insists on its inseparability from Becoming, which does not lead either to otherworldliness or reactionary viewpoints, and which is ethically and politically committed, then Burke's *praxis* Being, his dialectical, ecological Being, may be our best option. Perhaps we can at least cease widening and deepening the hole that we have dug for ourselves by uncritically accepting the Truth of Becoming, which, as Burke correctly insists, is the way to disengage from rather than engage in the perpetual struggle for the "good life."

The focus of attention shifts now from Burke's early philosophy to his late philosophy—defined here as everything from *A Grammar of Motives* (1945) on. The focus shifts, but we are not about to set rhetorical pragmatism and *praxis* Being aside, nor allow the early philosophy in general to drop out of the picture. Because, in contrast to Wittgenstein and Heidegger, there is no "early Burke" that a "late Burke" repudiates, we can draw freely on both at any juncture in our argument without much fear of misrepresentation. And so, for instance, the theory of comedy, developed in 1937, will figure prominently in my essay on *praxis* in the later philosophy. But while Burke's determination to grow by accretion allows us to move almost without restriction between his early and late thought, developments in the later philosophy carry us far beyond the purview of the early philosophy and to a significant degree supersede it.

Part Two

Four Essays on the Later Philosophy

5

On Discounting, Terministic Screens, and Dramatism

In Part One we followed Burke's development from antinomianism to rhetorical pragmatism, from a largely corrosive, deconstructive stance toward prevailing norms to the recognition that norms had to be insisted on and argued for in an intellectual environment given over too much and too uncritically to temporal modes of thought—to historicism, concepts of progress, and the Truth of Becoming generally. I showed that Burke began with an outlook akin to what we now call poststructuralism and postmodernism, and that how he worked his way through and out of it into a skeptical reconstructionism can help us imagine possibilities beyond postmodernism.

Part Two's approach to the later philosophy is not developmental. Rather than tracing the evolution of Burke's thought in detail, I have relied on more conventional *topoi* of common philosophical concern—hence, a series of essays about, in order, hermeneutics, philosophical anthropology, dialectic and dialogue, and *praxis*. Such an approach lends itself more readily than an intrinsic, book-by-book approach to a conversation with other recent philosophies.

Reading Philosophy PostPhilosophically

As a whole, the later philosophy amounts to an ambitious effort to reinterpret significant aspects of Western thought and culture for postPhilosophical use. In a moment we will consider Burke's motives for approaching the tradition as he does and its significance in the context of other postPhilosophical attitudes. But first, omitting the essay collection, *Language as Symbolic Action* (1966), which defies synopsis, I will offer a brief account of the other three major books as re-creations of the Western heritage.

A Grammar of Motives (1945) pries dialectic loose from its metaphysical entanglements in Hegelian idealism and Marxist materialism, returning it in a sense to what it was, to how it began in ancient Greece, as a *purely verbal* art. But Burke's dialectic is not Aristotelian—not, that is, a logic of propositions or syllogisms—and not Hegelian or Marxist, a logic of concepts. It is rather a logic of *terminologies* or nomenclatures, expressly designed to cope with what has been happening to language since at least the seventeenth century—that is, increasing fragmentation into specialized vocabularies, each more or less sealed in its own domain, and decreasing connection with "ordinary language." The result is a "new dialectic" ideally suited to the decentered postPhilosophical conversation and its fragmented cultural context.

Burke applies his new dialectic to reread not only Hegel and Marx but also an impressive cross section of Western Philosophy *as if it could be generated dialectically, purely by exploring the implications of key terms.* That is, Burke invites us to read Philosophy not as so many quests for the "ultimate foundation" or the "final synthesis"—the Truth—but rather much as it is often read now, as "merely" words. Burke calls into fundamental question Philosophy's pretense to Truth, but he also reshapes much of the contending traditions themselves into a set of what he calls "terministic screens," each capable of limited and provisional claims to truth. He deconstructs and reconstructs Philosophy, that is, rather than discarding it. The outcome is a *retrieval* of Philosophy as different from Heidegger's notion of retrieval as Burkean deconstruction is from Derrida's deconstruction.

A Grammar of Motives reinterprets Philosophy, organizing it into a metahermeneutic. In contrast, Burke claims that *A Rhetoric of Motives* is only "an accessory to the standard lore" (xiv). Rather than deconstructing traditional rhetoric, he draws so much into it that the seams of the inherited category begin to creak under the strain, bulge, and finally burst. By the time one finishes the concluding section, called simply "Order," one is so far beyond what preceded it, "Traditional Principles of Rhetoric," which itself ranged far beyond the traditional principles it purportedly explicates, that one can only say that the gentle accessory is actually perhaps the most violent appropriation of the standard lore we have. There is a deconstructing after all—by slow-motion explosion.

Tradition typically confined rhetoric to public speaking and later to such arts as the homily and letter writing, in effect acquiescing to rhetoric's subordination to more "substantial" disciplines, that is, theology, metaphysics, the sciences. But in Burke's hands rhetoric is no longer safely tucked away but has become "substantial" as Burke explained sub-stance in *A Grammar of Motives* (22–24): It "stands under," supports, makes possible not only the persuasiveness of its "betters" but also all human-made order itself. For, in Burke's vastly expanded sense, *as identification*, rhetoric designates the very process by which human societies are created, maintained, transformed, destroyed, and recreated.

Taken together, *A Grammar of Motives* and *A Rhetoric of Motives* bring off a reading of Philosophical culture as radical as any since. In Burke there is nothing more "substantial" than interpretation (hermeneutics), the logic of natural and artificial languages (dialectic), and persuasion (rhetoric). The so-called master or fundamental disciplines, Philosophy and/or theology (old style), elementary particle physics (new style), are all hermeneutical, dialectical, and rhetorical disciplines, all caught up in language and dependent on that which language enables, such as sophisticated tools and instruments, everything from the fulcrum to the particle accelerator. There is, consequently, no penetrating to the "thing itself," no matter how nuanced the interpretation, how subtle the dialectic, or convincing the rhetoric. We are still and forever filling out our interpretations, chasing down the implications of our own terminologies, and competing with one another to win adherents with whatever rhetorical skills we can muster. This—not Truth—is the human fate.

A Grammar of Motives and *A Rhetoric of Motives* carry us far into postPhilosophy, with its inversions and de-structions of Philosophical hierarchies and categories. But the most ambitious book is yet to come. In *The Rhetoric of Religion* (1961) he takes on onto-theology, the Jew-Greek synthesis at the center of the West, anchored in Jewish myth and history, and rationalized in the Philosophical struggle of Platonists and Aristotelians we know as Christian theology.

One way to understand what Burke is doing in *The Rhetoric of Religion* is to contrast his aims with a hermeneutical theorist who worked the same materials, Rudolf Bultmann. Since the "higher criticism" of the Bible became dominant in the nineteenth century, the tendency of most liberal theology has been toward some version of "demythologizing" (9–10). Bultmann and his many followers attempt to save the tradition by reading many of its less believable narratives as testaments of faith rather than history. From one point of view, demythologizing is the opposite pole to Vatican-style rigidification of dogma or Protestant Biblicism. From another, it is the "conservative" opponent to Derrida's uncompromising attack on onto-theology and all P/philosophy even distantly related to it, including Heidegger, Bultmann's primary influence. Derridean hermeneutics moves beyond demythologizing to desymbolization, that is, to depriving all symbols of meaning in the ordinary sense, reference or extension to extralinguistic existence, and therefore to any connection with or power to evoke the numinous. Deconstruction is indeed, especially with respect to the West's Jew-Greek synthesis, a cultural "scorched earth" policy (1), as Southwell maintains.

Burke's approach to onto-theology cannot be aligned with either Bultmann's or Derrida's. Unlike Bultmann's, Burke's position in *The Rhetoric of Religion* is explicitly uncommitted; as he says, he is not theistic, atheistic, or even agnostic (2). One's stance toward God's existence is simply irrelevant to logology *qua* logology, which means that it aligns easily with Burke's skepticism about claims to Truth. Consequently, since Burke makes no leap of faith, his project has nothing to do with Bultmann's effort to make Christianity more negotiable for modern intellectual horizons. However, Burke's motives are as tradition-conserving in their own way as Bultmann's: The former's proposal to study religion and theology in purely secular terms *for what they reveal about the motives of language itself*—that is, to study theology, "words about God," as logology, "words about words" (1)—makes virtually all onto-theology vitally relevant to the linguistic turn and, thus, to most contemporary philosophy. Demythologizing is relevant only to the believer or potential believer, desymbolization only to the purposes of negative hermeneutics; logology is relevant even to the avowed atheist and constitutes the constructive step beyond deconstruction. As long as we are interested in language, Burke suggests, we cannot cease turning the pages of religious and theological works, since they reveal with unusual clarity and profundity the motives inherent in symbolism.

From the standpoint of how traditional theologians read theology, logology is, as John Freccero contends, "essentially deconstructive of the theological edifices of the past" (53). Read as Freccero reads it, *The Rhetoric of Religion* does something similar to Derrida's work a few years before Derrida—an attractive thesis, no doubt, for some interpreters of Burke. However, one will not find in *The Rhetoric of Religion* Derrida's animus toward onto-theology, and whether we receive it as "essentially deconstructive" or not, we will certainly misread it if we take it as yet another effort in the vein of the radical Enlightenment to pass beyond or dispose of religion. Quite the contrary, Burke's aim being "to uphold the position that, in the study of human motives, we should *begin* with complex theories of transcendence . . . rather than with the [reductive] terminologies of simplified laboratory experiment" (5, my emphasis), he takes onto-theology as indispensable to understanding human being. To have language, to exist in a world rather than only an environment, is to find ourselves always already "beyond"—"transcendent" of—nonlinguistic existence. Hence, to ignore, dismiss, or deconstruct ontotheology is, willy-nilly, to play into the hands of scientistic reductionism.

I have commented at greater length on *The Rhetoric of Religion* because it exemplifies Burke's constructive deconstructionism. How he reads onto-theology, in other words, is paradigmatic of how he reads generally, via a hermeneutic he calls discounting. "By proper discounting," Burke maintains, "*everything* becomes usable" (*ATH* 244). But what exactly does Burke mean by "discounting"? Here is how it works in the less complex case of Burke's reading of dialectical materialism:

> [T]he statement that there is "a constant *interaction* between *spiritual* and *material* factors" would provide no grounds for taking materialism as the starting point, the "essence" of the pair. There is no "starting point" for an "interaction" . . . [I]t would be literally nonsense to say "This is both A and B, but it is only A." . . . The choice of *materialism* as the essence is not "logical," but "sociological." The word is a slogan, a comprehensive bit of shorthand. . . . [T]he church had taken "spirit" as the essence of the pair, Marx stressed the antithesis . . . in a way that could afford a new start. (*ATH* 245)

Or as Marx himself put it, he stood Hegel on his head ("Capital" 420), making matter rather than spirit the starting point or "essence" of the dialectic.

The hermeneutics based on discounting follows from Burke's antiformalistic view of discourse as symbolic action. A philosophy is not just a set of propositions. It is an act in a scene, a strategy for encompassing a situation. If we read it *only* formalistically, "in itself," or assess it solely by formalistic means—that is, logically—we are not only bound to misunderstand it as a response to a context but very likely to assess it only negatively, in deconstructive terms. We will perform like "those overscrupulous philosophers" Burke indicts as "bound to impoverish themselves by discovering that all thought is nonsense" (*ATH* 245–46). Some logical sophistication and ingenuity and the patience to scrutinize a philosophical text at length is all anyone needs to find incoherence of some kind. If mathematics falls short of full formal coherence, how could philosophy, relying for the most part on the polysemous symbols of natural language, possibly achieve it? Discounting, then, is designed in the first place to prevent wholesale rejection of our intellectual inheritance, the sort of cultural vandalism Burke saw going on among the logical positivists of his day.

Burke's hermeneutics is based in *caritas*, but he doesn't propose to arrest the analytical slide into wholesale massacre of past thought by *caritas* alone. Rather he reads philosophy both logically and sociologically, which is to say, rhetorically. Whatever its strictly logical shortcomings might be, Marxism, *read in context*—that is, interpreted as a strategy with definite rhetorical designs—is quite cogent, as the number of intelligent people past and present dedicated to or significantly influenced by it attest. In context the contradictions of Marxist thought become understandable, explicable. And so, simply by refusing to be hemmed in by formalism, Burke can discount any critique that ends merely in rejection or deconstruction, that rates the philosophical symbol at zero.

However, discounting does not reject logic or extol contradiction as a virtue. Burke discounts interpretations whose purpose is merely to debunk past thought, but he also discounts past thought. Tradition is not something to be swept away, but neither is it to be worshipped. Burke would avoid both cultural vandalism and book idolatry.

One way he discounts past thought is through logical critique. In the case of dialectical materialism, for example, Burke takes the interaction of spirit and matter *as an interaction*, resisting both the Hegelian and Marxist reductions. That is, on the one hand, he discounts materialism insofar as it would reduce symbolic action to an epiphenomenon of the brain or the forces of production. On the other hand, Burke takes symbolic action as never working independently of biology and economics. In this way he retains materialist insight without taking materialism as the Truth. He can also engage in formalistic critique without being trapped by its "all or nothing" mentality. A terminology does not have to be completely consistent to be insightful. But insofar as it is inconsistent or contradicts itself, it must be discounted, not taken, as the true believer takes it, at face value.

Burke also discounts via the most important concept in his hermeneutic, situational context. A philosophy is an act in a scene. As inscribed or printed, the act remains "the same" while the situation it was designed to encompass alters. No matter how well a philosophy copes with its original exigency, applied to a different set of historical conditions, it will be less apposite, more or less in need of revision. The naive ignore context or suppress its consequences and cling to "what the good book says"—hermeneutic fundamentalism, whether specifically religious or not—while iconoclasts are inclined to make pyres out of many good books, supposing that they have become wholly irrelevant or outmoded. In contrast, Burke "retrieves" past thought. He is not much concerned with what a philosopher did not or could not say, as Heidegger was, but rather with refurbishing old ideas and concepts, making that which most would consign to the history of philosophy usable again. As the "translation" of myth and ancient theology into logology, *The Rhetoric of Religion* is one sustained act of retrieval. Dramatism "brings back" act-centered thought, at least as old as Aristotle. Less spectacular examples abound in all of Burke's philosophy, making discounting-retrieval one of his most characteristic acts.

Finally, Burke also discounts pragmatically, by studying "how [a] doctrine behaved when released into a social texture" (*ATH* 245). The principle is ancient and unsurpassable: "By their fruits ye shall know them." But Burke resists any form of crude pragmatism, any simple-minded application of the "Does it work?" criterion.

When a philosophy or part of one is, to use Burke's term, "bureaucratized" (*ATH* 225), it is also typically "compromised," not necessarily in a bad sense, since innovative ideas have to be adjusted to social textures, or functional contexts, to stand any chance of working. But if rigidity usually means that a doctrine cannot be implemented or behaves badly when implemented, compromise means that reading the institutionalized "ism" is never a reading of it in "pure" form. Furthermore, bureaucratized doctrines rarely produce simply good or bad fruit, but typically good, bad, and indifferent simultaneously, making pragmatic discounting a highly relativistic judgment of proportions. For instance, Western capitalist theory combined with scientific-technical reason has produced great wealth for North America, western Europe, and parts of Asia but has also produced a legion of what Burke calls "unintended by-products" (*ATH* 139)—a massive underclass, dehumanization, loss of community, cultural destruction and trivialization, environmental degradation, and so on. Clearly only the very naive can still take capitalist-scientistic ideology at face value, but to rate "free" markets and technological innovation at zero is no less naive. How deep should the discount be? And exactly what needs discounting the most? These tend to be Burke's questions, not flat, global judgments of the thumbs up or down variety characteristic of vulgar pragmatism.

Although at the heart of it, there is more to Burke's hermeneutics than discounting and more to discounting than I have discussed here. But we have enough to get an adequate idea of what Burke is doing. He is merging interpretation and critique.

The more important question is *why*—Why does Burke want a hermeneutics that can at least in theory make everything usable? Having taken up an unmistakably postPhilosophical position by the mid-thirties, why does he spend much of the next thirty years transforming Philosophy into a hermeneutical pluralism, breaking traditional rhetoric out of Philosophical confinement, and developing a secular logology as elaborate and intricate as any Philosophical theology? Why tote all this baggage forward when one could, in the spirit of the Enlightenment, simply jettison it?

This question has several answers. As I have shown elsewhere ("*Auscultation*" 358–63), very early in his career Burke rejected the "*von Haus aus*" hermeneutical school, which wants a clean break with tradition and locates all hope in starting over, rebuilding from the ground up. Even if it were desirable, Burke argues, one cannot erase history as one erases a blackboard. Besides being impossible, starting over is undesirable. Had past horizons of meaning been *massively* in error, had those before us been unable to incorporate what they had learned from hard experience, even survival seems unlikely, much less the escape of sizable portions of the human race from a life nasty, brutish, and short. Burke would agree with Donald Davidson—massive error is unintelligible (167–68), which, of course, does not mean that considerable error is or that values functional in the past will remain so. By all means, as Burke said in his sketch of "the good life" in *Attitudes Toward History*, let us study the "Documents of Error"; but how can we if our approach is *von Haus aus*? We have swept out the very documents we would study. Even if we retained them long enough to deconstruct them, what profit is there in this? The "We-know-better" attitude characteristic of all negative hermeneutics—the attitude Burke satirizes as the arrogant, parochial notion that "everybody was a fool before November 14, 18——"—almost assures that we will learn much less than we could. "Our stupidities are ever born anew" is Burke's rejoinder to those who place all hope in messiahs, revolutions, new ages, and radical enlightenments (*ATH* 258–59).

Clearly, then, Burke rejects the whole rationale of hiatus hermeneutics. Much has been written about his concentration on "rebirth" (e.g., Rueckert, *Drama* 96–117), more or less significant reorganizations of our individual and collective life in response to private and public crisis. It is true that Burke sees rebirth as central to symbolic action. However, "rebirth" for Burke is always a metaphor, and a steeply discounted one at that. To echo Nicodemus, we cannot enter our mother's womb a second time and be born. We can alter our priorities, enlarge our horizons of meaning, even transvalue *some* of our values—but the process Burke calls "Saul-Paul reversals" in *Auscultation, Creation, and Revision* (90) are not only exceedingly rare but also not *really* a "dying" of the old self into a completely "new life." The old Pharisee of the Pharisees becomes a Christian obsessed with the law, and still entertaining other sources of his preconversion motives. If this is so of individuals, it is more so of groups, collective inertia being greater. Yet change, even significant change, which can certainly *feel* like rebirth, is possible, and may require symbolic acts to formalize it, as Burke holds; but as he also insists, a naive understanding of rebirth, an undiscounted one, distorts and distorts dangerously, encouraging people to believe that the past actually can be nullified and to cooperate unthinkingly with violent processes of change.

Another reason Burke rejects the Enlightenment assault on tradition has to do with the rhetorical turn. The provisional truths of rhetoric are quite distinct from Q.E.D. demonstrations; lacking compelling proof, rhetoric depends heavily on *topoi*, or commonplaces—that is, appeals to tradition. As Burke points out in *Permanence and Change*, one can only make the new appealing by resort to the unquestioned old (87), to what people already accept as true or desirable. Consequently, when Burke sought an alternative to the blandishments of scientific-technical reason, he "reached back" before the Enlightenment to action-centered or Dramatistic thought, which, as he says, "is sanctioned by a 'collective revelation' of long standing," represented by "such key terms as *tao, karma, dike, energeia, hodos, actus*—all of them words for action" (*LASA* 53–54). Burke is attempting to trump the appeal of mechanical or motion-centered scientistic images of human being, whose tradition is mostly recent and comparatively shallow, with an ancient and multicultural tradition whose persuasive resources may be sufficient to counter what Suzanne Langer aptly calls, in an ironic echo of Bacon, "the idols of the laboratory" (33–53). In short, Burke requires tradition as the source of Dramatism and most of the appeals he makes in its behalf.

Dramatism is new in the sense that it does not depend on the theology and metaphysics of ancient Dramatism, and new as well in incorporating, while discounting, the mechanistic metaphor itself—but the point is that it can draw on a "collective revelation" of deep and wide appeal. What Ricoeur calls the "hermeneutics of suspicion" ("Hermeneutics" 63–64) cannot. Pervasive hostility to one's own cultural inheritance drastically reduces the persuasive resources of a hermeneutic, and is thus, as Burke contends, self-defeating in the long run. It is far better to accept and discount than flatly reject or deconstruct.

Discounting is also better for the rhetorical turn's future. From Nietzsche on, negative hermeneutics has appropriated rhetoric for use against Philosophy, helping to fuel the turn itself. Increasingly Nietzsche and his most loyal followers (e.g., Foucault, de Man) are understood as allies in the contemporary revival of rhetoric, including rhetorical philosophy. At best this reading is a half-truth. Negative hermeneutics is friendly to rhetoric in only a very narrow way—typically to its own rhetoric and those likewise motivated by an animus toward tradition. In contrast, discounting, while *requiring* the negative critique (otherwise we read naively, taking philosophical symbols at face value), is in principle receptive to all rhetorics, past and present. Obviously, this openness, this continual search for the usable, is a far healthier and sustaining motivation for the rhetorical turn than the one-sided demolition work of Nietzsche's art of distrust.

It is also more consonant with rhetoric's function as, in Richard McKeon's phrase, "the architectonic art" (1): Through rhetoric claims come into being, that is, become articulate, come to stand. In the final analysis, no matter how useful it is for deconstruction, rhetoric is the art of construction and reconstruction. Rhetorical philosophy must ultimately "edify," using materials that have their source, like stone and concrete, in past sedimentations. Otherwise rhetoric cannot be itself and the rhetorical turn will turn against rhetoric.

It should now be clear why Burke resists the position we call negative hermeneutics and he called "debunking" (*PLF* 168) and why Burke refuses to discard the Philosophy and theology whose assumptions he has replaced with postPhilosophical ones.

The Linguistic Skepticism of Terministic Screens

As we discovered throughout Part One, what makes Burke's philosophy intriguing is that much of what he has to say is both germane to current concerns and different enough from current schools of thought to represent a distinctive voice in the dialogue. This is certainly true of his hermeneutics. Discounting engages a question at the center of contemporary controversy: What stance toward our intellectual inheritance ought we to take? His answer resembles neither of the two common alternatives we encounter now—the hermeneutics of trust or the hermeneutics of suspicion. It is too critical for the former, too ironic—too undercutting of modernist "superiority"—for the latter. Rather than opting for trust or suspicion, Burke preserves the tension between them, while locating hermeneutical virtue as Aristotle located ethical virtue—between a deficiency and an excess, between on the one hand no capacity for criticism and on the other a criticism too acute, that lets nothing stand.

Our question now becomes: Toward what general philosophical stance does discounting lead? While in practice Burke does not find a use for everything, one obvious consequence of the maxim, "Make everything usable," is that philosophical terminologies pile up more or less indefinitely. Deconstruction leaves no residual requiring further handling. But discounting is faced with the "problem" of what to do with a wealth of terminologies, all discounted, but nevertheless "there" to be coped with somehow.

We could decide to leave everything as hermeneutical affairs normally are anyway, at sixes and sevens. "Why make a problem," I could imagine a postmodernist such as Rorty or Lyotard asking, "out of a diversity of viewpoints, each represented by its own particular combination of terms?" We could just celebrate difference and diversity. "All the better for keeping the dialogue going," Rorty would say. "All the better for assuring dissensus," Lyotard would say. Only Philosophy, both would say, makes a problem out of Burke's ideal of "a dialectic of many voices" (*CS* xi), because it can be satisfied only with a monologue of Truth.

But Burke cannot be quite so *casual* about decentered fragmentation as some postmodern philosophy is. For him the accumulation of terminologies is a problem if only because he requires a rationale for the hermeneutic diversity that actually exists and for the *principled* organization of diversity, the pluralism, he espouses. The rationale for the former is what he calls "terministic screens." The general intellectual stance it implies is *linguistic skepticism.*

The concept designated by "terministic screen" can be traced to the treatment of "orientation" in *Permanence and Change* (see this study, pp. 45–46). But the following passage from "Definition of [Wo/]Man" is its *locus classicus* in the later philosophy. Having defined human beings as "typically the symbol-using animal," Burke asks:

> [C]an we bring ourselves to realize . . . just how overwhelmingly much of what we mean by "reality" has been built up for us through nothing but our symbol systems? Take away our books, and what little do we know about history, biography, even something so "down to earth" as the relative position of seas and continents? What is our "reality" . . . (beyond the paper-thin line of our own particular lives) but all this clutter of symbols about the past combined with whatever things we know mainly through maps, magazines, newspapers and the like about the present? . . . The various courses in the curriculum are in effect but so many different terminologies. And however important to us is the tiny sliver of reality each of us has experienced firsthand, the whole overall "picture" is but a construct of our symbol systems. To meditate on this fact until one sees its full implications is much like peering over the edge of things into an ultimate abyss. (*LASA* 5)

A terministic screen is this "whole overall 'picture'" of "'reality.'" It is part of ideology in the nonpejorative sense: We all have one or several screens just by being speakers of a certain language living in a certain time and place. It is also part of vocational or professional life, each way of earning a living developing its own more or less distinctive terminology or terminologies.

Each screen is like a template dropped over "reality"—but the analogy creates a misleading image because it conjures up a "reality" conveniently "there" for an overlay, whereas Burke insists that "overwhelmingly much of what we mean by 'reality' has been built up for us through nothing but our symbol systems." That which a terministic screen screens—that is, lets through and filters out—is also in very large measure constituted by the screen itself. Or viewed from the standpoint of the symbol-user, Burke claims that words

> in being a link between us and the nonverbal . . . are by the same token a screen separating us from the nonverbal—though

the statement gets tangled in its own traces, since so much of the "we" that is separated from the nonverbal by the verbal would not even exist were it not for the verbal. (*LASA* 5)

Now that much contemporary philosophy is dominated by "social constructionists," who see nothing but cultural *poesis* in truth claims; by hermeneuticists, who insist that there is nothing before or after interpretation; by devotees of "depth critique," who expose the ideology hidden in "objective accounts" of reality; and by deconstructionists, who say there is nothing outside the text—given this convergence in a symbolically constituted "reality"—perhaps the tendency is to receive what Burke said more than thirty years ago as "old news." Shrugging it off, however, misses the point implicit in the opening question, "Can we bring ourselves to realize just what the formula [symbol-using animal] implies?"

Decades later Rorty would ask much the same question: "Can the ubiquity of language ever really be taken seriously?" (57). The problem for both Burke and Rorty is not the sheer accumulation of terminologies, nor accepting the lack of fully authoritative centers. Given the global intermingling of cultures and the extreme social fragmentation of late capitalism, some version of linguistic relativism is inevitable. But can we really take seriously the implications of our own insight?

Burke says we can't. The abyss he speaks of opens up as soon as we recognize that words and things can never be identical: "Language referring to the realm of the nonverbal is necessarily talk about things in terms of what they are not" (*LASA* 5). The abyss is "ultimate" for human beings because there is no way out of language, no path "back to the things themselves." And so, while we may be able to suppress vertigo long enough to "peer over the edge of things into an ultimate abyss," we will also crawl away from the edge with relief and a will to forget the deeply unsettling experience. As the infant (i.e., the speechless) fears loss of support in the most literal, physical sense, so we speechful adults fear loss of symbolic support, resisting at a visceral level any attack on "good common sense" about language corresponding to "reality." We want to rely on it because we have to rely on it. And so Burke concludes, "[T]hough [we are] typically the symbol-using animal, [we] cling to a kind of naive verbal realism that refuses to realize the full extent of the role played by symbolicity in [our] notions of reality" (*LASA* 5). Rorty seems to believe that the problem is only taking seriously what we know to be the case—that language is ubiquitous. Burke's view is much less sanguine: The root of the problem is that when our theoretical guard is down—and it is down most of the time, whenever we are not playing the philosophy game (postmodern rules)—we revert instinctively and irresistibly to "a kind of naive verbal realism." *Everybody* does. He is not exempting himself. This is not some craven lack of intellectual courage, as Nietzsche thought. One cannot solve the problem by exhorting people to dance in joy at the edge of the abyss, any more than one can exhort an infant not to be afraid when the comforting arms are suddenly not securely beneath him/her. The ubiquity of language *cannot* be taken seriously—or if it can, only by cultivating a high level of sophistication and intellectual discipline. In all probability this means: It cannot be lived. It can only be thought, and then, in practical terms, "forgotten" when we return to quotidian activity where language is, as Burke says, "a set of labels, signs for helping us find our way about" (*LASA* 5). At this level it works tolerably well; for the most part the chasm between sign and signified, between, as Burke phrased it, the "sheer emptiness" of words "as compared with the substance of the things they name" (*LASA* 6), hardly shows itself. For the most part we can because we do function in the world as if the abyss did not exist.

There is in Burke's philosophy both an uncompromising commitment to linguistic enlightenment and a certain diffidence about its potential, a tension he shares, for example, with Theodor Adorno. He emphasizes, in much the same way Adorno does, the nonidentity of symbol and symbolized, together with all that it implies, especially a tragic estrangement of human being from the very world it founds and finds, especially from bodily or material existence. And like Adorno, Burke takes this alienation as a permanent condition, part of the being of human being, and therefore not reducible to specifically capitalist alienation. Consequently, again like Adorno, Burke is not caught up in the dialectic of the Enlightenment, with its promise of a progressive overcoming of all human limitations. Alienation can be ameliorated, but not eliminated.

Unlike Adorno, however, Burke sees little profit to residing within a purely negative dialectic. What approach, then, is livable, given the skepticism warranted by the absurd disproportion between symbol and symbolized and the relativism warranted by the sheer piling up of terminologies, each with its own following of "true believers"? Burke opts for the dialectic of "terministic screens," as summed up in the following formula: "Even if any given terminology is a *reflection* of reality, by its very nature as a terminology it must be a *selection* of reality; and to this extent it must function also as a *deflection* of reality" (*LASA* 45)." Terministic screens obviously affirm the hermeneutics of discounting: Insofar as a terminology has some power to reflect or "speculate" on "reality," we cannot simply discard it without diminishing our own options for "seeing"; but insofar as it also, and it must, select-deflect, we cannot simply take it as terminologies normally want to be taken, as synonymous with or adequate to "reality" itself. Keeping the identity of discounting and terministic screens in mind, let's ponder some of the implications of the formula itself.

"Even if any given terminology is a *reflection* of reality"—in this "even if" Burke recognizes the wholly negative possibility, that a terminology may be so distorted by malice, ignorance, blinding prejudice, and so forth, that it bends back only its own dis-ease. His opposition to a methodology of debunking does not mean that he cannot rate *some* terminologies at, or very near, zero. But in this "even if" Burke also recognizes the power of language to reveal the world selectively, which means rejecting poststructuralism's flatly anti-epistemic stance. For poststructuralism language is not a screen, a reflecting-deflecting of "reality," but a self-contained system lacking "speculative" power. "Reality" itself becomes *wholly* sign or symbol, wholly "textual"—a reduction Burke would construe as very drastic indeed, since symbols are "sheer emptiness as compared with the substance of the things they name" (*LASA* 6). To make reality wholly a text is to make it sheer emptiness—traces, and traces of traces.

On the one hand, then, Burke forecloses on epistemology. The alienation of word and thing makes all talk about correspondence at best a very superficial affair. On the other hand, he stands firmly against any effort to dissolve or even weaken the tension between symbol and symbolized. For Burke terminologies are certainly epistemic: As he says, they "direct the *at*tention" (*LASA* 45, Burke's emphasis), permitting us to "see"—observe, already an interpretation—what we would otherwise miss altogether. For example, where most of us would see nothing but rocks, the paleontologist, equipped with a terminology and the experience of working with others likewise equipped, sees little fragments of fossil bone. What we know is overwhelmingly de-term-ined, enabled-limited by our terminology. So much so that

> *[m]any of the "observations" are but implications of the particular terminology in terms of which the observations are made.* In brief, much that we take as observations about "reality" may be but the spinning out of possibilities implicit in our particular choice of terms. (*LASA* 46, Burke's emphasis)

We must not equate the "here" (the terminology) with the "there" ("reality" observed); Burke avoids the fallacy of the framework by refusing to *reduce* perception to language. "Many . . . much" but not *all* observations derive from our terministic screen. If all did, the anomalous could not arise. But since the "here" is already "there," directing the attention, and the "there" is already "here" as marked expectations of what we expect to re-view, there is also no separating them, no neo-Kantian urge to discriminate what language contributes to knowledge as opposed to "reality." No line can be drawn between differences so intertwined that no place remains for the drawing. We can never be certain, then, about the status of our observations, about what is "really there." We can, however, be certain of this: In directing the attention into some channels rather than others, a terminology will at best reveal "reality" selectively. As Burke put it in *Permanence and Change*, "[A] way of seeing is also a way of not seeing" (49).

Since we are all invested in our terminologies, a frontal assault on naive verbal realism—for example, Derrida's effort to eradicate presence—is not a very productive hermeneutical strategy. The danger is not in presence *per se* but in fanatical adherence to a single presencing. If a way of seeing is also a way of not seeing, then the best approach is to cultivate as many ways of seeing as possible. Burke's "dialectic of many voices" is a decentering that precludes fanatical adherence to any one presencing. It also precludes synthesis in the totalizing and potentially totalitarian sense that postmodernism would avoid at any cost. There will be no shortage of dissensus in a dialectic of many voices. But what matters most is that a dialectic of many voices is livable, and the life of it is dialogue, precisely the cure for human being's constant lapsing into naive verbal realism. If meditating the abyss is not sustaining, perhaps an endless conversation is, enlisting language against itself, screening the screens, draining the idol of its mystique, which makes dashing it against the temple floor an act of pointless vandalism.

Beyond Mere Relativism: The Dramatistic Screen

"Must we merely resign ourselves," Burke asks, "to an endless catalogue of terministic screens?" "In one sense, yes," for "we *must* use terministic screens, since we can't say anything without the use of terms; whatever terms we use, they necessarily constitute a corresponding kind of screen; and any such screen necessarily directs the attention to one field rather than another." Pushed to nominalistic extremes, our individual idiolects amount to so many terministic screens. "There will be as many different world views in human history as there are people"; we are "'necessarily free' to be [our] own tyrant, inexorably imposing upon [ourselves] the peculiar combination of insights associated with [our] peculiar combination of experiences" (*LASA* 50, 52).

To some degree we can escape self-imposed tyranny through dialogue, with its capacity to enlarge horizons and examine critically the terms we use. We can also deliberately cultivate a number of screens, increasing our options for seeing. Dialogical pluralism can save us from idolatry, from what Burke calls elsewhere "the mania of the One." But it delivers us from mania only to surrender us to "the delirium of the Many" (*CP* 41), apparently total linguistic relativism. The "endless catalogue" of terministic screens remains, "each of which can be valued for the light it throws upon the human animal, yet none of which can be considered central." Unwilling to settle for a decentering indistinguishable from intellectual fragmentation, near the end of "Terministic Screens" Burke offers an "attempt to avoid mere relativism" (*LASA* 52). It may also be read as an attempt by a postPhilosopher to preserve philosophy itself, and therefore highly significant in the context of current arguments about whether the end of Philosophy means the end of philosophy as well.

Commenting on an article by Dennis H. Wrong, "The Oversocialized Conception of Man in Modern Sociology," Burke claims that "the author's thesis really has a much wider application than he claims for it":

> [Since] all scientific terminologies . . . are designed to focus attention upon one or another particular field . . . would it not be technically impossible for any such specialized terminology to supply an adequate definition for the discussion of [hu]*man* [being] *in general*? . . . Any definition . . . in terms of specialized scientific nomenclatures would necessarily be "over-socialized," or "over-biologized," or "over-psychologized," [and so forth] . . . [I]f we try to correct the excesses of *one terminology*, by borrowing from several, what strictly *scientific* canon (in the modern sense of scientific specialization) could we adduce as sanction? Would not such an eclectic recipe itself involve a generalized philosophy of some sort?

By this reasoning Burke concludes that "the definition of [hu]man [being] in general would be formally possible only to a *philosophic* terminology of motives" (*LASA* 51–52, Burke's emphasis).

Burke's argument depends on a number of assumptions, all open to fundamental question. Most importantly, he assumes that the proper study of human being is human being, and that this study can yield a significant measure of self-understanding. In other words, to agree with him we must believe that a philosophical anthropology is both possible and worthwhile. As we will see in the next essay, his entire philosophy rests on these assumptions: If there is no "proper" to human being, if there is nothing we can say about the being of human being, then Burke's philosophy must be rejected. For all of it is the explication of a single proposition: Human being is typically the symbol-using animal.

If only for the sake of argument we can for now allow the assumptions to stand, I cannot detect any significant problem with what he has to say about the nature of scientific terminologies and their relation to philosophical terminologies. Even scientific anthropology, supposedly dedicated to the study of humankind as such, is really a collection of loosely related screens, each designed for highly specialized inquiry. No common understanding of human being in general arises from archaeology, physical anthropology, cultural anthropology, and so forth. From time to time we hear of efforts (or at least aspirations) to integrate physics with chemistry, both with biology, and biology with the study of culture (see, e.g., Gell-Mann), but so far at least the results have not been impressive as compared with the depth and sophistication of the individual sciences themselves. And the efforts at integration show, if nothing else, that no "strictly *scientific* canon" can be adduced to sanction the integrative effort itself. "An eclectic recipe" will bake a strange cake indeed in the absence of "a generalized philosophy" for putting ingredients together—without, that is, a "screen of screens." But science, especially in the English-speaking world, is checked by the fear of "contamination" by philosophy.

In arguing for the necessity of philosophy Burke takes care not to make Philosophical claims for philosophy in general or for his philosophy in particular. Philosophy is not the foundational or capstone discipline. Rather it is "higher" only in the sense of being more abstract than the special sciences, which makes a "definition of [hu]man [being] in general . . . formally possible." By "formally possible" Burke means only this: Whereas, for example, biology can only be biology by confining itself to biological terms, a philosophy can address what all terminologies have in common—their nature as linguistic or symbolic constructs. Philosophy can develop a terminology for discussing terminologies—not the same thing as linguistic science, of course, which is another set of specialized terminologies. In moving to this level one moves at the same time to the possibility of a definition of human being, since the vast accumulation of specialized nomenclatures as such confirms our species being as the symbol-using animal. As Burke puts it, in language obviously designed to distinguish his own view from older, honorific conceptions of human being:

> Whether such proneness to symbolic activity be viewed as a privilege or a calamity (or as something of both), it is a distinguishing characteristic of the human animal in general. Hence it can properly serve as the basis of a general, or philosophic definition of this animal. From this terministic beginning, this intuitive grounding of a position, many observations "necessarily follow." (*LASA* 52)

The "proof" of the position resides in the quality of the observations—whether a philosophic view that begins from a position as abstract as species being results in useful insight. If not, the cogency of Burke's logic is, in the worst sense, academic. But for now I would at least insist on its cogency: The existence of many specialized terminologies provides the incentive for studying terminologies *per se* and the animal that uses them. This study is *formally* a philosophic concern, not something science *qua* science can address. To the extent that we acknowledge a need for the kind of study Burke proposes, postPhilosophy cannot part with philosophy. To do so would be to give up all general views of anything and settle for "an endless catalogue of terministic screens," all valued equally, none valued in particular.

And yet, even if we recognize the function for philosophy Burke argues for, have we escaped relativism? By his own logic, "must we not concede that a screen built on this [philosophical] basis is just one more screen; and that it can at best be permitted to take its place among all the others?" (*LASA* 52–53). Dramatism cannot escape its nature as a screen; it too directs the attention into some channels rather than others and partakes in the dialectic of selection-reflection-deflection. It *is* "just one more screen" in being quite unable to claim any privileged contact with "reality" itself. Burke never defends it as a special revelation of Truth. The "special favors" he claims for it are not justified Philosophically. Rather, he claims that "we do make a *pragmatic distinction* between the 'actions' of 'persons' and the sheer 'motions' of 'things'" (*LASA* 53, my emphasis). "Even the behaviorist," Burke maintains, "must treat his colleagues as *persons*, rather than purely and simply as automata responding to stimuli" (*LASA* 53, Burke's emphasis). The Dramatistic distinction is not warranted by an appeal to ontology or epistemology but by an appeal to *praxis*—that is, as implied by the way we comport ourselves toward human beings as contrasted with things or even other animals.

Burke quite specifically abjures Philosophical intent in defending his *praxis*-based distinction between action and motion:

> I am not pronouncing on the metaphysics of this controversy. Maybe we are but things in motion. . . . For the sake of the argument, I'm even willing to grant that the distinction between *things moving* and *persons acting* is but an illusion. All I would claim is that, illusion or not, the human race cannot possibly get along with itself on the basis of any other intuition. (*LASA* 53, Burke's emphasis)

At the very least, then, Dramatism's insistence on "persons acting" is a necessary fiction, with heavy emphasis on necessary. Otherwise we cannot explain why we treat things and people differently. Otherwise we cannot account for our moral outrage when people are treated as things, or like insects or rats, as candidates for mass extermination: Much of the horror of the Holocaust resides in a *systematic* abrogating of the Dramatistic distinction. When the distinction is lost, all moral bearing is lost, and we enter the darkness at the heart of darkness. Something so indispensable to explaining why we behave as we do and why we condemn certain behavior that ignores the implicit rules can surely claim "special favors." Dramatism both is and is not "just another screen."

It is hard to doubt what Burke is saying here: Dramatism has a pragmatic-ethical rationale not a metaphysical foundation. What he says, however, is one thing; how we read him quite another. Interpreters invested in a metaphysics of action—Southwell and Lentricchia, for instance—will likely discount what Burke says as a cagey minimalism. He really believes in at least a limited human capacity for action, they will say, and expects us to believe in it as well. They have a point: Burke *is* being cagey here; why claim more than one has to to secure "special favors" for a terministic screen? And they are undoubtedly right to hold that Burke "really believes" in action, that any taking of it on his part as an illusion could only be "for the sake of argument." But what does "believe" mean here? It means, in his own words, "an intuitive grounding of a position"—not something one could know in the sense of epistemological certainty or undertake to demonstrate in the sense that mathematics or science understands demonstration. Burke's belief in action is, as you prefer, a postulate or an act of faith, a "belief" in the sense of the New Testament word translated as faith, *pistis*, "opinion." The fact that many people in many cultures have also held this opinion—part of the evidence Burke adduces in support of the Dramatistic distinction—lends a certain force to it, makes it more persuasive, but it does not make it True.

In a memorable phrase Burke called metaphysics "coy theology" (*LASA* 46). Is his pragmatic-moral argument for Dramatism a covert or "coy metaphysics," only another step removed from a full-blown theology? To say so is to refuse to recognize or to take seriously Burke's skepticism. Burke knows that he does not know whether his intuition is any more than an intuition. He points himself in "Terministic Screens" and elsewhere to examples of people just moving or being moved. He knows that many influential thinkers from Augustine to Freud (and before and after both of them) have denied, in some sense and to some degree, the assertion that "people act." The opinion is hardly universal or beyond dispute. So he plays the hand he has been dealt, taking maximum advantage of its strengths, but refusing to overplay it.

In sum, had Burke wished to write a Philosophy of the act, there was nothing to stop him from doing so and many examples, ancient and recent, he might have drawn on for his metaphysics. But he chose not to, and he chose not to because his skepticism precludes a metaphysics. If Southwell, Lentricchia, and other students of Burke wish to make the leap from pragmatics to metaphysics, we can wish them well, but we must deny that they can make the leap hand in hand with Burke. The pragmatic-moral argument is not a coy metaphysics; it is, rather, what one has left when one thinks there are no grounds and no compelling need for a metaphysics.

Burke opts for philosophy rather than Philosophy—this must be affirmed against those that wish to construct a metanarrative about Truth from his work. But it is precisely this opting for philosophy that postmodern interpretations of Burke must resist or ignore or downplay. They will be deeply suspicious of Burke's motivation for claiming special favors for Dramatism. Isn't Burke's argument only a harder-to-attack way of reinstating Philosophy? Doesn't it move dangerously close to Philosophical monologue or aspirations for overcoming otherness in yet another Philosophical synthesis? In short, postphilosophical readers of Burke may also assume that there is a coy metaphysics lurking somewhere in Burke's refusal to affirm a metaphysics. But instead of celebrating it, they will condemn it.

Postmodern thought is marked by a healthy regard for otherness, and consequently a pervasive animus toward "centricities," ego-, ethno-, phallo-, logo-, and so forth. The absolute value Burke attributes to dialogue and his view of language as terministic screens confirm the postmodern commitments of his philosophy. But Burke understands the dialectic of difference better than most postmodernists do. We can only encounter otherness from the horizon of our own prejudices, and no useful encounter can result without these prejudices: If we have no center, there is nothing from which to decenter, no assertions to make, and therefore no dialogue. Conversely, decentering is misunderstood if taken to end desirably in no center, in "mere relativism." Decentering is not dis-integration but rather a new or at least enlarged integration: To decenter is to move to a revised center. There is, in short, no escape from "centricity" *of some kind*, as there is no escape from terministic screens *of some sort*. The question is not, Shall we have a center? but rather, What kind of center shall we have? Once we acknowledge this, only the capacity and the courage to articulate stands between an implicit horizon of meanings and an explicit philosophy. Our general view of anything is our philosophy of it; our general view of "everything" is our philosophy. The rather transparent trick of "writing under erasure" makes no difference in this regard.

What Burke does near the end of "Terministic Screens" is acknowledge his center and acknowledge it for what all articulate and reasoned centers are or can become—a philosophy. He presents it as an effort to escape "mere relativism," but obviously the Houdini maneuver was already a *fait accompli*, and what he is doing is arguing for "dramacentricity." What kind of center is Dramatism? It is clearly humanistic in the technical sense of focusing on human being, but not in the Humanistic, self-glorifying sense that might be called species arrogance. Symbol-using happened to evolve in a certain species and became its most distinctive aptitude. If human being ceases to exist, so far as we know symbol-using will cease as well. In other words, Burke claims neither human being nor its language as the intent or culmination of Being or creation. Burke's humanism is decentered even from its centering in *homo dialecticus*.

Dramatism would avoid "mere relativism." But it would do this while being as broadly inclusive as possible. As his close study and use of behaviorism shows, he even proposes to take in whatever can be gleaned from *anti*-Dramatistic screens. Behaviorism rejects its other, denying categorically that persons act; Dramatism affirms its other, acknowledging that persons sometimes move rather than act, that there are "givens" or compulsory aspects in all action, and that all action depends on the sheer motions of the body, on its physics and chemistry, without being reducible to physics and chemistry. If Burke willingly admits the anti-Dramatistic to his dialogue of many voices, the only non-Dramatistic—most of the rest of science and some P/philosophy—poses no problems. No source of insight is omitted because of the source. In *Attitudes Toward History* Burke praises William James as "one who welcomed light from any quarter" (9). The same can be said of Burke. The Dramatistic center is always already decentered, relativistic without being "merely" so.

Finally, since so many of Burke's students speak of "the Dramatistic system" or "synthesis," we need to remember that he deliberately left the so-called system unfinished and that the synthesis—if the word can be applied at all to his work—is *not* Hegelian. For example, Burke's treatment of the "philosophical schools" in *A Grammar of Motives* is actually a certain organization of diversity around his Pentad of terms implicit in action: There is act-centered philosophy, scene-centered philosophy, agency-centered philosophy, and so on. Burke would use them all, throwing away nothing or as little as possible. He does not attempt to sublate otherness as Hegel did—that is, he does not claim that his philosophy embraces and reconciles all previous philosophy, as if Dramatism was the hidden *telos* driving the history of thought. Rather the various voices are left in conflict, each directing the attention in its own way, and making its own, limited claims to truth. The Pentad offers only, in his own words, "a system of placement" (xxii–xxiii), a way of grouping related terminologies and of seeing relationships among the groupings. As for Truth, the Dramatistic screen offers no metanarrative, no Truth of truths: Rather it "involves a methodic tracking down of the implications in the idea of symbolic action, and of [hu]man [being] as the kind of being that is particularly distinguished by an aptitude for such action" (*LASA* 54). Burke's resolve is to expose what his chosen screen can do—its pragmatic value—which should be sharply distinguished from foundational claims.

Dramatism poses no threat at all to postmodernism's salutary insistence on difference and shares its distrust of totality. But Burke also challenges postmodernism at its most vulnerable point, its tendency to collapse into an empty, omnitolerant anti-structure, all margins and no center, a mere negation of Philosophy, a "mere relativism." The challenge is, first, to admit that the intellectual life requires constructions, centeredness in something besides negative dialectic or deconstruction. Then, second, the challenge is either to accept Burke's "decentered center" or find another that can do more without compromising the dialectic of difference. We see again, then, this time in the context of Burke's later philosophy, that his thought leads not toward or away from postmodernism but rather through and beyond it to something that is neither Philosophy nor anti-philosophy but a workable postPhilosophy.

6

"Humility Without Humiliation": The Philosophical Anthropology

Always beneath the dance of words there will be the dance of bodies.

—Kenneth Burke, *The Rhetoric of Religion*

Introduction: Locating the Later Philosophy

Our task is to examine a single essay first published in 1963, "Definition of [Wo/]Man." For Burke it was a "breakthrough" (*LASA* 3), a kind of eureka moment. I see it as the gathering place of his philosophy. Most of the issues and ideas discussed in Part One converge here, and most of the later philosophy may be traced to or back to it. For Burke's mature thought is a philosophical anthropology, and its text of texts is "Definition."

The general implications of this claim are perhaps obvious to anyone familiar with recent Burke criticism and/or with what I have been calling the conversation after Philosophy. Cary Nelson, David Cratis Williams, and others have begun to challenge the consensus reading of Burke as a humanist. Their efforts are stimulating, a creative instance of Burke's "perspective by incongruity" (*PC* 88–92). Certainly Burke is not a traditional humanist—a Humanist, capital "H"—and the post-humanist readings have helped to make this clear. However, the perspective is also definitely incongruous; dissociating Burke from humanism is like reading Marx as if we were a closet idealist. And so the question that must be asked is, What kind of humanist is he?

To grasp what is at stake in the question, we turn again to Thomas McCarthy's "General Introduction" to *After Philosophy: End or Transformation?* "Cartesianism is something of a straw man in contemporary philosophy," McCarthy observes, because, after the linguistic turn, no one "regards the subject . . . as punctual, atomistic, disembodied," or "understands rational autonomy [as] total disengagement," or "appeals to immediate, intuitive self-presence as the basis of self-knowledge," or "regards full self-transparence as a sensible ideal of self-knowledge" (8). The real issue is what conclusion to draw from the demise of the Cartesian subject.

> For the end-of-philosophy thinkers the twilight of Cartesian-Kantian subjectivity means the end of "Man" and of the philosophical humanism that draws its life from that conception. For . . . other[s] . . . this situation represents rather a challenge to rethink our idea of the rational subject and to recast accordingly our received humanistic ideals. (8)

It is hardly surprising that the inspiration for the post-humanist interpretation of Burke is drawn from end-of-philosophy thinkers, especially Derrida. If Christine Oravec is right in claiming that these philosophers come together in "view[ing] . . . the individual as 'constructed' rather than 'constructing,'" as "determined by forces . . . nonproductive of uniqueness or 'identity'" (176), then it follows that they will also be indifferent or hostile to philosophical anthropology and contemporary humanism. "Constructed" human being has no being "in itself." "Human nature" is a mistake or a fiction or a fraud; we are entirely the product of "thrownness," the environmental and cultural conditions of our time and place.

The humanist reading of Burke has not responded adequately to Burke's firm and unambiguous rejection of Cartesian-Kantian subjectivity. Nor has the humanist reading connected Burke significantly with the ongoing effort "to rethink our idea of the rational subject and to recast accordingly our received humanistic ideals." Our choice is not confined to Descartes or Derrida, a reified subject or no subject. Rather, as McCarthy points out, we can turn to, among others, Ricoeur, Blumenberg, Gadamer, and Taylor, all hermeneutic neo-humanists whose motives for doing philosophy parallel Burke's. Taylor, for instance,

> argues that overcoming epistemology does not amount to overcoming philosophy *tout court*. It points, rather, to a continuation-through-transformation of the "tradition of self-critical reason." . . . [W]e are first and foremost embodied agents in a world. Our propositional knowledge of the world is

grounded in our dealings with it; and there can be no question of totally objectifying the prior grasp gained as agents within it. The task of philosophy is the unending one of articulating this background[,] . . . making partial detachment and revision possible. Philosophy . . . leads to a better understanding of what we are as knowing agents; it thereby provides insight into the anthropological questions associated with our moral concerns. (McCarthy 9)

I began this study by arguing against any simple assimilation of Burke to existing philosophical "schools." My opinion has not changed. However, Burke's later philosophy finds its strongest "family resemblance" among hermeneutic neo-humanists.

We have seen already that Burke "overcomes epistemology" with his action-centered view of knowledge without abandoning philosophy (see pp. 87–91). Burke's work, then, offers independent confirmation of Taylor's argument that overcoming epistemology need hardly imply overcoming philosophy *tout court.*

Burke and Taylor come together most strongly in the assumption that human beings are "first and foremost embodied agents in a world," a position they share with contemporary phenomenology in general and with Bakhtin and Merleau-Ponty in particular. There can be no question that Burke's philosophy aims at the "unending [task] of articulating [the] background" of action, "making partial detachment and revision possible." His later philosophy is so committed to hermeneutical reflection that if we hold with postphilosophy "that there is nothing there [in the background of action] that could be better understood," that the quest for meaning is to be "rejected on the grounds of the essential undecidability of meaning" (McCarthy 10), we can see no point in what Burke is trying to do.

Finally, in a distinctive way analogous to hermeneutics, Burke is committed to "anthropological questions associated with our moral concerns." Kant's philosophical anthropology and ethics are no longer live options, but his linking of the question, What are we? to the question, What should we do? hardly belongs to the past. Without invoking metaphysics or natural law, the "ought" of ethics has only philosophical anthropology left as a source of moral understanding. Put negatively: To deny being for human being amounts to either the abandoning of ethical thought or the complete assimilating of it to this or that cultural constellation of norms.

The question is, Is ethics entirely relative to regimes of truth? The "constructed" view of human being must answer "yes" and can point to cultural and historical studies for confirmation. Without denying either cultural diversity or alterations within cultures over time, Burke holds that regimes of truth cannot be the whole story it purports to be. Consequently, he seeks an "is"—a being for human being defensible after Darwin—within which an "ought" (*pace* Hume) can be derived—that is, a transhistorical, transcultural understanding against which to assess historical-cultural norms. This possibility is what he means when he says that "Definition of [Wo/]Man" is both descriptive and normative (*LASA* 20).

In sum, then:

1. While remaining skeptical in his attitude toward Philosophy, Burke's later thought finds its center in a philosophical anthropology.

2. Rather than deforming his thought to fit post-humanist outlooks, a more illuminating approach is to assess his philosophy within contemporary hermeneutic neo-humanism.

The rest of this essay deals with point one. But point two is no less important in addressing the question of Burke's philosophical identity, part of which is deciding how to locate his thought within the current intellectual scene. I claim him not only for postPhilosophy in general but also, more specifically, for its hermeneutical branch.

If Burke's loyalties are to postPhilosophy rather than postphilosophy, we cannot place him within poststructuralism or deconstruction. As we discovered in Part One, he *rethinks* the rational subject rather than abandoning or dismantling the category (see pp. 36–43). In this essay we will explore his effort to recast our inherited humanistic ideals, ideals that must be recast if we define human being as *embodied* agents in a world, in Burke's case, as symbol-using *animals*. But clearly Burke does not hold either that human being is indeterminate nor that humanistic values are merely "ideological" (i.e., illusory) or outmoded. Furthermore, again in sharp contrast to poststructuralism, Burke believes in the value of hermeneutical reflection and in its power to increase self-understanding.

These are significant motives for continuing to do philosophy that Burke shares with philosophical hermeneutics. In the next essay we will take up something else Burke and hermeneutics have in common—a profound commitment to the dialectical tradition.

To claim a family resemblance, however, is not to claim a simple identity. Burke is not an American version of Gadamer. In the last essay we could not equate Burke's hermeneutics of discounting with the hermeneutics of trust or tradition; the former has a critical function absent or underdeveloped in the latter. In this and subsequent essays we will uncover other points of difference, among them the following. Whereas hermeneutics seeks to overcome dualistic thought, Burke's very notion of human being entails an anthropological dualism; whereas hermeneutics contrasts truth and method, Dramatism does not; most importantly, whereas hermeneutics tends to limit praxis to self-understanding, Burke follows Marx in understanding it as more than self-interpretation.

These differences are fully as significant as the motives Burke shares with philosophical hermeneutics. In asserting a family resemblance, then, I am claiming only that they are close enough to make argument pointed, dialogue worthwhile. We should locate Burke in the hermeneutic branch of PostPhilosophy because the best potential for an extended conversation exists here—and with other philosophers also akin to hermeneutics, such as Bakhtin and Buber.

Humanisms, Traditional, Neo, and Post: A Typology

Humanistic philosophy embraces a number of meanings, each with its own complex history, none of which can be discussed here in detail. Purely as a context for thinking about Burke's "Definition," I offer the following sketch of five categories:

1. Static or traditional

2. Dynamic or Enlightenment

3. Finite or hermeneutical

4. Deficient or anthropological

5. Null or postphilosophical

The first two categories are Humanistic or Philosophical, grounded in metaphysics. Probably the clearest example of the first is the classical *zoon logon echon* or *animal rationale*. At least implied is the "great chain of being," a fixed hierarchy of creation. Human being is both animal, belonging to the sublunar world, and rational, partaking in the creative, ordering mind of God—a "quintessence of dust" and yet "like an angel," as Hamlet said. In one way, human being is a culmination—last created in the Genesis account and given dominion over the earth—in another way, a fallen and typically self-deluded creature, incomparably less than the heavenly orders, unthinkably less than the Creator.

Traditional Humanism belongs to the history of Philosophy in the sense that neither the universe nor anything in it can now be thought of in steady-state fashion. In the pre-Darwinian world individuals and peoples had a history, came and went, but the category, the human *zoon*, remained. In the post-Darwinian world, the *zoa* themselves have no permanence. Consequently, except as a habit of thought left over from Philosophical realism, one can no longer speak of Creation in the way that older cosmologies could, nor of human being as the pinnacle of Creation.

And yet we still define *per genus et differentia*, a heritage of what C. S. Lewis aptly called "the discarded image" of a fixed, hierarchical Being. Furthermore, the current sense of human being as finite, deficient, and even empty, passively fashioned from without, can be traced to Traditional Humanism. The so-called honorific conception of human being as rational always had its opposite, Dionysian ecstasy or the Greek-Jew understanding of human being as predisposed toward error or distorted by sin.

The dynamic conception of human being has its origin in Jewish historicism, in the destruction of Israel and the diaspora, redeemed as the last days approach by a new Israel conceived as a universal mecca for all humankind. Essence resides in the *telos* of history, in the perfection of the fullness of time that brings history to an end. Hegel, of course, is the great Philosopher of dynamic or Enlightenment human being, the unfolding of history toward Absolute Spirit being Philosophy's equivalent of the visions of Jewish apocalypse or the Christian Second Coming. Marxist faith in the eventual withering away of the state is the dialectical materialist equivalent of the moment that becomes permanent, and thus ends history. In popular philosophy throughout the West, belief in never-ending material, intellectual, social, and moral progress belongs to the dynamic-Enlightenment image of human being.

At first Darwinism reinforced Enlightenment human being, its understanding of more complex life forms developing from less complex ones cooperating with the Excelsior! mentality of the era. But evolutionary thought is really the negation of Humanism, static or dynamic, a profound decentering from doctrines of human specialness, whether conceived as here and now—the Kingdom of God is within you—or to come—the Kingdom of God is dawning. In any case, whatever remained of Enlightenment "Man" could not survive the War to End All Wars, succeeded by yet a still more devastating global conflict and the unimaginable misery of the Holocaust. The "triumph" of the latter half of the twentieth century is that our wars and holocausts have been relatively small and our once quite realistic fear that the world will end in nuclear fire has become a little less warranted. This is "progress." Enlightenment "Man" survives only in occasional rhetoric whose hollowness is apparent to all but the very young or the invincibly naive. Rushing to meet the future with open arms is hardly the spirit of our times.

And so where (and who) are we? What are the options after the collapse of both traditional and Enlightenment Humanism?

The closest to Philosophy is Ricoeur's "fallible man," his "ontology of finitude" (*Fallible Man* 18–24). Ricoeur emphasizes the tragic dimension of Traditional Humanism, human being as "fallen"—that is, alienated from Being, not in possession of self and world—and prone to error and misjudgment. Human being desperately needs God, yet inclines to a misplaced self-reliance. For all of its ties to tradition, Ricoeur's view is nevertheless postPhilosophical in its acceptance of Heidegger's "thrownness" (*Being and Time* 416) as a description of the human condition. "Thrownness" implies the absence of an assured grounding and thus removes Ricoeur from both static and dynamic Humanism. Radical finitude also implies rejection of the all-encompassing Philosophical project. Ricoeur is a Hegelian but denies the very possibility that human being can attain complete knowledge of self and world—that is, Absolute Spirit. We can understand ourselves better, but never completely. The ontology of finitude can imagine limited enlightenment, but not Enlightenment "Man."

In the place of rational animal, hermeneutic anthropology substitutes some version of Taylor's "self-interpreting animal," or "subjects of significance," or "beings for whom things matter" (Baynes 459–60). All derive from Heidegger's explication of human "ek-sistence" as "standing in the lighting of Being." Animals exist in the sense of being "lodged in their respective environments." But human beings ek-sist in a *world* made possible by language, "the lighting-concealing advent of Being itself" ("Letter" 205–6). In language Being and beings become present, meaning-full, no longer only the flux of fleeting sensation.

As a continuing through transformation of the ancient tradition of text interpretation, hermeneutical anthropology is humanistic in the sense of being rooted in the humanities. In contrast, the deficient view of human being draws from natural science. "[Wo/]Man is a creature who has fallen back out of the ordered arrangements that nature has accomplished" and thus lacks certain "pre-given, prepared structures to fit into." Human being is deficient in instincts, a "bare, forked thing" deprived of its natural home—a *Mangelwesen* ("creature of deficiencies"). As Blumenberg explains, "Actions have to take the place of the automatic controls that [s/]he lacks or correct those that have acquired an erratic inaccuracy. Action compensates for the 'indeterminateness' of the creature [wo/]man" (433). Whereas hermeneutical anthropology contrasts the human world with the creaturely environment, finding in the former what Blumenberg calls a "transcendent 'surplus,'" a richness of significance denied languageless animals, the *Mangelwesen* construction sees everything we are as a means of compensating for our exile from nature. The apparent richness of human being may be traced to actual existential poverty. Rhetoric (for example) is not the result of creative exuberance but rather "the effort to produce the accords that have to take the place of the 'substantial' base of regulatory processes in order to make action possible." Language is not the high-sounding "advent of Being itself" but only a humble "set of instruments not for communicating information or truths but rather, primarily, for the production of mutual understanding, agreement, or toleration, on which the actor depends" (433).

The creature of deficiencies may sound like postmodern despair about the human condition, but it has its sources in ancient commonplaces about this strange animal that fancies itself rational. Other animals are bigger, stronger, faster than we are; see, hear, and smell better, and so forth. Fragile and defenseless as we are, how did we survive, much less come to dominate the earth? The answer has to reside in a big brain and language, cunning and cooperation—and technology, of course, which enables a band of puny creatures to bring down a giant bison or a woolly mammoth, both creatures whose extinction our ancestors at least contributed to, perhaps even caused. The linking together of deficiency, action, and rhetoric in human being, then, has a not easily dismissed logic of survival and power behind it, as well as ancient commonplaces and modern scientific evidence for support. It also appeals for obvious reasons to those suspicious of the human tendency toward inflated self-interpretations.

It is a small step from *Mangelwesen* to no philosophical anthropology, from deficient human being to no being in human being. The difference between Blumenberg and Derrida, for instance, comes to this: Whereas the former takes our species as "indeterminate" *only* in a biological sense because we occupy no niche in an ecosystem, the latter takes us as indeterminate, period. "[T]he thinking of the proper of man," Derrida says in "The Ends of Man," "is inseparable from the question of the truth of Being." Derrida goes on to say that "this occurs along the Heideggerian pathways by means of what we may call a kind of magnetic attraction" (139). If we deny Being, claiming as Derrida does that it is an illusion of presence created by the word, then we also deny any presence, being, substance, or proper to "Man." This occurs along Derridean pathways by a kind of magnetic attraction also. Derrida concludes "The Ends of Man" with the question, "Who, we?" implying not that we urgently require an answer but that the question cannot or should not be answered. It cannot be answered because the meaning of human existence, like all meaning in poststructuralism, is undecidable; it should not be answered because any claim about the proper of "Man" pulls us back into the crypto-metaphysics of Heideggerian talk about the truth of Being.

Derrida does not say that the human animal is null or empty "at the core." His position is that the best position is no position. But the null or empty hypothesis nevertheless belongs to the attitudes and ideas that cluster around poststructuralism. It takes two sharply conflicting forms. The first is Nietzschean. If Being is an illusion, a set of fixed meanings not "there" but imposed on the flux of existence, then we are free to make and remake ourselves at will. The difference between "Man" and superman is that "Man" thinks that he is something definite, grounded in God or the inevitable progress of history, whereas superman thinks there is no source or grounding save one's own godlike self-making.

Too romantic for contemporary sensibilities, Nietzsche's self-creating "man" seems to have lost out among most poststructuralists to "man" as made by his environment, especially by language. The will to power shifts almost entirely to the pregiven. Freedom is illusory, responsibility hardly more than a convenient fiction to justify such spectacles as the Nuremberg trials. This is "bureaucratic man," the inhuman image of Bentham's Panopticon, the fruition of scientific-technological reason, the reflex of Nietzsche's mountaintop being. Did it believe in sin, its cry would be, "I am more sinned against than sinning." Resistance becomes self-consciously quixotic, the postmodern act that denies the efficaciousness of action itself.

What in general is there to say about these five humanisms, two Philosophical, three postPhilosophical? As never quite before, the question of human being is very much an open question, unsettled and unsettling. Philosophical "Man" has few adherents, but its influence remains; none of the postPhilosophical alternatives have as yet taken center stage. Probably we can also affirm Blumenberg's statement: "The varieties of what we now call philosophical anthropology can be reduced to one pair of alternatives: [Wo/]Man can be viewed either as a poor or as a rich creature" (429). Last, perhaps we can appreciate better why Burke sought "humility without humiliation" for his philosophical anthropology. Suspended between self-glorification, which now seems unreasonable, and self-abnegation, which seems both unpalatable and pointless, is there another way? Burke's "Definition" offers another way. In the context just offered, we shall now begin to examine it.

The Spirit of "Definition"

As one might expect a language-centered philosopher to do, Burke begins his essay with "a few words on definition in general" (*LASA* 3). Behind these few words are more than thirty pages on "Antinomies of Definition" in *A Grammar of Motives* (21–38). Getting into this would take us too far afield. What matters is that Burke is fully aware of the problems attending traditional *genus-differentia* definition. He therefore can use it without much risk of being used by it—without slipping into belief, for instance, in the fixed entities that such a mode of definition implies. Burke thinks there is heuristic value in the idealization we call definition, providing that we are able and willing to "discount" (see my discussion, pp. 122–25) our definitions *as idealizations*.

The purely dialectical problems of definition belong to the background of Burke's essay. Foregrounded in the opening paragraphs is Burke's insistence that we understand his essay *as a certain kind of performance distinct from scientific or "objectivist" uses of definition*. Definition, he says, is "the critic's equivalent of a lyric," a moment of illumination frozen in prose, involving deeply personal or what a scientist might dismiss as "subjective" tones and undertones. Burke acknowledges his own involvement in his definition. Like Kierkegaard, Burke values committed discourse, rhetoric in the fullest sense, an appeal from the entire humanity of the writer to the entire humanity of the reader. This separates him from the *persona* of the scientist and from Philosophy when it wants to be scientific.

Part of the appeal of science is its pretense of foregoing appeal, a virtually universal and steadfast refusal to acknowledge that its rhetoric is rhetoric. In contrast, Burke admits that "I am offering my Definition of [Wo/]Man in the hope of either *persuading* the reader that it fills the bill or of prompting [her/]him to decide what should be added, or subtracted, or in some way modified" (3, my emphasis). He is "up front" in announcing what he is doing, and while we might read this as also a ploy, it is quite different from the claim to objectivity and no rhetoric. Furthermore, in asking for dialogue, Burke turns away from the monologic ideal of "proof," a compelling or irrefutable argument. He is committed, yet open to correction—a stance comparable to sophisticated scientists, those who know that they are in the business of persuading.

But "Definition of [Wo/]Man" is a contribution to philosophy rather than to science. The performance is what Burke calls a "symbolic act," a discourse of the *full gesture*, melding the self-expression of the writer, persuasive intent directed at the reader, and a realistic desire to "chart" (approximate) what's "out there." It also involves the perfectionist urge to formulate completely and elegantly, for we are told that "a definition should have just enough clauses, and no more" and that "each clause should be like a chapter head, under which appropriate observations might be assembled, as though derived from it" (3). The likelihood that many of the observations came first and the certainty that we can never say how many clauses will be enough does not undermine the aspiration to "get it right." Nor does consummation contradict Burke's open stance but rather indicates how human motives are always tugging at one another in the symbolic act's miraculous synthesis. Purity of motive is not the point, but balance and integration—and a human act at ease with its humanity.

Finally, for those concerned with proof, we should remember this: The "proof" of Burke's definition *is* the performance itself. He is about to argue that the human animal distinguishes itself by a capacity for symbolic action. He represents this capacity in his own symbolic act of definition. We cannot call this act that confirms itself "circular reasoning," for Burke does not reason from his own act. Rather the act manages to be the meaning it urges, silently "demonstrating" its truth in a way that no demonstration could.

Clause One: "The Symbol-Using Animal"

"Granted," Burke says, immediately after proposing the clause, "it doesn't come as much of a surprise"—and he moves on immediately to an effort not so much to defend the clause itself as to explicate our immersion in language and symbols generally. We discussed the results previously (pp. 129–33). Accordingly, I would like to center attention here on the clause itself, quite apart from how Burke unfolds it in "Definition."

One of the places where Burke argues for his first clause is in the "Comments" appended to the essay, "Terministic Screens" (*LASA* 58–60). He is pondering the dialectic of continuity and discontinuity in the context of two articles, one stressing human specialness, our discontinuity from other animals, the other stressing evolution and continuity. Commenting on the Darwin-inspired author, Burke observes that he "could have appropriately quoted Darwin's shrewd remark, 'If man had not been his own classifier, he would never have thought of founding a separate order for his own reception.'" Noting that the Darwinist "sloganizes his position visually by opting for a model of 'man' rather than an image of 'Man,'" Burke says:

> My position would necessarily be that, in the very act of developing a structure of classifications, the human classifier (be he "man" or "Man"!) by the same token does establish his nature as a special class of being. For one cannot be the kind of animal that can study biology except by having a distinctive way with symbol systems. (*LASA* 59)

Characteristically Burke grounds his own position in the very arguments of those most resistant to acknowledging anything special about the human species. All the biological evidence one might imagine, including the now well-established fact that we share all but a few percent of our genetic information with chimpanzees, cannot call Burke's modest claim into question. It could only be refuted by finding another species either on earth or somewhere else with language—*not* a species that communicates with grunts, calls, moans, whistles, and so forth, but a species capable of doing what we can do with language, such as producing taxonomies. Short of this—and chimpanzee and porpoise "language" is well short—Burke's claim must stand.

We need not decree for ourselves a separate biological order to have a model of "man" as distinctive. Nor need we appeal to "Man"—to the Philosophical Humanism of the past. We need resort only to language, self-evidently present in *homo sapiens*, absent, so far as we know, in any other species.

If we say, as Burke usually does, that we are *typically* the symbol-using animal, which allows for infants not yet using language and the rare adult who never acquires it or loses it entirely through illness or injury, then we have a highly defensible claim about the being of human being. It is not vulnerable, as rational animal is, to a mountain of counter-evidence confirming that, for the most part, we are non/irrational.

Burke's symbol-using animal is obviously very close to Taylor's "self-interpreting animal" or "beings for whom things matter." The advantage, however, must go to Burke. We can easily imagine conditions—severe depression, for instance, or extreme deprivation—when things might well cease to matter to us. But this side of catatonia or coma or severe brain damage or deficit, we remain symbol-users.

Burke's definition has at least one other advantage over the hermeneutic "subjects of significance." The latter inclines toward Humanistic glorification of our species, the former does not. Alluding again to Darwin, Burke observes:

> His terministic screen so stressed . . . continuity . . . that he could view . . . discontinuity only as a case of human self-flattery. Yet . . . [w]e can distinguish [wo/]man from other animals without necessarily being overhaughty. For what other animals have yellow journalism, corrupt politics, pornography, stock market manipulators, plans for waging thermonuclear, chemical, and bacteriological war? . . . We don't need theology, but merely the evidence of our characteristic sociopolitical disorders, to make it apparent that [wo/]man, the typically symbol-using animal, is alas! something special. (*LASA* 50)

While obviously able to do both, Burke is not here *merely* outwitting Darwin or playing the ironist with traditional Humanism. Rather he is calling attention to a dialectic richer and more complex than the "creature of deficiencies." We are only too proficient at symbol-using, proficient enough to make us always turbulent animals, perhaps to destroy ourselves. Our very proficiency is deficiency so that no concept of what we are can possibly be sufficient that opts for either a "rich" or "poor" view of human being. Our concept of human being should encourage us to contemplate both the "up" and the "down" side of symbolism, the inherent ethical ambiguities of language as power.

Everything depends on how we use language and in how it uses us. The passage just cited is not a casual piece of cleverness at the expense of biology or theology. His entire philosophical anthropology is meant to get beyond the pointless logomachy of Darwinist and Biblicist to expose the problem of problems for symbol-using animals, how to attain a measure of understanding and control over our own symbol-driven motives.

This concern is the center of Burke's *praxis*, as we will see later; for now the point is that "man" need not opt for humiliation to achieve humility, nor revert to species arrogance to achieve self-respect. Our falling out of the ordered arrangements of nature confirms that we are clearly not merely a species amid species. To invoke a little of the "other side" of the dialectic of symbolism: What other animal dwells in rich cultural spaces, creates civilizations, stockpiles knowledge, mounts massive relief efforts to help other members of its species devastated by famine and war? But the case for specialness gains nothing by self-flattery or claims to transcendent status. All we have is "a distinctive way with symbol systems," nothing more, nothing less. Everything else special about us derives from this. The trouble is that if we are typically the symbol-using animal, we are also, as Burke insists in his expanded version of the first clause of "Definition," the typically "symbol-*mis*using animal" (6, my emphasis). If we use symbols in deliberate and responsible acts, we are also used by symbols, the victims of motives we would otherwise not have. Much of the human misery we derive satisfaction from alleviating would not exist without the symbol-driven motives, for example, of racism and empire. As we discovered when we explored Burke's view of the nonrational and irrational in Part One (pp. 43–51), Dramatistic "man" exists in a state of profound and perpetual self-conflict and self-contradiction.

Instead of Heidegger's "thrownness," Burke's understanding of human being emphasizes "tornness." We will discuss this concept in connection with another clause in "Definition." But the mention of Heidegger's concept suggests a question we need to ask now: What is the status of the symbol in Burke? Does it have or lack a grounding?

In *A Rhetoric of Motives* Burke claims that "nature must be more-than-verbal. For . . . it encompasses verbal and nonverbal both; and its 'nonverbal' ground must have contained the 'potentiality' of the verbal, otherwise the verbal could not have emerged from it" (*LASA* 290). In other words, nature is not simply other-than or less-than-verbal, for the symbol-using animal has a natural history, an origin in nature. The very existence of a language-using animal indicates that nature has the potential for producing a being that can comment on nature itself.

Under the impact of naturalistic assumptions, the tendency is to hold that language, along with everything else that exists, is fortuitous, the result of a chance confluence of forces in themselves lacking purpose or meaning. We "read" the universe this way, just as our ancestors often "read" it as a marvelous design, implying a Designer yet more excellent.

Burke's point is that there is no particular justification for assuming that language is an accident. All we can reasonably claim to know is that language *did* emerge from natural processes and that therefore the potential for language must have been somehow implicit in the Big Bang. The assumption that "it didn't have to turn out that way" or, conversely, that "it had to turn out that way" are just and only that—assumptions. We don't know, probably can't know: The skeptic in Burke insists on keeping the question open rather than allowing naturalistic assumptions to slip into the status they too often have now, Truth itself. It is *possible* that nature has some inner *telos* that results in symbol-using animals— and therefore in culture, intellect, personality, everything that would not exist without language. Were we to make contact with other symbol-using animals on other planets, the *telos* construction might well enjoy a revival.

Almost thirty years after *A Rhetoric of Motives*, in an essay widely accepted as representative of his "final" views, Burke seems to opt for naturalism:

> If all typically symbol-using animals . . . were suddenly obliterated, their realm of symbolic action would be correspondingly obliterated. The earth would be but a realm of planetary, geologic, meteorological motion, including the motions of whatever nonhuman biologic organisms happened to survive. . . . The realm of motion . . . preceded the emergence of our symbol-using ancestors; and doubtless the time will come when motions go on after all our breed will have vanished. ("[Nonsymbolic] Motion" 811)

All talk about nature as the source of language has dropped away. Here "motion" (the phenomena studied by physics, chemistry, and biology) clearly has primacy; our species, like Macbeth's "poor player," "struts and frets his hour upon the stage/ And then is heard no more." In the context of a four-billion-year-old earth, our coming and going hardly seem to matter at all.

We could explain the differences between these two passages based on context. In the first he is clearly resisting making a decidable out of an undecidable, a dogma out of naturalistic assumptions. In the second he is presenting his views synoptically so that even those holding naturalistic assumptions should find little cause for resistance. The content is different, then, because Burke's purposes are different.

We need not invoke context, however, to reconcile the two passages. It is quite possible to hold, on the one hand, that language is part of nature because language emerged in an animal, one of nature's beings, without holding, on the other, that human being or the human use of symbols is "ultimate," nature's inner *telos*. The first is hard to doubt; the second, given what we know and surmise about the history of the universe and of life, is very dubious. Holding the first while not holding the second is Burke's position on the question of a grounding for language. Without opting for naturalism, Burke "grounds" language in nature, not, as Philosophical Humanism does, in an eternal *Logos* or in some version of "Man" as the fruition of Absolute Spirit. His philosophical anthropology, then, is a theory of "man" rather than "Man"; it is not homocentric in the way, for example, that Southwell's neo-idealist reading of Burke would make it (65–68). Burke's thought remains intensely humanistic without requiring that our species be the favored darling of the universe—without, that is, the metaphysical supports of Humanism. Making this work is the key to "humility without humiliation" and the primary challenge confronting contemporary neo-humanism generally.

Given the pragmatist bent of Burke's interests, he is less interested in grounding language than he is in what language grounds—in his view, an entire realm of motivation totally absent or only very crudely present in speechless animals. We shall have more to say about this shortly. At present, however, precisely because it doesn't surprise us and we are therefore apt to pass over it too quickly, we need to appreciate the philosophical importance of the first clause of Burke's definition.

In a famous statement from his influential "Letter on Humanism," Heidegger claimed that "[e]very humanism is either grounded in a metaphysics or is itself made to be the ground of one" (202). Already fallen on evil days by 1947 when "Letter on Humanism" was published, humanism has since suffered much from Heidegger's claim, as many saw in it the ultimate justification for consigning humanism to outmoded thought. To opt for humanism was to opt for Philosophy. Heidegger's claim is certainly true in the context of what I have called Traditional and Enlightenment Humanism, and a good case could be made for Ricoeur's "ontology of finitude" and Taylor's "subjects of significance" as more subtly entangled with homocentricity. If Ricoeur and Taylor incline toward idealism, the *Mangelwesen* notion inclines toward naturalism—so perhaps Heidegger's claim applies to most of contemporary neo-humanism as well.

Because Burke grounds language in nature, the temptation is to associate "symbol-using animal" with the metaphysical commitments of naturalism—or, recalling the apparently similar *animal symbolicum* of Cassirer (23–26), with the metaphysics of neo-Kantian idealism. Burke explicitly rejects both linkages.

In the 1952 "Preface" to *Counter-Statement*, for example, he claims that "[n]aturalism has served as deceptively in the modern world as supernaturalism ever did in the past, to misrepresent motives that are intrinsic to the social order" (xv). That is, we sometimes "explain" human brutality as a legacy of the animal's struggle to survive, whereas most of it derives from economic, national, racial, and ethnic ambitions, from social or symbol-driven motives. In this regard, we need to remember that the metabiology of *Permanence and Change* is a *meta*biology, not a biological reductionism (see my discussion, pp. 110–12), and that in *The Rhetoric of Religion*, Burke claims that we must begin with complex notions of transcendence rather than with positivistic laboratory experiment (see my discussion, pp. 121–22). In short, when our species became symbol-users, we did not cease to be animals, but we did pass beyond the explanatory power of naturalism. Far from entailing a naturalistic metaphysics, Burke's humanism explicitly rejects it.

His stress on the radical difference between an animal with language versus an animal without it obviously has idealistic implications. Aware of this, Burke explicitly dissociates his view from metaphysical idealism in the 1966 "Foreword" to *The Philosophy of Literary Form* (xvi). Furthermore, he distinguishes "symbol-using animal" from Cassirer's formulation by pointing to the latter's epistemological commitments (*LASA* 23). The statement "Human beings are typically symbol-using animals" owes nothing to Kant or Kant's tradition. It is an empirical generalization that provides a "taking off point" for a philosophical anthropology, for a humanism that escapes altogether Heidegger's claim that "every humanism remains metaphysical." Burke's isn't. His is a humanism for postPhilosophy, one that can be held apart from any metanarrative about Truth.

This is its philosophical significance: to give the lie to Heidegger's linkage without falling into Derrida's skepticism about being in human being. Burke answers the Who, we? question in a way that clearly preserves intact his own lifelong doubt about the human capacity to know the Truth.

Clause Two: "Moralized by the Negative"

Burke's explication of the negative amounts to two key points:

1. Apart from the symbol-using animal, "there are no negatives in nature"; the negative, both as "it is not" and as "thou shalt not," is "solely a product of human symbol systems." "To look for negatives in nature would be as absurd as though you were to go out hunting for the square root of minus one" (9).

2. The hortatory or ethical negative (thou shalt not) is developmentally prior to the propositional negative (it is not).

Almost without exception P/philosophy has ignored the hortatory negative and dealt with negation formalistically, as a logical function applicable to propositions. "The negative," however, "begins not as a resource of definition or information, but as a command, as 'Don't'" (10). Children encounter "no-no's" long before they have any capacity to understand propositional negatives. Their world, and therefore our world as adults shaped by childhood experiences, are "negatively infused" (11).

Nothing mystical is intended here; in Burke's philosophy there is no equivalent of *le Neant*, which he dismisses as a "sheer[ly] linguistic trick of treating no-thing as an abstruse kind of something" (10). What Burke means by "negatively infused" is this: Whereas, for example, a mature, healthy male animal will normally attempt with little or no ceremony to copulate with a female in estrus, all of it, including the "ceremony," instinctive behavior triggered by hormones and pheromones, for the heterosexual human male the female is a vast "repository" of negation. There is the fear of rejection—"Will she say no?"—and the fear of acceptance—"Should I say no to myself, refusing to become involved?" And of course there are the thou-shalt-not's having to do with marital status and sexual ethics in general, hardly a concern for languageless animals. Ceremony in our sexual arrangements is not a metaphor, as when we speak of "courtship rituals" in birds, but a reality, always fraught with symbols "negatively infused," patently or latently.

"Moralized by the negative": What is Burke claiming exactly? "Our character is built of our responses (positive or negative) to the thou-shalt-not's of morality." No negative, no character. No character, no action, as the following passage Burke cites from his earlier *Rhetoric of Religion* confirms:

> *Action* involves *character*, which involves *choice*—and the *form* of choice attains its perfection in the distinction between Yes and No (shall and shall-not, will and will-not). Though the concept of sheer *motion* is non-ethical, *action* implies the ethical, the human personality. Hence the obvious close connection between the ethical and negativity, as indicated in the Decalogue. (*LASA* 11, Burke's emphasis)

The negative, character, action, personality, ethics—each term implies the others; all belong to the family of Dramatistic terms. Furthermore, take away the negative and the human "life world" goes too, for "we necessarily approach life from the standpoint of our personalities"; hence "*all* [human] experience reflect[s] the genius" of the negative (11, my emphasis).

We see, then, just how much Burke means by the phrase "negatively infused"; even something so "positively there" as my house exists by virtue of the negative. "'[M]ine' equals 'not thine'; insofar as property is not protected by the thou-shalt-not's of either moral or civil law, it is not protected at all." Not only is the negative "basic to [hu]man[s] as moral agent[s]," but it is also "hidden behind a realm of quasi-positives," latently at work when no moral question is immediately at issue (11).

We glimpse in Burke's explication of the negative a little of the vast domain of motives we would not have without symbols. Take away language, and morality, together with the stubborn philosophical problems summed up in the term "ethics," disappears. Is Burke, then, attempting to dissolve the problems posed by ethics by tracing morality to a purely linguistic resource, the hortatory negative? Is he saying that ethics is a figment of symbols? If we cannot affirm a transcendent ground for morality and "there are no negatives in nature," isn't ethics an insubstantial affair, basically arbitrary, an affliction that human beings impose on themselves? Or if, as Burke affirms, "language and the negative 'invented' [hu]man[ity]" (9), can't we "reinvent" ourselves, as Nietzsche advocated, free from our own self-confinement?

Burke does not pose any version of these questions in "Definition," but it is not especially hard to see how he would answer them. Far from any desire to dissolve the problems posed by morality and ethics, Burke insists that *human existence is moral existence*. Whereas Heidegger's "man" deemphasizes ethics by subordinating *Dasein* to Being, Burke's Dramatistic "man" is *primarily* a moral being. Burke's philosophical anthropology emphasizes ethics even more than Traditional Humanism does: For Burke reason is a precarious achievement, a kind of triumph against the odds in a creature more non/irrational than rational, whereas the negative is an all-pervading social necessity, and therefore a much stronger candidate than reason for what classical metaphysics understands by "essence."

It is true that Burke "grounds" morality in language in the sense that morality could not exist without the negative. After Wittgenstein we are inclined to take any problem generated by language as a pseudoproblem. Are all ethical problems, then, basically without substance or moment?

In the first place, to hold that morality could not exist without the negative is *not* to take the reductive position that morality is nothing but the negative. For Burke, as for all contemporary ethicists working without a transcendent ground, morality is unthinkable apart from cultures and societies, arrangements that are certainly more than language even if they could not exist without language. Furthermore, morality is entangled in the animal, in bodily needs and desires. There is a world of difference—a negatively infused world of difference—between an animal "marking off its territory" with scent deposits and a human being posting "no trespassing" signs, but both indicate the bodily requirement for a dwelling place. To the extent, therefore, that societies and bodies are "substantial," morality is also "substantial."

In the second place, even if morality could be reduced to the "merely linguistic," Burke would not allow that it would then be insubstantial. "Symbol-using" *is* our "essence," as close to an unchanging universal as anything we could predicate of human being. The "merely linguistic" therefore is "substantial" for us, never without moment, and symbol-engendered problems are our fate. As we have seen, Burke certainly recognizes the existence of pseudoproblems (see pp. 37–38), but ethical problems cannot be dissolved short of a literal "end of man."

It follows that any notion of "post-ethical man" is for Burke a contradiction in terms. Individual persons may be amoral, able to resist or ignore all moral injunctions and prohibitions—we call them psychopaths—but human being would simply cease to be human being without ethics. Instead of interpreting morality as only something that confines or distorts natural energies, Burke sees it on the whole as not only necessary but even beneficial: "By saying no to himself," Burke observes in one of his aphorisms, "he gave form to his life" (*CP* 89).

A keen observer of and ironic commentator on the human struggle to cope with moral conflict and contradiction, he often calls attention to the negative's destructive power—the need for scapegoats, for instance, to cope with the burden of failure and guilt. Nevertheless, in Burke's view, morality not only forms private life but must inform public life as well, especially in an age given over to the essentially amoral rationale of technological manipulation. The "powers developed by the new technology . . . are deadly indeed," Burke warns, "unless we make haste to develop the controls (the negatives, the thou-shalt-not's) that become necessary, if these great powers are to be kept from getting out of hand" (*LASA* 12–13). Rather than turning from ethics we must turn to it ever more insistently to combat the amorality of "bottom line" and scientific-technical reasoning. "Post-ethical man" is a threat, not a promise, another holocaust-in-the-making rather than a deliverance from arbitrary bondage. Surely our current preoccupation with ethics in government, education, business, medicine, religion, and so forth—desperate as it may be, and perhaps largely ineffectual—amounts implicitly to the rejection of post-ethical man.

By grounding morality in language, Burke accomplishes two aims central to his philosophy. Most importantly, he demystifies morality, depriving it of transcendental or natural status. This in turn opens it to critique in the vein of Nietzsche, Marx, or Freud. For example, the following exchange between The Lord and Satan in Burke's comic dialogue that concludes *The Rhetoric of Religion* illustrates my point well. The Lord is explaining what will happen after he creates the world:

> TL. In the course of governance many kinds of inequity will develop.
> For instance, some of the Earth-People will be able to accumulate

        more property than they could intelligently use in a myriad lifetimes, short as their life span is to be. And many others will starve. In brief, there'll be much injustice.

S.   It's revolting!

TL.   Hence all the more need for "sanctions." In the course of "proving" that such inequities are "right," sanctions will pile up like bat dung in a cave. (And bat dung, by the way, will be quite fertile.)

Out of the offal of systematic injustice sprouts the dense undergrowth of "sanctions"—customs, unwritten moral codes, laws, ingenious legal arguments, and so on. To approach an ethics apart from history and social structure—apart from the form of life it reflects and supports—is not to understand it at all. Hence the necessity for a demystifying critique.

But it is easy to draw simple-minded conclusions from such critiques. And so the dialogue continues, with Satan, who is cast as a young admirer of The Lord, quick-witted but "over-hasty, mercurial" (276), generalizing to a categorical indictment of all "sanctions":

S.   Then "sanctions" are just symbol-systems that justify injustice?

TL.   No, my lad. It's much more complicated than that. The range of language being what it is, the very propounding and treasuring of such sanctions will lead in turn to the equally persuasive questioning of them. And all these matters will come to a head in man's theology, metaphysics, political theory and the like, in short the higher criticism that grows out of such venerable piles. (287)

That which germinates out of rot is not reducible to it, just as morality, while dependent on the negative, is more than the negative. Sanctions necessary because of injustice will eventually be shaken by the very injustice it perpetuates. Language, which makes a negatively infused world possible as a way of justifying power ("They will use language to rule over one another" [287], TL tells us), also provides the means for undermining a particular regime of power. "Sanctions" *per se* are not the issue but rather the form of life an ethic supports. Nor is morality *merely* a device of repression in the service of the will to power of a class, gender, or race. It is much more complicated than that. A social animal with language cannot create or recreate worlds without "sanctions"; if all is permitted, no characteristically human order can exist.

What can we say in sum about the second clause of Burke's "Definition"? Taken in itself, "moralized by the negative" is a *formalistic* account of the linguistic source of ethics. It explains the connection between symbol-using and morality in such a way that ethics becomes "substantial" without recourse to natural or supernatural groundings. Moreover, in grounding morality in language, Burke implies that ethics is ineluctable—and therefore that ethical reflection, while it may go in and out of fashion, can never be transcended or rendered pointless by metaphysical determinisms. Even the behaviorist, for example, cannot escape questions about the ethics of animal experimentation or the ethics of applying behavioristic research in human settings.

However, if in Burke's account ethics is about as permanent as anything human can be—if an ethics *of some sort* will be detectable in any human community—it is also the case that no *particular* ethical system is either "substantial" or ineluctable. Put another way, "moralized by the negative" is not offered as an answer to How should we live? or What should we do? and cannot answer these classical ethical questions. Like Kant's categorical imperative, Burke's hortatory negative is quite contentless, offering no specific ethical guidance at all. But whereas there is no escape from abstract formalism in Kant's ethics, Burke's ethics are social, relative to culture and historical circumstances. As we have seen already in scrutinizing his comments on the good life in *Attitudes Toward History* (see pp. 113–15) and will see again when *praxis* becomes our theme later, moral reflection in Burke can and does become quite concrete and specific, as do the aims, the social goods, it pursues.

Clause Three: Tornness and Burke's Dualism

"Separated from [our] natural condition by instruments of [our] own making"—so reads the third clause of Burke's definition of human being. He makes the following key points in explicating it:

1. The clause "is designed to take care of those who would define [hu]man[s] as 'tool-using animal[s].'"

2. There is a "close tie-up between tools and language," especially in the "second level" dimension of both, the use of tools to make tools and of words to talk about words. Some nonhuman animals use tools and signs, but not in this "second level," reflexive way.

3. Although "the human powers of symbolicity are interwoven with the capacity for making tools" so that we cannot say which is primary or more significant in evolutionary terms, it is best philosophically to stress symbol-using over tool-using. For

   those who begin with the stress upon *tools* proceed

> to define language itself as a species of tool. . . . But though instrumentality is an important aspect of language, . . . Edward Sapir's view of language as a "collective means of expression" points in a more appropriate direction. (*LASA* 13–15)

In other words, by beginning with symbol-using, we avoid the temptation of reducing language to instrumentality. Language is much more than a tool—we cannot, for instance, pick it up and set it aside at will.

All three points are significant, especially the last, which rejects Dewey's equation of language with tools and reaffirms the language centeredness of Burke's own thought. However, I would like to direct a spotlight on a single word in the third clause, "separated."

One of the more salient postmodern themes, easily detectable in both art and philosophy, is that human existence is irremediably incomplete, beset by contradiction and conflict, and best characterized by metaphors not of wholeness and stability (i.e., groundedness) but of fragmentation and unbridgeable rifts. We have in effect "rediscovered" an ancient *topos*, expressed in myth by a "fall" from some primal unity and in philosophy by various formulas of bivalence such as the struggle between reason and desire, soul and body. Burke believes that he can trace all notions of bivalence to the hiatus implied by "symbol-using animal." Citing again from the dialogue that concludes *The Rhetoric of Religion*, The Lord is explaining the sources of human motivation to his attentive student, Satan:

> Purpose will have its origins in bodily desires, most notably the appetites of food and sex. In this respect it will be grounded in man's animality. But it will attain an immaterial counterpart in the principle of communication. Hence, purpose will have a secondary grounding in man's symbolicity. (305)

With symbols come all sorts of motivations having to do with "transcendence," attempts to rise above the limitations of the body, of temporal and material existence generally. Among these symbol-driven motives, The Lord points out, is the desire for empire, for thousand-year Reichs, one mode of the will to power that one way or another drives all human beings. Yet, The Lord declares, "even in its fullness it cannot be satisfying," this desire for transcendence—at which point Satan asks, "Why can it not be satisfying even in its fullness?" to which The Lord replies:

> *Because the parts do not fit.* By the tests of sheer animality, the "deathless essences" of sheer symbolicity will be a mockery. Yet, by their own tests, they really will transcend the sheerly material realm of corruption and death. The fall of all the

trees in the world will not bring down the meaning of the
word "tree." (305, my emphasis)

Caught between material existence and "spiritual essence"—that is, the
meanings and motivations of our symbol systems—human being is necessarily a composite organism, irremediably at odds with itself.

"The parts do not fit"—at its simplest, this is Burke's understanding
of human being, a condition he did not name, but which I call "tornness." It is not enough to say that our species has fallen out of the ordered
arrangements of nature and into a world of action and rhetoric to compensate for instinctual poverty. We still must explain why our motives
reach so far beyond bodily needs and why we seek in religion, art, theology, Philosophy, and in a host of other ways the fullness and reconcilia-
tion that nevertheless typically eludes us. Likewise it is not enough to
point, as almost everyone in the dialectical tradition has pointed, to bivalence. If not the symbol-driven struggles of an animal whose parts do
not fit, what is the source of this sense of division and struggle?

Burke does not offer a unifying ground for human existence; rather
he explains why we long for it even (perhaps especially) in the midst of
postmodern sophistication about Truth and language. It is not just the
undertow of modernism that pulls us out to sea; we are drawn toward
the abyss by language itself, by a drive to transcend our creatureliness
that can never be satisfactory. We find this drive in the oldest expression
of humankind and in every culture and circumstance. Alienation is not
simply a theme of existentialists or a temporary condition of "alienated
labor," but as permanent as anything human can be. As long as we are
symbol-using animals we will also be "separated"—biologically, from
our natural condition; psychologically, from ourselves; and socially, from
each other.

Implicit in "Definition" and all of Burke's later philosophy is a defense of dualism in general and of his dualism in particular. In an article
published in 1979, Burke defends dualism by dissociating it from Cartesian metaphysics and pointing to the consequences of rejecting dualisms
in principle:

> [W]hen I read of hermeneutic experts who congratulate them-
> selves that the traditional Cartesian split between subject and
> object, thought and extension, is being avoided, I would note
> that there are two quite different ways of considering any such
> development. . . . Descartes' dualism . . . is in trouble. But we
> should not let any reservations regarding the *Cartesian* for-
> mulation . . . serve . . . to discredit the dualistic principle
> itself. For if we do so, we are in effect implying monism, either

by smuggling in undeclared vestiges of idealism, or by willy-nilly subscribing to the "materialistic" oversimplification of behaviorism. ("Theology" 184)

Of course, turning from dualism does not *entail* turning to monism—one could, for instance, opt for pluralism. Burke's point is not logical but rather historical: In the past and at present most of the attacks on dualism have come from monistic thinkers. Since the metaphysical question cannot be settled, Burke points to the consequences of monism, a reductionism that distorts self-understanding by either denying mind and underrating the importance of language or by denying the body and underrating the importance of economic struggle. Above all, Burke wants to preserve a *tension* between "symbol-using" and "animal," which means resisting the monistic satisfaction of resolving apparent tension via some underlying, unifying principle. For this reason primarily, Burke insists on the *practical value* of dualism as a way of avoiding reductionism—not the same thing, of course, as proposing a dualistic metaphysics. Burke's defense of dualism occurs in the context of anthropology, not metaphysics. He defends dualism as an approach to human being, not as a necessary postulate about existence generally.

Burke's vigorous defense of the dualistic principle in general is matched by an equally vigorous defense of *his particular version* of what he calls "the basic polarity." Instead of "the traditional pair[,] *res* and *verba*," Burke argues for "nonsymbolic motion" and "symbolic action," claiming that this pair is "at the root of such distinctions as mind-body, spirit-matter, superstructure-substructure, and Descartes' dualism, thought and extension" ("[Non-Symbolic] Motion" 809). By "at the root" Burke means that the more familiar Philosophical polarities may be traced not necessarily to the nature of things but rather to the nature of human being as an organism compounded of both motion and action. On the one hand, as an animal, our very existence depends on autonomic processes such as the immune system, respiration, and digestion—on, that is, what Burke would call "sheer motion." In this respect we are no different from other organisms or from the inorganic processes that support life. Body, thing, matter, extension, the substructure—all are comprehended by "nonsymbolic motion," a realm characterized as either necessity or chance, but at any rate apparently lacking in purpose and apparently indifferent to human constructions of meaning. It "just is" and moves and is moved.

On the other hand, there is "symbolic action," the so-far-as-we-know uniquely human capacity, as J. L. Austin put it, "to do things with words." But symbolic action as Burke uses the term takes in much more than speech acts: To some degree all utterances and all texts are purposeful and involve choice. All symbol-using is symbolic action—not just ritual, ceremonies, social pageants, and the like, the usual meaning of "symbolic action." So understood, how is symbolic action "at the root" of such traditional categories as mind, spirit, ideology, and thought?

By now the notion that mind or thought is language or at least inseparable from language has become so commonplace that few would dispute it. We hesitate not over the modifier, "symbolic," but rather over the noun, "action." Much more than at any time in the past, we have become aware of the mind as overwhelmingly preconscious or unconscious, more a matter it would seem of "symbolic motion" than symbolic action. For Burke, however, even dreams or the "repetition compulsions" of neurotics are symbolic acts when interpretation can reveal or construct meaning or purpose—the issue for Burke is meaning or purpose, not consciousness or awareness of acting as such. Consequently, symbolic action "covers" what Philosophy typically means by mind and thought—conscious reflection and even consciousness of reflection—as well as Freud's unconscious and the largely nonconscious web of cultural meanings and purposes that Marx taught us to call the superstructure or ideology.

With regard to ideology and "spirit," I cite the following passage from "Definition of [Wo/]Man":

> Do we simply use words, or do they not also use us? An "ideology" is like a god coming down to earth, where it will inhabit a place pervaded by its presence. An "ideology" is like a spirit taking up its abode in a body: it makes that body hop around in certain ways; and that same body would have hopped around in different ways had a different ideology happened to inhabit it. (*LASA* 6)

This passage, together with Burke's discussion of the "second analogy" between words and the Word in *The Rhetoric of Religion*—that is, "Words are to the nonverbal things they name as Spirit is to Matter" (16–17)—indicates how symbolic action can be "at the root of" a traditional concept like spirit. Short of faith in "another world," we can only trace spirit to language, to the symbols that inhabit us, like gods come down to earth, or like the meaning of a sentence that exists somehow "beyond" the sounds or marks that comprise the individual words themselves. When we became the symbol-using animal, we also became spiritual, haunted by the "disembodied" meanings of our symbols and driven by the motives of transcendence.

Perhaps we can now see why Burke asserts that nonsymbolic motion/symbolic action is "the basic polarity." So far Burke's claim has barely been noticed, much less disputed or deconstructed. Attacking it will not be easy. We would have to deny that "animal" is part of our essence, as

Heidegger in fact did in "Letter on Humanism" (204–5), and/or deny that humans are typically symbol-users. The first can only be maintained in ignorance or willful neglect of everything modern biology and ecology tells us about the human condition; the second would entail a frontal assault on the linguistic turn. Neither is likely to prove persuasive in the current climate of opinion.

Finally, Burke's dualism is not vulnerable to the "two worlds" critique that did so much damage to Descartes's thought and extension. Whereas Descartes so sharply dissociated the members of his pair that interaction between them was impossible, Burke insists that symbolic action depends on nonsymbolic motion, the neurophysiology of the human body, without which no word may be uttered or inscribed. Nor does Burke conceive the body as merely a passive support system for symbolic action. Symbolic action is "the dancing of an attitude" (*PLF* 9), and the dancer *is* the body, our assertions being as much a total posture as a string of phonemes or graphemes. Our action in the world is always already a synthesis of motion and action.

Clause Four: "Sickly O'er With the Pale Thought of Caste"

> If, to seek its level,
> Water can all the time
> Descend,
> What God or Devil
> Makes men climb
> No end?
>
> —Kenneth Burke, *The Rhetoric of Religion*

"*Goaded by the spirit of hierarchy*" is the actual phrase Burke uses in "Definition"—or "if that sounds too weighted . . . 'Moved by a sense of order.'" Perhaps we should prefer the more weighted phrase, for if nonhuman social animals clearly have "pecking orders"—a kind of nonsymbolic "caste system"—they are not *goaded* as we are by motives connected with who is "up" and who "down," who is "in" and who "out." As Burke explains:

> Here [our] skill with symbols combines with [our] negativity and with the tendencies towards different modes of livelihood implicit in the inventions that make for divisions of labor, the result being definitions and differentiations and allocations of property protected by the negativities of the law. (*LASA* 15)

Put more simply, an animal that can classify will have classes; economic,

cultural, and historical conditions dictate how much a society is strati-
fied and the degree to which its members are goaded by the motives of
rank and privilege, but no human society can function without hierarchy. "[H]ierarchy is inevitable" (*RM* 141).

Given modernist egalitarian utopias, such as Marx's classless society, and postmodern antipathy to authority and hierarchy in general, we
should expect that the fourth clause would draw fire from Burke's critics. "If human beings prize order, so too do they prize disorder; if they
possess the spirit of hierarchy, so too do they possess the spirit of equality, spontaneity, and rebellion." So claims the sociologist, Joseph R.
Gusfield, who goes on to say that

> [t]he anthropologist Victor Turner has given valuable insight
> into society with his contrast between *structure*—the hierar-
> chical, role-allocative side of life—and *communitas*, the sense
> of human similarity and solidaristic feeling. A great deal of
> ritual celebrates the spirit of equality rather than the dividing
> order of hierarchy. It is strange that so dialectical a thinker as
> Burke should turn hierarchy and order into ultimates. (49)

It is quite true that Burke takes the hierarchical *principle* as an *anthropological* ultimate. It is implicit in all "systematic thought" and "embodied in the mere process of growth, which is synonymous with the
class divisions of youth and age, stronger and weaker, male and female,
or the stages of learning, from apprentice to journeyman to master."
Rooted, therefore, in language, biology, and productive forces, hierarchy *of some sort* is as ineluctable for Burke as regimes of power are for
Foucault. The latter would have enjoyed the irony of Burke's hermeneutic advice: "[O]n hearing talk of equality, [we should] ask ourselves,
without so much as questioning the possibility that things might be otherwise: 'Just how does the hierarchic principle work in this particular
scheme of equality?'" (*RM* 141).

We must be clear about exactly what Burke is saying. First, his
claim is for the principle of hierarchy, not for any particular hierarchy.
"[T]he crumbling of hierarchies is as true a fact about them as their for-
mation" (*RM* 141). Particular hierarchies come and go, but the motives
of hierarchy are "eternally recurrent." Burke's defense of the hierarchical principle, then, is not a defense of the current order of things—or for
that matter, taken in itself, of any order.

Second, human beings can only "prize disorder" or rebelliously prize
a counterorder within an established hierarchical system; moreover, the
very assertion of *communitas*, of a shared common humanity, only makes
sense and has resonance within a scheme of inequalities. Order and disorder (or counterorder) are what Burke calls "dialectical terms" (*RM*
184–85), concepts that always imply opposites and require opposites to

have meaning. Turner's structure and anti-structure are also dialectical terms, and a careful reading of Turner will confirm that he agrees with Burke that social structure is primary. "Planned" anti-structural rituals (such as the annual Saturnalia) and "spontaneous" liminal events (celebrated in and by some postmodern art) have point and efficaciousness only in relation to quotidian structure. Gusfield's idea that there are two independent "spirits," the one structural (Apollonian?), the other anti-structural (Dionysian?), is the undialectical conception; Turner and Burke come together in construing the motives represented by the two gods as inextricably intertwined.

Third, we must never forget that Burke's definition was not offered in the spirit of scientific detachment and neutrality. "Goaded by the spirit of hierarchy" obviously implies a negative judgment, a moral reflection, on human motivations. It is pointless, therefore, to raise counterexamples of human societies past and present that are minimally hierarchical and relatively immune to what Burke elsewhere calls the "hierarchical psychosis." For this "norm" is exactly what Burke seeks, a human society "moved by a sense of order" rather than "goaded by the spirit of hierarchy." The "good life" for Burke is impossible without a liberating exposure and critique of the drive to possess the insignia and power of privilege—but the freedom he seeks is not anarchic, rather pragmatic or therapeutic, analogous to the freedom gained when we overcome a compulsion or phobia. The Scramble for the Top, the mania of a society that overstresses competition in all human activity, is the object of Burke's critique, and happiness resides not in denying its appeal but in rejecting it as the be-all and end-all of human purpose.

Unlike the first three clauses, how we respond to the fourth depends in the last analysis on faith, which to some degree reaches beyond argument to prophesy and vision. Clearly Burke did not live in expectation of the Kingdom, whether imposed "from above" as a sudden, divine descent or emerging "from below" as the "natural" outcome of social evolution. Instead of progress toward some great society, Burke sees us as permanently caught up in "the incentives of organization and status," including the close "relation between social hierarchy and mystery, or guilt":

> Here we encounter secular analogues of "original sin" . . . [T]o the extent that a social structure becomes differentiated, with privileges to some that are denied to others, there are the conditions for a kind of "built in" pride. King and peasant are "mysteries" to each other. Those "Up" are guilty of not being "Down," those "Down" are certainly guilty of not being "Up." (*LASA* 15)

These connections, explored in considerable detail in *A Rhetoric of Mo-*

tives and *The Rhetoric of Religion*, reveal the kinship of Burke's anthropology to Ricoeur's "fallible man," the latter's emphasis on fault "in the geological sense: a break, a rift, a tearing" (Kelbey xxiii) corresponding to the former's emphasis on mystery and guilt. But whereas in matters of faith Ricoeur's anthropology owes much to Christian scripture and theology, Burke's does not—"secular analogues" to Christian hermeneutics mark the extent of his commitment to our dominant religious tradition.

Consequently, whereas Ricoeur can and does hope for ultimate deliverance from the human condition he calls *dechirement* (a tearing), Burke remains within the less sanguine, therapeutic (Freudian-Wittgensteinian) position. There is no cure for hierarchy, only, at best, a certain limited potential to cope better with a dis-ease deeply rooted in human being itself.

The fourth clause of "Definition"—together with other developments in Burke's later philosophy—constitute a fundamental challenge to all utopian thought, including certain postmodern anti-structural ones, such as Rorty's PostPhilosophical culture (see my discussion, pp. 5, 7–8). If Burke is right—if hierarchy is rooted in symbolism, biological development, and divisions of labor—then it cannot by any means be rooted out. And yet, properly discounted (i.e., criticized), Burke has no quarrel with the utopian imagination. We require a vision of the good life even as we know that reality will fall well short of the lion of power laying down with the lamb of the powerless. If hierarchy is inevitable, no particular hierarchy is, and Burke's *praxis*, though hardly driven by Enlightenment "Man," owes enough to the Enlightenment to have a limited faith in an imperfect deliverance from the *goads* of hierarchy. Like the American philosopher he probably admired most, William James, Burke is a meliorist, not a pessimist or a cynic.

Clause Five: "And Rotten With Perfection"

Burke glosses what he calls the "wry codicil" to his "Definition of [Wo]Man" as follows: "The principle of perfection is central to the nature of language as motive. The mere desire to name something by its 'proper' name, or to speak a language in its distinctive ways is intrinsically 'perfectionist'" (16). The codicil occurred to him as an afterthought, he says (*LASA* 16), perhaps by reflection on his own perfectionistic drive to have a definition of human being with "just enough clauses, and no more" (*LASA* 3). After Derrida's lessons in the dynamics of centers and margins, we should not be surprised if this "mere addendum" turned out to be at least as important as any of the other four clauses, especially when we remember that the most common meaning of codicil is a clause added to the end of a will that can have the effect of altering it significantly.

The fifth clause has much in common with the fourth. In decidedly negative terms, both designate symbol-driven motives characteristic of our most unnatural being-in-the-world, motives common to all human beings even when they are most enlightened and benevolent. "Hierarchy" and "perfection" sum up a vast array of motives that bear watching, that require from us constant vigilance if we are not to be "goaded by" or "rotten with" them—if, that is, we are to use language with wisdom rather than being used by it.

"Symbols are in the saddle and they ride humankind" might well be Burke's motto, and his aim, especially in this fifth clause and its predecessor, is therapeutic, a way of coping with ourselves as we are rather than hoping for some magical transfiguration. Symbols ride us expertly, so much so that the "action" in symbolic action becomes questionable in every given instance. Only by reflection, by understanding what symbols do to us, can we make the rider's course less headlong and heedless, less darkened by self-ignorance, and less malevolent by default, by just not thinking—in short, more an act and less a compulsion.

But if the last and penultimate clauses have much in common, one key difference separates them: Whereas we can detect "class structure" in social animals as primitive as ants, "perfection" is altogether a symbol-driven motive. The most beautiful and elegant natural architectures—the double helix, for example—apparently evolved by chance mutations, without Aristotle's entelechy, which as Burke reminds us, means "possessing *telos* within" (*LASA* 17). In contrast, any use of language or symbols always has intrinsic purposefulness; for example:

> A given terminology contains various *implications*, and there
> is a corresponding "perfectionist" tendency . . . to attempt
> carrying out those implications. Thus, each of our scientific
> nomenclatures suggests its own special range of possible de-
> velopments, with specialists vowed to carry out these termin-
> istic possibilities to the extent of their personal abilities and
> technical resources.

Of course, as Burke goes on to point out, this "terministic compulsion" (*LASA* 19) is hardly confined to science. To varying degrees we find it in every field and in all symbolic enterprise: We strive for the "perfect" poem, the "just so" ritual performance, the theory of everything; we fight the "war to end all wars," seek the ideal energy source, the last word, and so on, *ad infinitum*. Once one grasps what Burke calls the "'entelechial' principle" peculiar to symbolism, one finds it in all human activity.

It is tempting to characterize Burke's attitude toward perfection as an ironic reversal of Enlightenment faith in the perfectibility of "Man." Perfection has its benign aspects, as well as merely silly or comical dimensions, long a favorite subject of satirists. But Burke dwells on the darker aspects of perfection, pointing, for instance, to the symbolic goads that converge in creating the "'perfect' enemy":

> The negative helps radically to define the elements to be victimized [e.g., Aryan as purely "not Jew," wholly "untainted" by "Jewish blood"]. And inasmuch as substitution is a prime resource of symbol systems, the conditions are set for catharsis by scapegoat [e.g., by "overcoming" capitalist disorders through eliminating "Jewish finance"]. And the unresolved problems of "pride" . . . intrinsic to privilege also bring the motive of hierarchy to bear . . . [with] many kinds of guilt, resentment, and fear [requiring] a sacrificial principle such as . . . a political scapegoat [e.g., the collective failure of the "master race" to prevail in the First World War can be blamed on "Jewish traitors"]. (*LASA* 18–19)

Clearly what disturbs Burke is "perfection in this dangerous sense" (*LASA* 18–19), which continues to victimize people all over the world almost half a century after we allegedly conned the lessons of the Holocaust. In effect Burke explains why the lesson is never learned or always forgotten: Too much of our symbol-driven motives converge in what he elsewhere calls the "cult of the kill" (*RR* 5); furthermore, "there seems to be no principle of control intrinsic to the [perfectionistic] ideal" (*LASA* 19)—no "inner check" such as prevails in natural ecosystems to maintain or restore balance. So far as the unnatural order of things is concerned, our falling out of nature was a free-fall into the abyss of language-engendered perfectionism—not perhaps a special problem for most of human history, but now ominous indeed as technology (itself symbol-driven and highly entelechial) makes systematic dehumanization and destruction ever more easy and efficient. Our perfectionistic dreams have converged with the "perfect" means to dispose of the "perfect" enemy—and the victims are all around us, on distant battlefields, in the third world of our inner cities, in the high-speed violence and frenetic activity of daily life, in exhaustion, ennui, and emptiness, and in the most fateful victimization of all, the probably inexorable devastation of the environment.

Burke's message, however, is not merely counter-Enlightenment, not reducible to "Down with perfection." His stance is much more complicated than this. On the one hand, he wants to undermine and disperse the appeal of perfectionism. Instead of one vocabulary pursued with the single-minded zeal of the specialist, he would teach us to use many terminologies and to play them off one another. If language has us rather than we it, yet we can at least choose a dialogue of vocabularies that should prevent bondage to only one. Another closely related strategy, as Southwell points out, amounts to a characteristically Burkean act of prudence: "Get off before the end of the line" (85). That is, if we can become aware of the entelechial compulsion, then we can also to some extent loosen its hold on us, as we can with Freud's repetition and destiny compulsions that Burke alludes to early in his discussion of perfection (*LASA* 17–18). Instead of "going with it," we can resist it, through self-reflection becoming wary of our own motives.

Mention of self-reflection brings us to the other hand: If Burkean therapies counter Enlightenment faith in human perfectibility, Burke also shares somewhat in Habermas's aim of pushing the Enlightenment forward, this time with the critical center in language and discourse rather than a pervasive distrust of tradition. Reason can only "perfect" itself by becoming critical of its own discursiveness, part of what Burke hopes to do in developing "a 'comic' theory of education" (*LASA* 20). "[I]f enough people began thinking along the lines of this definition," Burke says, placing some hope in enlightenment—if, that is, and here Burke frankly acknowledges his own perfectionistic aim—"such an approach could be *perfected* by many kinds of critics and educators and self-admonishers in general," then perhaps "things might be a little less ominous" (*LASA* 21, my emphasis). "A little less ominous": Even as Burke imagines perfection, he gets off well before the end of the line, well short of any delusion that becoming aware of our symbol-driven motives provides The Answer.

Conclusion: The Significance of the Philosophical Anthropology

Even after we have disseminated its clauses into traces of past formulations, Burke's "Definition" remains as a whole startlingly original, not much like anything else in the humanistic tradition. How, in sum, might we characterize its uniqueness?

We can say, first, that it represents a sharp and radical departure from Philosophical and scientific objectivism, with its pretense to neutrality and timelessness. Burke's anthropology is a passionate act, authentic, deliberately provocative; he is not above or apart from but *in* the formulation.

We can say, second, that Burke's anthropology seems almost a rejoinder to Heidegger's linking of humanism with metaphysics. As he breaks free of objectivism, he also eludes the magnetic attraction of Humanism and metaphysics. To accept Burke's anthropology we need only believe in bodies and language, neither of which are secure or secured.

Third, we can say that because of his emphasis on the body, on the *animal* in symbol-using animal, his philosophy can locate human being in nature, which, for example, Heidegger and Wittgenstein fail to do. At the same time, by shifting stress to *symbol-using*, Burke can also insist on our separation from nature. We are composite creatures whose existential condition is tornness. We belong both to nonsymbolic motion and symbolic action; the "permanent" "synthesis"-tension between them cannot be resolved by any economic or political order.

Yet, fourth, we should also say that Burke does not participate in the tragic overdignification of "man" we find in Nietzsche, Heidegger, and many of their followers, especially among the existentialists. "Tragedy is too eager to help out with the holocaust," Burke believes, and "too pretentious to allow for the proper recognition of our animality" (*LASA* 20). In contrast, comedy shifts attention away from *amor fati* and toward the study of our "foibles and crochets," toward "understanding [the] 'natural temptations' towards kinds of turbulence" peculiar to the symbol-using animal. As the essay on *praxis* shows, Burke explicitly advocates a "cult of comedy" (*LASA* 20) as a way of exposing and defusing our "naturally" negative-driven, hierarchy-driven, perfection-driven need for self-respect through victimage. He thereby articulates an emerging consensus in postmodern thought: a comic pragmatism instinctively suspicious of the overcommitted.

Last, we can say that Burke's anthropology "responds" in fruitful ways to the entire humanistic tradition, including voices that came along after "Definition." Although he understands "essence" differently, he shares with classical Humanism a faith in determinate meaning and insists that human being has a unique place in a *relatively* stable ecological order.

Shifting our attention to postPhilosophical anthropologies, Burke's definition clearly encompasses Ricoeur's emphasis on finitude and *dechirement*, while resisting the ontological commitments of Philosophy. His definition exemplifies what Taylor means by "self-interpreting animals," but he moves beyond Taylor and hermeneutics generally by developing a *critical theory of the motives inherent in symbolism*. In this respect he draws near to Habermas's effort to fuse hermeneutics and critical theory, but whereas the German theorist seeks a transhistorical normative pragmatics, Burke's scope is larger—a "grammar of motives" for the symbol-using animal.

Most interesting, perhaps, is the converging-diverging of symbol-using animal with the "creature of deficiencies." Betraying the bias of its source in Philosophical idealism, hermeneutical anthropology tends to slight body and biology. Burke and Blumenberg come together in exposing and resisting the Philosophical embarrassment with the body and with the stubbornly "arational" doings of matter generally. They also merge in taking language as action and strategy, as rhetoric, rather than the workings of Mind or *Logos*. But they differ sharply in several crucial ways. In resisting idealism, Blumenberg flirts dangerously with a biological reductionism. In contrast, Burke's emphasis on linguistic "transcendence" allows him to recognize an entire realm of motives that amount to much more than compensation for instinctual loss. It also results in a quite different conception of deficiency. It is our very proficiency with symbols that makes us deficient, which means that any rich versus poor dichotomy misconceives our condition and potential. If we are inherently a creature of deficiency, there is nothing to be done, but if we are deficient because we have not yet learned to cope with the Frankenstein monster of language, there is much to be done toward rendering us less deficient.

If there is to be a conversation after Philosophy about and with Kenneth Burke, we would do well to return often to "Definition." The challenge remains what it has been since Socrates asked the Who, we? question, but with this difference primarily: We must now muster faith in the answerability of the question and take responsibility for whatever answer we give. Burke understands the care and anxiety of "decreeing essence," that the whole venture is risky and beyond securing in a tranquil certainty. But he also insists that the question must be posed and reposed, that we cannot turn away from the question itself or leave it without an answer. Even after metaphysics and epistemology, self-understanding remains a vital issue. The sense of wonder about our strangeness may even survive Weber's "disenchantment of the world" (350).

7

Dialectics Within
the Dialogue

I asked Burke, "Why didn't you call *A Grammar of Motives*
a 'Dialectic of Motives'?"
  He answered, "I could have named all my stuff dialectic."

—Robert Heath, *Realism and Relativism: A Perspective
on Kenneth Burke*

When the conversation ends, the war begins. Conversations,
dialogues . . . keep us in the middle realm of comedy . . . and
away from the tragic abyss. . . . To take [Burke] as a model is
to commit oneself to the principle of, the value of, dialogue
and dialectics.

—William Rueckert, "Some of the Many
Kenneth Burkes"

My view throughout this study amounts to a reversal of how Kenneth
Burke has been received by many contemporary intellectuals: Instead of
seeing him as the forerunner of this and the anticipator of that, I take
him as belonging not to the past but to the future. As we continue to
think through postmodernism and seek ways to escape the cul-de-sac
of poststructuralism, my wager is that he will belong to "the conversation" more vitally than he ever did in his lifetime. We will not "go back"
to Burke; we will find him instead "out there" ahead of us, where we

continually rediscover the best minds of any generation. His immediate relevance, however, may be greater than most, for, as I argued in Part One, he began with what we now call negative dialectic, negative hermeneutics, and deconstruction, working his way past them to a hermeneutics of discounting-retrieval and eventually to such ironic affirmations as "Definition of [Wo/]Man"—all without losing the skeptical edge of his early philosophy.

In the previous essay we scrutinized his philosophical anthropology. Here we shall examine a closely related postPhilosophical theme, the fate of dialectic, inseparable from dialogue and from intellectual activity conceived as an ongoing conversation.

The Fall of Dialectic and the Rise of Dialogue

We can gain a sense of what is at stake by linking Burke with Mikhail Bakhtin. In their excellent book on the latter, Katerina Clark and Michael Holquist observe that Bakhtin "rejects the prejudice of post-seventeenth-century European culture that only the neat formulations of isolated categories are valid or 'scientific.'" Then, because Bakhtin was relatively unknown in the English-speaking world when they were writing, Clark and Holquist compare him with a more familiar figure:

> In many ways he is close to . . . Kenneth Burke. One parallel between the two thinkers is their emphasis on what Burke called "perspective by incongruity," the ability to see the identity of a thing not as a lonely isolate from all other categories but as a contrasting variable of all other categories which might, under different conditions, fill the same position in existence.

In other words, instead of heeding method's "abstract and isolate" imperative, Burke and Bakhtin are contextualist thinkers fundamentally at odds with "the essentially mechanistic or mentalist impulse of Structuralism" (7).

Both share the "organic predilection" of Romantic philosophy, stressing

> performance, history, actuality, and the openness of dialogue, as opposed to the closed dialectic of Structuralism's binary oppositions. Bakhtin [and Burke] make *the enormous leap from dialectical, or partitive, thinking, which is still presumed to be the universal norm, to dialogic or relational thinking.* (7, my emphasis)

I underscore Clark and Holquist's sharp contrast between dialectic and dialogue because it represents an evaluation widely shared by postmodernist thinkers.

Dialectic is suspect. It is associated with inflexible method and dogmatism. Like some enormous, unrelenting amoeba, it wants to assimilate otherness rather than converse with it. Immodestly, with an arrogance blind to human finitude, it aspires to totality and nurtures totalitarianism. Since at least Karl Popper's tract on "the open society and its enemies," dialectic—whether Platonic or Hegelian—has been on the wane. It now seems virtually eclipsed by metaphors of conversation and community. The common view is that dialectic belongs to Philosophy, dialogue and dialogics to postPhilosophy. The implication is clear: Make the leap or remain mired in modernism, structuralism, and Philosophical commitments to metaphysics and epistemology.

Clark and Holquist's attempt to link Burke and Bakhtin, philosophers of the same generation but belonging to vastly different worlds and traditions, is certainly stimulating. Few would dispute what they say about Burke. He is clearly a contextualist thinker, whose central metaphors are organic and dynamic. His view of language as symbol action, as "strategies for encompassing situations," is enough to confirm this, also enough to separate him from structuralism, even if his fundamental differences with such theorists as Levi-Strauss and Noam Chomsky were not well known. He not only makes the leap to relational thought—for example, as Rueckert points out, the Pentadic ratios (act-scene, scene-agent, etc.) "make it impossible not to think relationally" ("Some" 11)—but also defends dialogue as an unqualified good and advocates a dialogic approach to the "speechless assertions" of nature (see my discussion, pp. 97–99).

But if Burke is committed to dialogue and dialogics, he is also equally committed to dialectic. We could easily confirm this claim by tracing dialectic in his work from the tension in *Counter-Statement* between the psychology of form and the psychology of information to his last essays on logology, which expose and contemplate the symbol-driven motives of the animal he calls *homo dialecticus* in *A Rhetoric of Motives* (232). His criticism and critical theories often dwell on "the fusion of opposites" in art and the conflicting imperatives of the critic, who must (for instance) "let the text speak" *and* do violence to the text in seeking to reveal what it did not or could not say. Even Burke's novel, short stories, and poetry are dialectical. For him dialectic was not merely an intellectual instrument, but a *modus vivendi*.

And so we must confront two hermeneutical problems.

1. How are we to understand Kenneth Burke, the dialectician?

Can our postPhilosophical reading of Burke encompass what may be the most pervasive of his many roles? If we ignore or underplay dialectic in his work, we misrepresent him; but if we acknowledge its full weight and force, we risk an association with Philosophy.

In the last essay I argued that Burke's philosophical anthropology shares a family resemblance with views of human being associated with philosophical hermeneutics. Burke also draws near to hermeneutical thinkers in featuring a dialectical approach to neo-humanistic philosophy. I shall argue here that *Burke retrieves dialectic for postPhilosophical use.* How he does this is distinctive, quite different, as we shall discover, from Gadamer's retrieval of Hegel's dialectic as hermeneutical dialogue with a text (*Hegel's Dialectic* 99).

2. Assuming that we can understand Burke's dialectic, how can we relate it to dialogue, no less important to him?

We will examine how Burke understood the relationship in due course. But we can't relate them (except by contrast) if we allow the sharp dichotomy between dialectic and dialogue we find in Clark and Holquist to go unquestioned. As in part an aspiration for synthesis, dialectic is not always or necessarily partitive, nor is dialogue, especially as it approaches eristic, always or necessarily relational. "The leap," therefore, may not be across an unbridgeable chasm. The very metaphor of "leaping" may be misleading—why not a movement back and forth not only from dialectic to dialogue but also vice versa? Nor need we assume that a dialectical approach to a given intellectual problem is always inferior to a dialogical one. Perhaps a less partitive and more relational approach to the distinction itself is called for.

But there *is* a distinction that must also be preserved. When Burke defines dialectic as study of "the *dis*position and the *trans*position of terms" (*GM* 402, his emphasis), he means "in *texts*" and according to the close scrutiny that textualization both permits and in a sense demands. In a late essay he clearly recognizes the "print-mindedness" of his dialectic ("Theology" 174). According to Ong and Havelock, despite its taking the form of dialogue, dialectic was from the outset, at its origin in ancient Greece, bound up with literacy (Ong 33–35; Havelock 208–9). Whatever cultural forces entered into the mix that resulted in the "invention" of dialectic, it would not have happened without writing. Dialectic belongs to the people of the book.

If this is so, then we may understand the contemporary attraction to dialogue and dialogics as partly driven by a longing for the communal, embodied, "living" word of speech, of face-to-face human interaction. If the letter kills, perhaps dialogue gives life. As contrasted with chirography and especially with print, dialogue despatializes the word and restores discourse to its primal dynamic, someone saying something to someone else in immediate expectation of response.

If, instead of Clark and Holquist's partitive view of dialectic and dialogue, we take the relational view that dialectic is to dialogue as literacy is to orality, then we can easily imagine a back and forth between them—a both/and relationship rather than a Kierkegaardian either/or. Such an understanding opens a way to Burke, who is both dialectician and dialogist, equally at home in both.

My phrase for expressing the relationship between dialectic and dialogue in Burke is "dialectics within the dialogue," which reverses the order in the title of Norman Levine's book on the history of Marxist thought, *Dialogue Within the Dialectic*. My rearranging of Levine's title and the addition of a crucial "s" to dialectic is meant to sum up a number of basic points. For Burke's generation the great informing experience was the Depression, when a significant portion of the American intelligentsia, united by the threat of Fascism, moved decisively (if in some cases only temporarily) to the left. *The* dialectic for Burke, consequently, is Marx's—not because he became a dialectical materialist but rather because his struggle with dialectic is necessarily, given the times, a struggle with Marx and Marxisms. His rejection of *the* dialectic for dialectical pluralism can best be understood in the context of dogmatic, classical Marxism. His subordination of dialectics to dialogue is likewise best understood in the same context: to borrow a phrase from Habermas, of "revolutionary self-confidence and theoretical self-certainty" ("Reply" 222). If both, as Habermas claims, are now gone—if, that is, Philosophy has truly given way to philosophy—then we have good reason to listen to and learn from a man who staked everything in dialogue and dialectic, while remaining skeptical of all versions of *the* dialectic. Amid the decline of dialectic and the rise of a conversational metaphorics, perhaps Burke's "dialectic of many voices," his dialectical dialogics, is exactly what we need.

Why Dialectic?

> Any terminology is suspect to the extent that it does not allow for the progressive criticism of itself.
>
> —Kenneth Burke, *The Rhetoric of Religion*

Much of this essay is concerned with the nature and function of Burkean dialectics, especially with how he disentangles dialectic from Philosophy, retrieving it for postPhilosophical purposes. But if our primary question is, How does Burke reclaim dialectic from Philosophy? restoring it to what it apparently was for Socrates, an art of inquiry rather than an instrument of dogmatics, clearly a question logically prior to this one must be answered first: Why retrieve dialectic at all?

Burke answers this question in many ways, but all of them converge in *homo dialecticus*: Dialectic is indispensable and unsurpassable because dialectic belongs to the being of human being. We are symbol-using animals, and dialectic is inherent in symbols. Consider, for example, the following passage from *A Rhetoric of Motives*:

> [R]everence, God, hierarchy are . . . the ultimates of the dialectical process. Call them the "basic errors" of the dialectic if you want. That need not concern us. We are here talking about ultimate dialectical tendencies, having "god," or a "god-term," as the completion of the linguistic process. . . . Language being essentially a means of transcending brute objects, there is implicit in it the "temptation" to come upon an idea of "God" as the *ultimate* transcendence. (275–76, his emphasis)

"We are not discovering 'God' here, in the theologian's sense," Burke goes on to say, for "God . . . must be much more than an 'Idea' dialectically arrived at" (276). Rather than discovering God, Burke is explaining the necessity for dialectic, arguing in effect for the "eternal" recurrence of the neo-Platonic "upward way."

Were there any need to do so in the current intellectual environment, we could deconstruct Plato and Platonisms. What we cannot deconstruct are the motives inherent in language, in this case, the motives of transcendence. If we have, say, a word such as "bison" for designating all instances of this particular animal, we have already "transcended" this particular bison in front of us, if only because the word itself may be applied to all instances of the species. More than this, we have transcended any need for a referent at all, since bison would still be with us "in spirit" (as meaning) even had we succeeded in destroying the whole tribe of brother bison.

We can extend the fellowship that links the human tribe to the bison tribe by a word designating, say, all animals we depend on for survival. From there, we could climb the ladder to all animals, thence to all living things—or if organic and inorganic is not a distinction we make—to the great web of life embracing earth and heavens, brought to completion and unity in, pervaded by, the Great Spirit (not the same as the personal God of the Judeo-Christian tradition, *Lord* God, source of all dominion and giver of dominion—nor equivalent to Being Itself, the Philosopher's "god," so ultimately abstract as to be empty of anything concrete, such as holy regard for a species and a way of life).

The point, of course, is that while there are many paths of abstraction, many ways of reverence, many gods, many hierarchies, there is no escape from *some kind* of abstraction, reverence, god, and hierarchy. Our abstractions may be the "pure reason" of mathematics, our reverence idolatry of the machine, our god the worship of power (or money, or sex), our hierarchy the organizational chart of a university or a corporation, but regardless of how secular our "upward way" may be, the drive to transcendence rooted in symbol-using is detectable in all human organization and activity. "*Empirically*, I sanction dialectic, which giveth and taketh away," The Lord tells Satan in Burke's "Epilogue: Prologue in Heaven," "[f]or such is time, and The Development"—

> And the dialectic . . . is never without . . . a principle of transcendence, an Upward Way that, when reversed, interprets all incidental things in terms of the over-all fulfillment towards which the entire development is said to be striving. (*RR* 303, my emphasis)

Upward Ways imply Downward Ways: The deconstruction of Platonism hardly deconstructs dialectic, indispensable and unsurpassable purely on empirical grounds, without recourse to anyone's metaphysics. Call, if you will, reverence, God, and hierarchy the basic errors of the dialectic—postmodernism rests on the radical Enlightenment's suspicion of all three—and nothing has changed at all. Dialectic and its motives remain. We cannot even pursue the "errors" of the dialectic without recourse to dialectic. We cannot pass beyond dialectic because we dwell in a symbolically constituted world.

Providing we remember that Being for Burke is *praxis* Being (i.e., not eternal or immutable [see my discussion, pp. 101–2]), we can call the above argument his "ontological proof" of dialectic's necessity. Transcendence is only one aspect of it; in *A Grammar of Motives* he also treats "merger and division" and what Chaim Perelman calls "philosophical pairs" (i.e., the dominant conceptual distinctions of a culture [*Treatise* 415–18]) as interrelated aspects of his defense of dialectic (*GM* 402–20). We need not concern ourselves with the details of his exposition to discern its answer to the question, Why dialectic? We cannot turn from dialectic without turning away from language. Dialectic and the linguistic turn are inseparable.

Put another way, not every culture "invents" dialectic, making it an art or science, a self-conscious practice. However, because there is no other way to think and act, every culture thinks and acts by mergers and divisions and by its characteristic ways of transcendence. All cultures are dialectical whether or not they "have" dialectic in the sense of an art or science. Our respect for cultural diversity should not lead us to neglect the motives all people have as symbol-using animals. It follows that any postPhilosophical culture that takes language as the primary source of its understanding of human being must turn or return to dialectic—or else fail to grasp the implications of its own project.

We can understand Burke's defense of dialectic in at least one other way, historically, in the context of modernity and postmodernity. He read the critiques of Hegelian dialectic in Kierkegaard, Nietzsche, Marx, and others. Burke himself belongs to this anti-Hegelian tradition inasmuch as he read Hegel's logic in an un-Hegelian way, as a fascinating meditation on the key terms of western Philosophy, without sympathy for Hegel's metaphysical claims. But like Marx and in a spirit akin to such contemporary Hegelians as Ricoeur, Gadamer, and Taylor, Burke insisted that dialectic must not be discarded in rejecting Absolute Idealism. Dialectic will survive all the discarded "isms" with which it has been associated, for its "ground" is symbols, not Philosophy.

Decentering Dialectic

Before Permanence and Change, in Auscultation, Creation, and Revision, written in the early thirties, Burke was already dissatisfied with the dialectic of his time: "I seek to develop methods of interpretation beyond Marx," he claimed, and as I have shown in an analysis of Auscultation, Creation, and Revision, he got beyond Marx by "de-[con]struct[ing] the bourgeois/proletarian antithesis, and with it, Marx's deterministic view of history and the whole process of 'conversion' via a radical shift from individualism to collectivism" (358). Burke's "methods of interpretation" (of history and anything else he studied) remained dialectical and retained the economic-material critique. But he saw many lines of conflict besides that between social classes and found more than conflict in class relations; he consistently refused to take symbolic action as an epiphenomenon of productive forces; he believed in the value of what he called "prophesies after the event" (i.e., efforts to understand, explain, and apply lessons gained from the study of what has happened) but steadfastly refused to believe that either individual human acts or historical events were entirely "necessary," and hence, entirely predictable. In other words, his assimilation of Marx was via the hermeneutic we discussed previously, discounting (see my discussion, pp. 123–25). He did not reject Marx, but he also did not take him as Truth or holy writ.

Burke's approach to Marx is an early example of a pervasive strategy he pursued throughout his career in retrieving dialectic for post-Philosophical application. Meaning to evoke some of the implications it has in Piaget, I call the strategy "decentering." Let's examine some aspects of it in the later philosophy.

We might begin by asking, What is dialectic for Burke? "By dialectics in the most general sense we mean the employment of the possibilities of linguistic transformation. Or we may mean the study of such possibilities" (*GM* 402). In other words, regardless of intent, we function as dialecticians when we unfold the implications of a chosen vocabulary, as I have done here with a cluster of terms connected with my key concept, "postPhilosophical." A book reviewer or critic who analyzes my terminological "moves"—for example, distinctions made or denied, patterns of association and dissociation—would also, in Burke's view, be functioning as a dialectician.

Burke's definition obviously broadens or democratizes dialectic. Since Plato, dialectic has generally been conceived as an art requiring special cultivation, the instrument of that leisure class of professional thinkers, Philosophers. But for Burke Philosophy or philosophy (especially as theology) only uses dialectic in an especially intense, thorough, self-conscious way. Dialectic belongs, however, to the symbol-using animal, not to P/philosophy or any other discipline or profession. Human beings are spontaneously dialecticians as they are rhetoricians.

Already we see in Burke's democratizing of dialectic a profound decentering from traditional concepts. Dialectic is not the preserve of Philosopher-Kings, nor a privileged way to Truth or wisdom. It is certainly not *Logos*, or even what we study in "Introduction to Logic" classes. It is not the intricacies of the syllogism, or the hair-splitting debates of medieval schoolmen, or Hegel's almost unreadable *Science of Logic*, or the oxygenless abstractions of symbolic logic, or the unearthly logic of possible worlds, and so forth. It is the use and study of terminologies, a reconceiving of dialectic as a tool for coping with the explosion of specialized nomenclatures characteristic of both modernism and postmodernism. Burke offers a decentered dialectic, then, for a decentered culture of specialists.

Another way Burke decenters dialectic is by limiting it to "*linguistic transformation*." Dialectic for Burke is a purely verbal affair. It is not a reflection of or on *Eidos*, the eternal essence of things. It is not Hegel's Spirit or the Marx-Engels dialectic of nature and human productive forces. Burke does not claim, as do some Philosophers from the ancient Greeks to contemporary physicists, that God is a mathematician, a symbol-user, and that therefore by study of the dialectics of mathematics we draw near to the Mind of God. None of these grand, more-than-linguistic notions of dialectic infect Burke's humble art of vocabularies and how people think with them. Dialectic in Burke assumes not only an irreducible diversity but also a finite and fallible human being—equivalent to saying that Burke's decentering of dialectic marks the end of dialectic's striving for totality.

I will discuss only one more way Burke decenters dialectic: namely, by recognizing a plurality of meanings and applications for the word,

which amounts to turning away from any concept of *the* dialectic in
favor of dialectics. As we have seen, "dialectic in general" in Burke's
philosophy designates only two activities: "employment of the possibilities of linguistic transformation" or study of "the *dis*position and the
*trans*position of terms," both dependent on textuality (*GM* 402, his emphasis). But dialectics in Burke is not so confined. For example, Burke
offered a well-developed dialectic of history in *Attitudes Toward History*. He described it informally and ironically as follows through the
Impresario of the comic conversation, "Epilogue: Prologue in Heaven":

> [T]he talking animals' way of life in civilization *invents* pur-
> poses. Rationalized by money (which is a language, a kind of
> purpose-in-the-absolute, a universal wishing well), empires
> arise. Such networks of production and distribution, made
> *possible* by language, become *necessary*. So, they raise prob-
> lems—and many purposes are but attempts to solve these
> problems, plus the vexing fact that each "solution" raises fur-
> ther problems. (Confidentially, that's "the dialectic.") (*RR* 275,
> Burke's emphasis)

"The dialectic," of course, was supposed to have some grand design to
it, an entelechy, a fruition in Absolute Spirit or the withering away of
class and state structures—hence the irony of the Impresario's paren-
thetical comment. This dialectic is no version of "the dialectic," for it
has no end or necessary sequence, promising only an endless struggle
with our own self-generated, symbol-driven problems. But whether we
enjoy the irony or not, the point is that dialectics in Burke has a range of
meanings and applications, not all of them, in any usual sense of the
word, textual. Burke decenters from his own concept of "dialectic in
general" to a pluralism of dialectics.

And yet, while refusing to play the Philosophical game of reduction
to univocal meaning, all forms of dialectics in Burke share common
ground. Consider only one more example, the dialectic of order developed at length in *A Rhetoric of Motives* and *The Rhetoric of Religion*
and summarized in the following lines:

> Here are the steps
> In the Iron Law of History
> That welds Order and Sacrifice:
>
> Order leads to Guilt
> (for who can keep commandments!)
> Guilt needs Redemption

(for who would not be cleansed!)
Redemption needs Redeemer
(which is to say, a Victim!).

Order
Through Guilt
To Victimage
(hence: Cult of the Kill). . . .

(*RR* 4–5)

This dialectic differs from the Impresario's in being all-too-predictable, all-too-necessary, the ellipsis that concludes the poem designating, not open-endedness, "solutions" generating more or less unforeseeable problems that in turn must be "solved," *ad infinitum*, but rather the gloomy prospect of an endless repetition of "the same." But they come together in the focus of the last essay, Burke's philosophical anthropology, in the symbol-using, misusing, and used animal, *homo dialecticus*. They also come together in the focus of the next essay, *praxis*, which for Burke requires something that "the dialectic" has always somehow missed—a critique of our symbol-driven motives, crucial to understanding the dialectical impulse itself, as well as the purposes required by the talking animals' way of life in a civilization.

Burke's decentering of dialectic, then, is also a centering, a repositioning of the art for a new critical task. Dialectic becomes the discipline Burke named logology, which, as we will see in the next essay, takes us a crucial step beyond the reflexiveness of ideology critique.

For now, the key point is this: We need not choose between some version of "the dialectic" (Platonic, Hegelian, Marxist, or whatever) and the rejection, neglect, or deconstruction of dialectic we find in Nietzsche, Heidegger, and Derrida, respectively. We can opt instead for Burke's decentering of dialectic, which delivers the art from everything that arouses postmodern suspicion—that is, inflexible method, dogmatic scientism, an all-swallowing synthetic, an immodest aspiration for the Whole, the Truth, totality, totalitarianism. Burkean dialectics belong to the open society. They return dialectic to its original purpose—study, inquiry. They are only so many tools for coping, not the instruments of a "master thinker" who would either dominate or collapse.

If we can opt for a plurality of dialectics and thereby opt out of Philosophy's quest for "the dialectic," why extend the postmodern attack on dialectic any further? What would we gain? And why, now that the "basic errors" of the dialectic are widely understood, deprive ourselves of so useful a set of tools? If, as Burke claims, dialectical motives and tensions are inherent in the symbol, how can philosophy after the

linguistic turn part with dialectics? The postmodern animus against dialectic seems misdirected in the context of Burke's postPhilosophical retrieval of the art.

Hermeneutics and Dialectical Pluralism

I have been explicating Burke's strategies for retrieving dialectic for post-
Philosophical use. Here are the key points thus far:

1. Against dialectic's detractors, Burke argues that dialectic is always
at minimum implicit in the motives peculiar to symbol-using—for example, abstracting or "transcendence." When our species developed language, we were, so to speak, doomed to dialectic, and it remains part of
our fate so long as we survive and remain symbol-users. In this sense,
"symbol-using animal" and *homo dialecticus* are synonymous.

2. But if we are doomed to dialectic, we need not be confined to any
particular version of it. Burke points to the many meanings dialectic has
had in the history of our culture as confirmation (*GM* 403), invents his
own conception of dialectic in general, and develops a pluralism of dialectics for understanding the dynamics of history, the logic of victimization,
and for a host of other hermeneutical purposes. He disputes thereby
the Philosophical conviction that "the dialectic" is lurking, waiting to be
discovered, somewhere "underneath" or "above" its multiplicity of uses.
By democratizing dialectic, he also responds to what has become the
most salient postmodern criticism: that dialectic has been typically in
the past a tool of dogma, an instrument of hegemony and repression,
usually tied to the interests of a privileged class. Finally, if we follow
Burke in decentering from all notions of "the dialectic," we decenter
also from the symbol-driven yearning for "perfection" (see my discussion, pp. 169–72), which drives dialectic toward totality in theory and
totalitarianism in practice.

As we move now toward dialogue and the relation of dialectic to
dialogue in Burke, we must explore his "dialectic of many voices" in
more detail. Developed at length in Part Two of *A Grammar of Motives*
("The Philosophical Schools" 127–320), it complements his pluralism
of dialectics with a dialectical pluralism, in Burke a reasoned organization of hermeneutical perspectives around the term "act" and its implications. The resulting "dialectic of many voices" completes the first phase
of his retrieval of dialectic; it also exemplifies logologic (a spinning out
of the implications of a terminology) and anticipates many of the concerns of logology, both important extensions of dialectic in his work
after *A Grammar of Motives*.

Perhaps the best way to appreciate Burke's retrieval of dialectic is to
contrast it with Gadamer's more Hegelian effort. In *Hegel's Dialectic*, Ga-

damer claimed that "dialectic must retrieve itself in hermeneutics" (99). Burke's dialectic of many voices implies the reverse of Gadamer's claim: *Hermeneutics must retrieve itself as dialectic*, specifically, as dialectical pluralism. We will explore both claims.

As I have explained elsewhere,

> by retrieving dialectic Gadamer means holding on to Hegel's phenomenology but discarding his metaphysics. Hegel's descriptions of the process of increasing self-understanding are very close to Gadamer's dialectic of experience, in that "assertions" (horizons of meaning) are constantly challenged by the anomalous and by other, conflicting horizons, resulting optimally in a dialogical process akin to *Aufhebung*, a modifying-enlarging of horizons to encompass "new matter." (*Hermeneutics* 83)

That is, Gadamer thinks that the only vital and defensible concept of dialectic for post-metaphysical thought is hermeneutical dialogue. Against method's ideal of a blank, "objective" observer, Gadamer holds that we actually encounter "the Other" as historical beings caught up in tradition, which is to say, prejudice or prejudgment. To be "the Other," our interlocutor must inhabit a horizon of meanings in significant respects at variance with our own. The encounter is initially, therefore, a clash, or at least a dissonance. Dialectic becomes hermeneutical argumentation, the struggle to transform the clash into a new concord, the dissonance into a new harmony, as our prejudices are challenged by the Other, and the Other's prejudices by ours. Optimally dialogue results in what Gadamer calls a "fusion of horizons" (*Truth* 273–74), an experience analogous to Hegel's *Aufhebung*, where both parties are transformed, brought together in a common understanding, and yet still different, still in tension. Clearly the dialogical process as Gadamer conceives it is akin to Hegel's dialectic, but hegelian in being endlessly recurrent and unpredictable, without any necessary sequence or ultimate fruition in Absolute Spirit. Hence Gadamer can claim with some plausibility that his notion of hermeneutics "retrieves dialectic" for what I have been calling postPhilosophy.

Burke would find much to celebrate in Gadamer's retrieval of dialectic. He rejects method's claim to omnicompetence as firmly as Gadamer does (see my discussion, pp. 73–76). He would construe Gadamer's commitment to hermeneutical dialogue as similar to his own, broader commitment to Dramatistic processes, which includes, as we have seen, advocacy of dialogue as an unqualified good (see my discussion, pp. 97–99). His own anti-epistemological view of knowledge as a tragic process gained through the trials of *praxis* (*GM* 38–41) differs little from Gadamer's dialectic of experience. Clearly, as David Damrosch was the first to point out, much in Burke and Gadamer correspond (224–25).

But if Burke wants to retrieve dialectic quite as much as Gadamer does, his understanding of hermeneutics differs crucially from Gadamer's. As far back as *Auscultation, Creation, and Revision*, Burke was calling attention to the enormous proliferation of interpretive vocabularies, including those we now call "depth hermeneutics" and "critical theory," developments over the last century or so that have altered hermeneutics fundamentally. We no longer dwell only in horizons of meaning made possible by language and culture in general; many of us have also internalized one or several specialized nomenclatures, professional jargons, typically drawn from a subdiscipline within one of the sciences. We commonly recognize economic, political, social, psychological (etc.) interpretations of the "same thing" or, within a single discipline (say, psychology), psychoanalytical, cognitive, behavioral, sociopsychological (etc.) interpretations of the "same thing." As Burke pointed out in *Permanence and Change*, the explosion of nomenclatures has irretrievably fragmented hermeneutics, making a perspectival, relativistic understanding of interpretation a practical necessity (117–19).

Mainly because Gadamer wants to release truth from the stranglehold of modernist method, he pays insufficient attention to the problem of nomenclatures that preoccupies Burke from the early thirties on. Gadamer believes he can still appeal to a *sensus communis*, while Burke points to the hermeneutical muddle of late modernism. Gadamer urges us to join in the *spiel* of dialogue, letting the *logos* lead us toward truths that will suffice, whereas Burke takes the dialogue itself as a struggle among terministic screens, each with its own version of "the truth," each seeking adherents with all the rhetorical skill it can muster. As the tendency to be overdetermined by our terms, the *logos* typically leads us too much. Difference must be cultivated to escape de-"term"-inism, idolatry of our own interpretive vocabulary. Gadamer holds that difference can be partially overcome, that horizons can "fuse" and disagreements can yield to consensus; Burke hopes only to "purify war," to confine the conflict of horizons to a permanent argument.

Clearly, from Burke's point of view, hermeneutics poses greater difficulties than dialectic and is itself in no condition to retrieve anything. Burke "solves" the problems posed by "the dialectic" (i.e., dialectic as the Hegelian-Marxist tradition understands it) quite early in his career by decentering from it—by, in effect, denying both its claim to totality and to foreknowledge of the *telos* of history. Thus deprived of its Philosophical pretension to Truth (but not to insight), Burke has declawed the tiger and disciplined its all-devouring ambition to the point that even the most chary postmodern sensibility can lay down with it in peace.

But the problems of interpretation pursue Burke far beyond the thirties, perhaps to the end of his career, certainly as far as the "invention" of logology in *The Rhetoric of Religion* (1961). In logology Burke found his "ultimate" rationale for hermeneutics: to understand our symbol-driven motives so that we might be less driven by them. However, finding one's own project is not tantamount to "solving" the hermeneutical problems posed by the disintegration of *sensus communis* under the combined assault of occupational specialization and method's great fertility in spawning a seemingly endless brood of interpretive nomenclatures. What are we to do with the modernist legacy of hermeneutical fragmentation?

For the most part postmodernism has chosen to do nothing, sometimes even to resist consciously the desire to do anything. Its "solution" comes to "negative capability" made absolute. But this strategy of acquiescence only cooperates with hermeneutical fragmentation by renaming "confusion," which no one wants, with a term everyone wants, "diversity." Gadamer's way was to turn away from method, which was also a turning within—toward the humanistic tradition of hermeneutics itself, where he found a rhetorical notion of truth of ancient provenience, "to convince and illuminate without being able to prove" ("Rhetoric" 279). But this solution, however valuable it may be, only served to bifurcate hermeneutics still further, hardening the Enlightenment-Romantic split into the sharply opposing "hermeneutics of tradition" versus "hermeneutics of suspicion." We had the Gadamer-Habermas debate and the struggle of Ricoeur in its aftermath to rejoin the two via critical hermeneutics ("Hermeneutics" 63–64, 87–100).

As I have argued elsewhere, Burke's way is neither typically postmodern nor comparable to philosophical hermeneutics ("Neither" 85–88). The flaccid eclecticism that left Lentricchia wondering exactly what the point of conversation might be among postmodernists (15–16) was not an option for Burke. One had to reckon with a dialectic *of many voices*, but it had to remain a *dialectic* of many voices, critical, principled, and willing to ask and re-ask the question, What exactly are we trying to understand and why? For this reason, Burke invented a dialectic, not of concepts, but of terms, designed to explore interpretative vocabularies. For this reason he advocated a hermeneutics of discounting, which made any voice in the dialogue "response-able" to critique. And for this reason he sought a pluralistic ordering of the voices rather than eclecticism. On the one hand, then, Burke's attempt to cope with confusion/diversity is not typically postmodern. Postmodernism embraces one of the options Burke rejects in "Dialectician's Prayer": "the delirium of the many" (*CP* 41).

On the other hand, while remaining, as we have seen, within postPhilosophical neo-humanism (see my discussion, pp. 141–44), Burke never sought, as Gadamer did, to set method and its many critical theories aside. There is no *systematic* contrast in Burke between "truth" and "method."

On the contrary, it is precisely method's multiplying vocabularies, the competing interpretations of "depth hermeneutics," that Burke hopes to cope with via the Dramatism of *A Grammar of Motives*. The contrast with Gadamer could not be greater. By comparison with Burke, Gadamer is a purist, turning away from methodical hermeneutics to an intense scrutiny of humanistic hermeneutics. His terminology *excludes* and is deliberately designed to exclude. Burke opts for a humanistic terminology— drama, action, and their implications—to create a dialectical pluralism that *includes*, that takes in even *anti-Dramatistic* modes of interpretation. Under the rubric of "Scene," for instance, Burke treats an array of materialisms, among them the classic Hellenistic Stoics and Epicureans, Hobbes's rather crude mechanistic version, and Darwin's theory of natural selection (*GM* 127–70). These perspectives are all more or less deterministic, unwilling or unable to respond to the "grammar" of action, scenes implying acts, and vice versa. Yet these anti-Dramatistic voices find their place within Burke's Pentadic dialectic, as does the far more complicated and more Dramatistic dialectical materialism of classical Marxism, which he construes as "grow[ing] out of idealism by antithesis" (200).

Whether one agrees or not with Burke's readings of this or that Philosopher, the general strategy that unfolds in "The Philosophical Schools" section of *A Grammar of Motives* should prove persuasive as a way of coping with our "postmodern condition." We are obsessed with "the Other"; how, then, does Burke treat Otherness? He does not exclude it, as Gadamer does. Nor does his dialectic "swallow up" the Other, reducing all the voices to Dramatism's act-centered terminology. He does not synthesize; rather he *places* and *relates*, leaving the voices themselves intact and at odds. His respect for the Other, however, does not end in "the delirium of the many." We can see all hermeneutical vocabularies in relation to the Pentadic grammar, as if derived from the implications of Act, Scene, Agent, Agency, and Purpose. *As if*—Burke is not claiming, as Hegel did, that all Philosophy is reaching completion in his dialectic. He is offering a scheme and knows that he is offering a scheme for relating past, present, and future voices, a way to have the One without the alternative to delirium he also would avoid—"the mania of the One" (*CP* 41). Burke allows us to see the implicational logic by which Scenic voices are interrelated, and the pathways by which Scenic perspectives can be connected, say, to Agent-centered ones, without believing that he has The Answer. Dramatism, rather, takes its place among other Act-centered philosophies. It is only one of many voices, and simultaneously one voice around which a dialectical pluralism can take shape.

There is no point in disputing that Burke's appropriation of Philosophy, his transformation of it into a dialectical pluralism, is in its own way violent—to transform is always to deform. Dialectic is always civilized aggression, a purification of war. But even those most deeply suspicious of dialectic's attenuated violence must recognize the advantages of

Burke's retrieval of hermeneutics as dialectical pluralism. When Gada-mer encountered Habermas's criticisms, he contended that philosophical hermeneutics does not preclude depth hermeneutics ("Scope" 288–89). This may be true, but the terminology Gadamer developed in *Truth and Method* nevertheless does not provide for it either. Burke's does and thereby avoids the most serious criticism leveled against philosophical hermeneu-tics. Burke also avoids Habermas's rather awkward hybrid hermeneutics, which attempts to graft critical theory onto the humanistic hermeneuti-cal tradition. Burke's hermeneutics has the critical function that Haber-mas considers essential without any need for grafting of any sort. We can "deduce" both humanistic and methodical hermeneutics from the ter-ministic resources of the Pentad, and do so seamlessly, without any need for the elaborate justifications Habermas requires. The power and economy of Burke's dialectic is remarkable.

If we understand *A Grammar of Motives* as the reverse of Gadamer's strategy for retrieving dialectic and if we place it in the context of the Other in postmodern thought, its virtues and significance become ap-parent. It is immediately obvious, for instance, that Lentricchia's read-ing of *A Grammar or Motives* as a "cold-blooded structuralism" (68–69) misses altogether what Burke was doing. *A Grammar of Motives* is Burke's first essay in logologic, the quizzical exploration and application of a terminology. It is not structuralism at all, but a self-critical dialectic, rich, supple, and full of surprises and by-the-by insights. Burke's dialec-tic of many voices does not anticipate structuralism but rather our cur-rent struggle with hermeneutics, offering an approach at least the equal of anything else we have. His dialectical pluralism not only saves us from idolatry of any single interpretative vocabulary, including Dramatism, but also resists the hermeneutical fragmentation and dissociation that modernism produced and postmodernism seems powerless to address.

Integrating Dialectic and Dialogue

> [Burke] dedicated his first book of poems to "My sparring partners" saying . . . "and long may we spar without parting."
>
> —William Rueckert, "Some of the Many Kenneth Burkes"

Our first hermeneutical question was, How are we to understand Ken-neth Burke, the dialectician? My answer in sum is as follows:

1. Burke "grounds" dialectic in symbol-using, which means

that dialectic cannot be discarded or overcome so long as
the symbol-using animal exists.

2. He decenters from any concept of *the* dialectic, which
means that his various concepts of dialectic, his dialectic*s*, are postPhilosophical—in the spirit of the open
society and against its dogmatic, totalizing enemies.

3. His notion of "dialectic in general" as the study of the
"disposition and transposition of terms" is a text hermeneutic, which means that Ricoeur's criticism of hermeneutics—that is, that it fails to consider texts as texts
(*Interpretation Theory* 22–32)—does not apply to Burke.

4. Burke retrieves hermeneutics as dialectical pluralism,
which means *both* preservation of the Other as Other
and a certain principled organization of contending
voices into related groups and into relations among
the groups, *as if* all hermeneutic perspectives (whether
humanistic or methodical) could be derived from the
implications of "drama" and "action."

In short, Burke shows us both how to escape from Philosophical
appropriations of dialectic and what can be done with dialectic "after
Philosophy." The turn to dialogue need not—for Burke, *must* not—be a
turning away from dialectic.

And so we arrive at our second hermeneutical question, How exactly does Burkean dialectics relate to dialogue? The key text for answering this question comes from "The Philosophy of Literary Form."
Near the end of this monograph-length essay, Burke is attempting a synopsis of his understanding of the relation between texts (for Burke, a
subcategory of symbolic acts) and what he calls "verbal action in general." First, he reminds us again of his more-than-formalistic position:

> [E]very document bequeathed us by history must be treated
> as a *strategy for encompassing a situation*. . . . when con-
> sidering some document like the American Constitution, we
> shall be automatically warned not to consider it in isolation,
> but as the *answer* or *rejoinder* to assertions current in the
> situation in which it arose. . . . [For example,] our Constitu-
> tion is to be considered as a rejoinder to the theories and prac-
> tices of merchantilist paternalism. (*PLF* 109, his emphasis)

In other words, texts for Burke have the same status as propositions for
Gadamer (cf. the latter's "What is Truth?" 42): Both are answers to ques-

tions, or responses to other answers to questions. They are not the self-contained entities they appear to be. Rather, they are always already caught up in an argument, fragments of a dialogue, so that dialectical examination of a text in isolation (i.e., analysis of its key terms and propositions as such), however fruitful, cannot constitute understanding. We can only understand a text as part of a conversation—that is, dialogically (or, in Burkean parlance, Dramatistically, as an act in a scene).

So understood, "[W]here does the drama [that is, the symbolic act or text] get its materials?" Burke asks. Clearly,

> [f]rom the "unending conversation" that is going on at the point in history when we are born. Imagine that you enter a parlor. You come late. When you arrive others have long preceded you, and they are engaged in a heated discussion, a discussion too heated for them to pause and tell you exactly what it is about. In fact, the discussion had already begun long before any of them got there, so that no one present is qualified to retrace for you all the steps that had gone before. You listen for a while, until you decide that you have caught the tenor of the argument; then you put in your oar. Someone answers; you answer him; another comes to your defense; another aligns himself against you, to either the embarrassment or gratification of your opponent, depending on the quality of your ally's assistance. However, the discussion is interminable. The hour grows late, you must depart. And you do depart, with the discussion still vigorously in progress. (110–11)

We could unpack this conceit at considerable length, for it expresses with great economy concepts philosophical hermeneutics has made familiar—finitude, historicity, thrownness, ungroundedness, open-endedness, and so on. In these few lines Burke draws very near to Gadamer—and at the same time, draws away, for whereas Gadamer characteristically stresses the reconciling capacity of dialogue, its potential to "fuse horizons," Burke characteristically stresses its drama, unreconciled and unreconcilable conflict—which is to say, difference, otherness. In Gadamer dialogue *transcends* drama; in Burke dialogue *is* drama, that is, dialectic in one of its meanings, face-to-face argumentation. We will see in a moment one of the reasons why Burke stresses conflict rather than transcendence of difference.

But the point that most concerns us now, as we seek to understand how Burke integrates dialectic and dialogue, literacy and orality, is this: "The materials of [the] drama [not only texts, but commonly texts] arise from this 'unending conversation'" (111). Not only does understanding a text depend on a dialogical context, but also, more fundamentally, no

text could exist without the "unending conversation" of history. Texts
are utterly dependent on dialogue. Without "verbal action in general,"
textual symbolic acts would have nothing to work with—no being at all.
    However,

> verbal action [is not] all there is to it. For all these words are
> grounded in what Malinowski would call "contexts of situa-
> tion." And very important among these "contexts of situa-
> tion" are the kinds of factors considered by Bentham, Marx,
> and Veblen, the material interests (of private or class struc-
> ture) that you symbolically defend or symbolically appropri-
> ate or symbolically align yourself with in the course of making
> your own assertions. (111–12)

We see immediately why drama or conflict is so emphasized and so beyond permanent resolution in Burke's understanding of dialogue, for
"context of situation" embraces class interests and economic struggle in
general, motives endemic to civilized existence. No amount of "good talk"
can overcome this kind of difference. "Context of situation" alone goes
far in explaining why the unending conversation of history is unending.
    We also see another crucial point of difference with Gadamer. Ga-
damer overlooks or ignores "context of situation" in the sense of the
material interests that always condition human interaction. It is precisely this "blind spot" (no doubt traceable to Gadamer's Hegelianism)
that Habermas seized upon in his critique of *Truth and Method*: The
domain of work and political-economic struggle plays no significant role
in Gadamer's hermeneutics ("Review" 272–73). Consequently, his understanding of dialogue is idealistic in both the general and philosophical senses of the word. Burke not only recognizes the role of material
interests in symbolic action but also allots them something like the status of "substructure" by treating them as the most significant aspect of
context of situation. At the same time, he rejects the economic determinism that usually accompanies the notion of "substructure": "These [ma-
terial] interests do not 'cause' [the] discussion; its 'cause' is in the genius
[of] *homo loquax*. But they greatly effect the *idiom* in which [we] speak,
and so the idiom by which [we] think" (*PLF* 112). *Effect, condition*, but
not determine or cause: Dialogue has its own dynamic, not reducible to
context of situation, but also not comprehensible apart from it either.
Verbal action is not all there is to it. There is much outside the text, and
more to human interaction than the play of words. Again we see how
consistently Burke rejects idealism as we typically encounter it now—
that is, as linguistic reductionism.
    Schematically Burke's vision of discourse amounts to three interac-
tive "levels," so intertwined with one another and so difficult to conceive
in a rigid hierarchical fashion that the quotes around "level" require

special emphasis. In the "middle," so to speak, is verbal action in general, all the arguments in all the parlors that sustain the unending conversation of history. Since as individuals we are a part of many ongoing dialogues and not a part of most of them, this "level" is by nature decentered, "de-seminated," influenced by what we read and write but beyond the control and discipline of texts, conditioned mainly by past discussions (mostly unknown or forgotten) and by the "level" "beneath" it—context of situation and its associated idioms. The unending conversation, then, is hardly free play, for like the all-enveloping ocean it may be likened to, it is gathered into bulges by the pull of lunar gravitation and shaped into currents by prevailing winds.

Texts may be compared to the detritus that the waves discharge upon the beach, husks that the life has left, a portion of which we accord special value by gathering them into the morgue-like, reverential silence of our libraries. Burke the dialectician likens himself to a beachcomber, possessed by a certain "pruritus of detritus" (CP 122) engrossed in tracing the intricate designs of the shells we call texts. Elsewhere he claims that all texts are like scripts for a play, directions for a performance ("Theology" 174), whose life resides not in the deep freeze of print but only as enacted by some reader. In this sense, the text is not the symbolic act, only that portion of it chirography and print can preserve. Put another way, a text draws not only its materials from unending conversations but also its vitality and continuing impact—outside the conversation, when no one is thinking with it or talking about it, a text is as obscure as an empty shell lying half-buried on a beach. "In itself" a text is very little more than nothing at all. But understood as arising from the conversation of history and as part of the conversation, texts enjoy a potent mode of being indeed—as "fixed" reference points for discussion, bearers of tradition with special authority, reservoirs of knowledge that release the mind from some of the burden of memory, records of past "strategies for encompassing situations," and so on. As Walter Ong and others have shown, textuality is no mere addition to human ways and means, but a transformation of human-being-in-the-world (35–53).

Conclusion: The Rhythm of Dialectic and Dialogue

As we have before with other themes and issues, we must locate Burke's understanding of the relation between dialectic and dialogue by contrast with other better known but less comprehensive and balanced stances. Burke confronts formalism in general, structuralism, textual fundamentalism or idolatry, and Derrida's attempt to undermine the primacy of the spoken word—all of which may be lumped together under the rubric "hyperliteracy"—with certain hard-to-dispute observations about textuality. Texts are fragments of the decentered conversation of humankind. They cannot be understood apart from the conversations in which they arose nor apart from their place and function in the conversations going on now. They cannot exist without the materials supplied by verbal action in general. They have little being and no efficaciousness "in themselves," as abstracted from the ongoing conversation that sustains their life. We can see the truth of these observations easily: Suppose that the human race ceased to exist; what would our libraries and all the books they house "come to" then? What would they be but wood, brick, steel, concrete, paper, and ink on the way to dust, like the ruins of an ancient abandoned city?

Hyperliteracy is the dead burying the dead. We see it in colleagues who love books more than the people that read them or the conversations they stimulate.

There can be no question that dialogue is alpha and omega for Burke, "first" insofar as we can speak of firsts, "last" insofar as we can speak of lasts, but always primary so long as the symbol-using animal exists, insofar as we can speak at all. And yet dialogue is hardly all there is, nor is it the free *spiel* of *logos* in some unprestructured search for the truth. We can, as Gadamer says, give ourselves over to the joy of the conversational game, the back-and-forth of dialogue, but in doing so "context of situation" is typically covered over. We forget the source of our idioms in "the material interests" we "symbolically defend or . . . appropriate or . . . align" ourselves with (at least implicitly) in making our assertions. We forget also certain disturbing facts, such as Lentricchia's point about how hard it is to get into even a small part of "the conversation" and harder still to remain part of it for very long (16). Many—most—are excluded, and some conversations matter (have more practical effect on the world) than others. The idealism that is so obvious in some exponents of dialogue—not only Gadamer but also, for example, Buber, and sometimes even Bakhtin—is absent in Burke. Dialogue has an absolute value for Burke, but it is not absolute, because "verbal action [is not] all there is to it."

We cannot leave dialectic behind or leap past it for at least two reasons: We cannot cope with texts as texts without it, without study of the disposition and transposition of terms and the unfolding of propositions, all of which must be questioned; and we cannot "get at" context of situation without pondering "the kind of factors considered by Bentham, Marx and Veblen." We need dialectic in both positive and negative forms as hermeneutical tools for coping—with texts, the situatedness of all talk, and with what Burke calls "naive verbal realism" (*LASA* 5), the belief that our idioms capture "reality" as it "really is." If the art of hermeneutics resides, as Gadamer says, in finding what is questionable (*Hermeneutics* 13), dialectic is its instrument, the means of opening up (or out) from the text's illusion of closure, finality, ultimate authority. Dialectic transforms "It is written" into "We must discuss it."

But whatever questions we find and whatever answers we advance through dialectical inquiry are always already part of a dialogue and never any more than contributions to an ongoing conversation. Our dialogues with texts, if they are to be anything more than the exercise of private curiosity, must become dialogues with others, our questions and answers challenging other participants and being challenged in turn. Dialectics within the dialogue: The analytical moment "within" projected "without" to the drama of interpretation, partitive thought giving way to relational thought and returning again—this is the rhythm of dialectic and dialogue Burke practiced and advocated as he sought to retrieve hermeneutics as dialectical pluralism, as "a dialectic of many voices." *It is the dialectical-dialogical rhythm and the drama of interaction that is vital*, lost in the metaphorics of the voiceless trace, impoverished by postmodern rejection of reason, and romanticized by taking metaphors like "the fusion of horizons" too literally.

8

Toward "Complete Sophistiction": The *Praxis* of Comedy, Logology, and Ecology

Definition, Focus, and Themes

As Nicholas Lobkowicz's study of the history of the concept from Aristotle to Marx shows, *praxis* has a range of meanings, none of them exactly equivalent to the current meanings of the English cognate, "practice." Rather than review the intricate history of the term, I shall simply stipulate what it shall mean here. "*Praxis*" in Burke means *any* act whatsoever, including symbolic action (i.e., expression, whether artistic or discursive), in behalf of a better life. Because Burke "hold[s] firmly to the basic Marxist axiom that all expression is equally a form of praxis," because he insists everywhere in his philosophy on "the correlation between discourse and action, between hermeneutics and power" (Gunn 76), he takes the commonsense distinction between "mere words" and "doing something" as too blunt, too unsophisticated to be helpful. Whoever controls our "readings" controls our attitudes and actions.

We encounter, therefore, at the outset perhaps the greatest problem in taking up the subject of Kenneth Burke's *praxis*—namely, if we understand it as Burke does, all that he wrote is *praxis*. I have tried to make the subject manageable by reducing it to three interrelated concepts. As early as *A Grammar of Motives*, Burke authorized my reduction by describing his philosophy as "an attitude embodied in a method" (441), to which I would add "with definite aims or ends in mind." In brief:

1. The attitude is *comic*.

2. The method is *logology*.

3. The aim is *ecological balance*

As an overview, I will comment on each in order.

The comic attitude is developed most fully in the early philosophy, especially in *Attitudes Toward History*, but carried forward intact into the later philosophy. It is actually an attitude embracing many attitudes: toward the self and its ambitions, the stance is humble and ironic; toward other people, it is open and charitable, generous without being gullible; toward the human condition in general, with its endless problems and perpetual conflicts, it requires a stance Burke identifies with wisdom, "fear, resignation, the sense of limits" (*ATH* 42), which in no way implies indifference to human suffering or inactivity on behalf of constructive social change; and toward the natural world, it is filled with wonder and respect, an almost religious sense of gratitude.

In part the point of Burkean comedy is to transcend or transmute our irritation, frustration, and anger with ourselves, other people, and social institutions by becoming interested in them, in much the same way that chronically ill people "make peace" with their afflictions by becoming engrossed in causes, symptoms, and treatments. Hence what Burke calls "hypochondriasis" (*CS* xii–xiii; *GM* 443) belongs to the comic attitude. The human race is chronically "dis-eased"; there is no cure because our neuroses and psychoses are rooted in what we are—symbol-using animals, beings whose "reality" is largely the product of a not-very-reliable language that drives our thinking and action in ways often disconnected from and sometimes flatly at odds with existence in bodies, with social existence in the body politic. But while there is no cure, there may be ways to approach our condition with less agitation and confusion. Hence, Burke's project: "By and through language, beyond language" (cited by Gunn 87).

Rightly understood, Burke's slogan could provide a rallying cry for much philosophy after the linguistic turn. If we go "by" and "through" language, we remain within it. The modernist sound of the slogan, suggesting the hubris of mastery, is undercut by postmodern irony: We remain enmeshed in the very thing from which we wish to extricate ourselves; the way out is the way in—but with a difference, a gain in self-awareness, which makes being "in" also equivalent to a way "out."

The phrase encapsulates the "ultimate" reflexiveness of logology. That is, all the human sciences are reflexive, "ologies" designed to study ourselves. They are words about some aspect of human being or human history. We may doubt that there is or could be any unity of understanding within any one of these sciences, much less among them all, but we cannot doubt that they all share the common condition of being "ologies," words about something. Hence the reflexive step beyond words about *psyche*, or *socius*, or *archaio* (etc.) is logology, words about *logos*, words about words. This step, which amounts to reflecting on the very means of reflexiveness, is a beyond-which-not: Apart from faith in a divine *Logos*, we cannot conceive a level of abstraction beyond words about words. Logology is "ultimate" not because it attains complete, unrevisable Truth, but rather because, in Burke's extended notion of it, metalanguage carries secular thought as "high" as it can go.

Logology is also a without-which-not: How can we understand, say, *socius-logos*, words about companions, without first understanding *logos*, how words themselves behave and how we behave because we "have" language? If language is the very medium by which human relationships are created, sustained, terminated, and studied, understanding it "comes first" even if we can never understand it completely.

In logology Burke discovered a method of "ultimate" reflexiveness— as we will see, a critical theory of critical theories. In ecology he found an "ultimate" frame of reference for his own *praxis* and also its end or purpose, ecological balance. As noted before (see pp. 112–13), "ecology" and "ecological balance" both appear as such in the early philosophy. But the *necessity* for an ecological context for *praxis* only becomes completely clear much later, as implied by his definition of human being as "symbol-using *animals*," or "*bodies* that learn language."

As animals, as bodies, we are, of course, wholly dependent on the earth, on the relatively narrow range of conditions that permitted carbon-based, air-breathing life to evolve. Conditions do not have to alter much to bring all or most life on earth to, in geological terms, a very speedy end.

Hence, an ecological context is "ultimate" in the sense of limiting *praxis* itself—if we alter ecology too much, all human activity ends. As Burke sees it, the basic problem is that with language came also a capacity to elaborate tool-using far beyond what any other animal can achieve.

Burke has much to say about the false god of the Machine and what he calls Counter-Nature and its relation to symbol-driven ambitions in general and specifically to the symbolism of money, capital-driven exploitation of people and the environment (see especially "Variations," passim). We will explore some of these connections. But so far as *praxis* and philosophy are concerned, the *precedence of ecology as context* matters most. Enlightenment philosophy touted freedom as the goal of *praxis*, especially liberation from outmoded ideologies. We still heed its call insofar as we work toward the liberation of women from sexism or of gays and lesbians from homophobia. But all talk and action in the cause of liberation obviously is secondary to preserving the very conditions of human existence, without which we have no choices and therefore no freedom.

In resisting the logic of ecology, we often invoke freedom itself, making the very rhetoric of the Enlightenment a threat. In our time *praxis* without an ecological context cannot be enlightened. It thrusts aside the greatest challenge we face, truly the "last frontier"—self-control.

Those of us who knew Burke in his "natural habitat"—a farmhouse in western New Jersey, near Andover—can testify that he was serious about his ecological commitments and tried to live them. Yet he also belonged to Metropolis, one of the great symbols of Counter-Nature, New York City, where he commuted almost daily in the early years of his career. Burke's *praxis* is hardly Amish-like, separated from the world, a deliberate opting out of the way of living sophistication has fashioned. Rather, willy-nilly, he belonged and knew that he belonged to high sophistication, part of which is automobiles, electric lighting, modern plumbing, and photocopiers, all of which, despite recurrent moments of resentment and guilt, belatedly found their way into his world. In this world, power lawn mowers (sometimes broken down and abandoned without apparent concern precisely where they had broken down) coexisted with organic gardening and birdhouses for his beloved wrens. He lived and knew he was living the contradictions and ironies inseparable from sophistication.

Amish *praxis* appeals in part because it reduces the tensions inherent in sophistication. But the problem with "Here we shall stand" or "back-to"-ism is that from *homo habilis* on to us, as Burke put it, the human "entelechy is technology" (Rueckert, "Kenneth Burke's Encounters" 199). In the West especially we are so caught up in and carried forward by sophistication that alternatives seem quaint at best, ineffectual as protest, a little perverse, and in any case engulfed by the technological society it rejects. Burke chose Hegel's route, courting contradiction and irony rather than seeking to lessen or eliminate tensions. Instead of some version of Romantic neo-primitivism, Burke advocated what he called "complete sophistication" (*ATH* 168).

Reading Burke from a neo-Marxist perspective, Lentricchia argued that "the confrontation with history . . . conferred identity upon his career" (55). Reading Burke from a postPhilosophical perspective, I find that his struggle with sophistication comes closer to defining his identity. For embedded (literally) in the general notion of sophistication is sophistic, and the end of Philosophy is tantamount to the rehabilitation of sophistic. Philosophy after Philosophy, in the absence of foundations, must understand itself as rhetoric, specifically, sophistic rhetoric, which held that all we have to guide *praxis* is persuasion, that which we can make likely, convincing, moving. After Philosophy the issue is not whether to accept or reject sophistication. PostPhilosophers are all sophists, in attitude toward claims to the Truth closer to Protagoras than Plato or Aristotle. Consequently, they aspire to "convince and illuminate without being able to prove" ("Rhetoric" 279), as Gadamer said. The issue, rather, is whether we learned enough from the old sophistic to make a "new sophistic" possible.

The key question is, How shall we use our sophistication? Some of the ancient Sophists apparently viewed rhetoric solely as an instrument of power, a way of getting what we want or more of what we want. For Burke a "new sophistic" must ally sophistication with wisdom, which is wary of power in general even as it grants the necessity for it. Wisdom must ask, Should we want what we have been taught to want? Is more of the desirable actually desirable? Rorty and other postmodernists might argue that Burke's wisdom is simply another name for Philosophy. What we want is what we want, and who is to say what we "should" want unless the critic believes he has the Truth or knows the Good?

Wisdom, however, is hardly equatable with Philosophy. Wisdom came before Philosophy and can come after it as well. No claim to Truth or the Good is required to hold, as Burke did, that "humane enlightenment can go no further than in picturing people not as *vicious*, but as *mistaken*" (*ATH* 41, Burke's emphasis). One needs only an ability to think through the implications of words to assent to the proposition. If we picture people as vicious, there is nothing to be done. We must become hermits and pray for the end of our species. But if we picture ourselves and others as prone to error, there is much to be done and human interaction becomes the great imperative, a good (but not *the* Good, since to make such a claim we would have to know whether our decision to *picture* people as mistaken is correct. We might actually be vicious.) We can't know the Truth about human beings. We can, however, be wise enough to see that we must picture people as mistaken rather than vicious to sustain human society. And without society, we are nothing.

Burke's *praxis*, then, is postPhilosophical, in Simons's words, a "brand of 'new sophistic' . . . that . . . offers a humanistic alternative to an unreflexive objectivism and a self-debilitating nihilism" (13). It is, Simons implies, the *praxis* to come, after scientism and the idolatry of the Machine, after postmodernism's celebration of the abyss, after deconstruction's negative dialectic have played themselves out. Perhaps we can glimpse a little of the future by investigating Burkean *praxis* in more detail.

The Case for Comedy

Only two of Burke's recent critics have insisted on the centrality of the comic in his work. The first was William Rueckert, who emphasized its inconclusiveness:

> [B]y comedy Burke means the whole range of possibilities intrinsic to this term, from the joke, through social comedy and the stage play, to *The Divine Comedy*—and beyond, if that is possible, . . . to some . . . cosmic comedy, conceived . . . in the manner of Vonnegut's *Slaughterhouse-Five*. [So understood] [i]n many ways, Burke's vision is more comic than anything else. (Rueckert, "Some" 5)

The second was Giles Gunn, who connects comedy directly with *praxis*, claiming that "Burke's method for turning cultural criticism into an instrument of social change is fundamentally . . . comic." "To deprive Burke of his jokes, his puns, and his sly winks, to say nothing of his burlesques of the serious and his parodies of the banal, is to rob him of much of the machinery that makes his thinking radically critical and his criticism radically social and political." Gunn thinks that Burke has been robbed by some of his best and most influential recent critics; he singles out Frank Lentricchia especially for "leav[ing] all the humor out of the Burke he presents to us" (80). Actually, however, Lentricchia is not only, as Gunn allows, "undoubtedly sensitive" to the comic in Burke but also critical of it. He does not so much omit the comic in Burke as regret its presence, both in Gunn's sense as humor and in Rueckert's as a literary form or strategy. The comic mask, Lentricchia believes, is the wrong persona for the serious business of furthering social change through criticism.

Even if we associate Burke's version of comedy with its "higher" manifestations, as Rueckert does, we may well feel that there is something odd, incongruous, about a comic *praxis*. According to Richard J. Bernstein, *praxis* in Aristotle "signif[ies] the sciences and arts that deal with the activities characteristic of . . . ethical and political life" (ix); and *praxis* in Marx designates all forms of sensuous, material activity, including revolutionary action. What could be more serious, more worthy of Philosophy, which, when it is comic, is usually so unintentionally? With a world of possible stances to choose from, why did Burke opt for comedy in *Attitudes Toward History* and stick with it for more than half a century thereafter?

This question could be answered in many ways, but our approach to it must be philosophical, in terms of comedy as a multifaceted idea. When Burke says in *Attitudes Toward History* that "whatever poetry may be, criticism had best be comic" (*ATH* 107), he is not announcing a merely arbitrary, personal preference but making a philosophical claim that can be understood and assessed as such claims normally are.

Why comedy? We need to recall that Burke sought in *Permanence*

and Change a *humanistic* corrective or source of resistance to the scientism dominant in the West since the seventeenth century. For reasons
we have discussed before, this meant for him, not poetry or literary art
per se but a *philosophy* of poetry, an *art of living* (see my discussion, pp.
35–36) rather than art in the Kantian, aesthetic tradition. Burke wanted
a philosophy of art that would be indistinguishable from *praxis*.

It is hardly surprising, therefore, to find the Burke of *Attitudes Toward History* engaged in a survey of traditional literary genres as, in a
phrase he used later, "equipment for living" (*PLF* 293). If all understanding is symbolically mediated (probably the most widely shared postmodern assumption), which of our many cultural "narratives" or inherited
"stances" offers the most serviceable overall attitude for living and the
most resources for criticism?

Burke holds with Schopenhauer and William James that we have a
basic choice to make at the outset: to "accept the universe" or to "protest against it"—acceptance or rejection, *Bejahung* or *Verneinung*. Faced
with "the problem of evil"—"anguish, injustice, disease, and death" (3)—
one must decide whether to affirm or condemn the conditions of existence as a whole. Burke had already made his choice, opting for James over
Schopenhauer, when, at a crucial moment in *Permanence and Change*, he
equates "life, activity, cooperation, and communication," adding that
"even the Schopenhauerian philosopher inevitably proclaims their
goodness by the zeal with which he frames his[/her] message" (236). One
may or must reject specific, historical conditions of existence, such as Fascism or the capitalist reduction of human motives to competition or the
technological reduction of *praxis* to manipulation, but rejection as a global
judgment, a totalizing attitude or stance, is self-contradictory. The nega-
tivist or absurdist position refutes itself in acting or communicating at all.

Burke does not go so far as James, who called rejection "an insin-
cere *pis aller*" (*ATH* 3), but he does contend that rejection is derivative,
only the reflex of acceptance (21). What one rejects only makes sense in
the context of what one accepts as valuable or desirable.

Burke's rejection of *Verneinung* as a totalizing attitude is based on
commitment to *praxis* itself. If we begin with *Verneinung* and mean it,
we end either in the myth of Sisyphus, in a life of activity we know to be
pointless, or in a Buddha-like discipline designed to extinguish the very
desire that motivates action-in-the-world. *Verneinung* makes *praxis* in
either Aristotle's or Marx's sense a folly or a defiant gesture.

Sorting out traditional literary genres as tending toward either *Verneinung* or *Bejahung*, Burke takes us through a process of elimination
that ends in comedy as the best overall stance for *praxis* (*ATH* 34–107).
I will not summarize his entire argument here but rather concentrate on
the key conflict, his hesitation between tragedy and comedy.

Burke is convinced that tragedy deals with recurrent motivations vital to an understanding of why people do what they do. In *Permanence and Change*, for example, Burke points to *sacrifice* as the act that accompanies value, and the greatest sacrifice, of course, is human, whether on an altar, a cross, or a battlefield. Thus, he calls attention to a strategy resorted to over and over in history—"recommending by tragedy" (195–97)—demonstrating the great worth of something (e.g., liberty, justice) by showing how many people have died and are willing to die for it. Tragedy is the great dignifier of action, especially concerted, collective action.

Later, in his many efforts to expose and understand the dialectics of social structure, Burke concludes that the scapegoat is essential to the dynamics of human congregation. Our unruly impulses must be managed somehow, and tragedy "deals *sympathetically* with crime. Even though the criminal is finally sentenced to be punished, we are made to feel that his[/her] offence is our offence" (*ATH* 39). The tragic hero functions somewhat like the escape goat of the ancient Jews. Through him or her we "slay" or "banish" our own temptations to transgress, gaining thereby both an imaginative expression of the forbidden and absolution from it.

The scapegoat has also a less sympathetic but no less permanent function as "them"—the enemy "out there"—by which we distinguish who "we" are. Such is what Burke calls "factional tragedy" (*ATH* 188–90), the tragedy of war or the mostly psychological violence of electoral dramatics, most "moving" when a once-popular party and its candidate are resoundingly defeated and the winner joyously inaugurated as the nation's savior (*PLF* 132–37). Such is the to-varying-degrees dreadful process of "cleansing," whether with actual or symbolic blood, whether organized ethnically, racially, religiously, or by some other contrast of "us" versus "them." The sobering thought that Burke returns to over and over again is that the very process of identification requires sacrifice—that victimage is inseparable from human congregation and the values by which life is lived meaningfully.

Careful study of everything Burke has to say about tragedy—a large body of texts indeed, whose implications take us far beyond what I have mentioned here—will yield at least one conclusion hard to doubt. Burke advocates comedy because he believes he has good reason to fear that history has a tragic denouement, a "repetition compulsion" requiring an endless line of victims that, short of eliminating the symbol-using animal entirely, can never absolve or cleanse. We begin to understand why comedy was necessary for Burke's *praxis*, why he insists that "criticism had best be comic." His valuing of comedy over tragedy, which inverts the traditional genre hierarchy, is neither perverse nor quixotic: Rather the comic perspective and much of Burke's *praxis* as a whole is designed to do one thing primarily, break the spell tragedy has over human motivation and create a comic persuasion as powerfully appealing as the mimesis of sacrifice itself.

Everything Burke tells us about comedy should be read with this purpose in mind. For instance, Burke cites Meredith's statement that comedy "is the most civilized form of art" (*ATH* 39). By "civilized" he has in mind not only the common meaning of the word but also its Latin root, for we are told a few pages later that "comedy deals with [hu]*man*[s] *in society*, [classical] tragedy with the *cosmic* [hu]*man*," while Hardy's post-Darwin kind of tragedy features "[hu]*man*[s] *in nature*." The classical emphasis overdignifies human being, invoking a cosmic significance for our affairs increasingly implausible after Copernicus, whereas naturalistic tragedy is reductive, depriving human being of the *civis* in favor of the jungle. "In classical tragedy the motivating forces are superhuman, in romantic-naturalist tragedy they are *inhuman*." But "comedy is essentially *humane*" as "the best of Bentham, Marx, and Veblen" are essentially humane (42, Burke's emphasis); that is, the motivating forces are "just human," the context society, usually the *civis*. It is precisely this context, of course, that *praxis* in both Aristotle's and Marx's senses both imply and require. *Praxis* is not the work of God or the gods nor merely the instinctual or conditioned behavior of animals. Comedy and *praxis* belong together in sharing the same context.

They also belong together because the comic mediation offers the most civilizing attitudes and resources for *praxis*. In concentrating on human folly rather than crime, comedy moves us away from the mimesis of sacrifice dominant in tragedy. Comic victims are exposed as pretenders or obsessives, made to endure embarrassment, sometimes threatened with the lash, but not usually beaten, much less imprisoned, banished, or killed. We are encouraged to view them and through them ourselves and most people as mistaken rather than vicious, capable of correction and reform, of being, in the end, included in society rather than, as in tragedy, excluded from it.

Burke completes his basic case for a comic *praxis* in the following contentions:

> [T]he comic frame [is] the most serviceable for . . . handling human relationships. It avoids the dangers of euphemism that go with the more heroic frames of epic and tragedy. And thereby it avoids the antithetical dangers of cynical debunking, that paralyze social relationships by discovering too constantly the purely materialistic ingredients in human effort. The comic frame is charitable, but at the same time it is not gullible. It keeps us alive to the ways that people "cash in on" their moral assets, and even use moralistic euphemisms to con-

> ceal purely materialistic purposes—but it can recognize as
> much without feeling the disclosure to be the last word on
> human motivation. (106–7)

Burke found in comedy much the same thing that Northrop Frye would later call "pragmatic freedom" (169), an invitation to act unencumbered by the fatalism of tragedy or conversely by antiheroic images of human degradation and failure so common in recent literature. But instead of calling the comic attitude "pragmatic freedom," Burke called it "complete sophistication."

In pondering what Burke means by "complete sophistication," we discover the political implications of a comic *praxis*. Noting "the incentives to take Fascism as a way out of bourgeois-commercialist confusions, and the antiheroic difficulties that go with the *delegated* authority of parliamentary procedure," Burke holds that "the cult of Kings is always in the offing." Via the charisma of a leader not merely elected but installed by God or Fate, we transform confusion into personal loyalty to a figure "above" the impersonal struggle of market forces and of class interests represented by a parliament or congress. The temptation is greatest under the constraints of late capitalism, as

> we near the "Malthusian limits" of its opportunities. The sense
> of frustration that accompanies the narrowing of these op-
> portunities leads to a naive sense of guilt, for which a *Fuhrer*,
> made "heroic" by the tremendous resources of modern propa-
> gandist organization, is the simplest remedy. (*ATH* 167–68)

"The comic frame must detect [and expose] the lure of such incentives." The only way to dispel the magic of a Napoleon or a Hitler is to understand the sources of frustration and guilt in the economic system itself and why we yearn for the hero that will make everything right and simple and unified again. "Democracy can be maintained only by *complete sophistication*" (168, Burke's emphasis), which in turn depends on the kind of awareness that the "high comedy" of Bentham, Marx, and Veblen represent.

In sum, then, why comedy? The answer is not primarily the therapeutic and strategic resources of humor. For Gunn the "underlying purpose" of the comic in Burke "is . . . to create an intellectual idiom supple and quixotic enough to resist the seductions even of its own performance." In this obviously postmodern reading, comic *praxis* amounts to resisting "the temptation to reify or essentialize our own insights . . . by learn[ing] how to laugh at our own foibles" (79–80). Self-directed humor is salient among Burke's strategies for coping, but he actually

insists on "an important distinction between comedy and humor . . .
disclosed when we approach art forms . . . as 'strategies' for living":

> Humor is the opposite of the heroic. The heroic promotes ac-
> ceptance by *magnification*, making the hero's character as
> great as the situation he confronts . . . ; but humor reverses
> the process: it takes up the slack between the momentous-
> ness of the situation and the feebleness of those in the situa-
> tion by *dwarfing the situation*. It converts downwards, as the
> heroic converts upwards. Hence . . . it tends to gauge the
> situation falsely.

He goes on to link the humorist with sentimentality and with "self-pro-
tection" via "the attitude of 'happy stupidity' whereby the gravity of life
simply fails to register" (*ATH* 43, Burke's emphasis). No matter how we
respond to Burke's distinction, clearly he wants to dissociate comic *praxis*
from humor. He would presumably resist both Gunn's tendency to equate
them and the reduction of comedy to a strategy for overcoming reification.

We need not look for some "underlying purpose" for the comic perspective; Burke is quite explicit about its primary function—that is, it
"should enable people *to be observers of themselves, while acting*. Its
[goal is] not . . . *passiveness*, but *maximum consciousness*," a "maximum opportunity [to exercise] . . . the resources of *criticism*" (171, 173,
Burke's emphasis). It promotes criticism (necessary for a thoughtful *praxis*
and a form of *praxis* in its own right) because it is the most *civis*- and
polis-centered of literary mediations. Tragedy deflects criticism by "conversion upwards," by encouraging a mystique of *amor fati* grounded in
a supernatural or natural metaphysics, whereas comedy, with its social,
"only human" context, and its tendency to decenter from the overdignified
and overdetermined, encourages us to see our problems as self-generated
and therefore open to *praxis*. Criticism had best be comic, then, because
praxis ought to be. We live in a century that will certainly be remem-
bered for slaughter and destruction on an unprecedented scale, whose
narrative logic thus far turns overwhelmingly on human sacrifice and
self-victimization. What hope we might have for a different story cannot
but increase by a *self-consciously* comic attitude in all forms of action
and interaction.

Comedy and the Limits of *Praxis*

In an age whose *praxis* is dominated by the allegedly neutral and objective ideal of technical mastery, Burke's singling out of attitude for attention and his effort to explain and justify a comic attitude to human relations
is itself noteworthy. Who else in contemporary philosophy has called

our attention to the importance of attitude in *praxis* so forcefully or argued for a specific *ethos* for *praxis* so persuasively? And yet the comic attitude has been largely ignored, misunderstood, or rejected. With so much at stake, we must try to understand why Burke's comic vision has met with so much diffidence and hostility.

The most important recent critic to reject Burke's comic *praxis* is Frank Lentricchia. "We need to distinguish this Burkean theory of comedy from its classical forefathers," he urges, for

> [w]hereas Aristotle . . . relegated to comedy the representa-
> tion of man as worse than he is, more frail, more prone to
> error . . . Burke . . . pushes the comic deviation to normative
> status by declaring in effect that comedy is the representation
> of man as he really is. The Burkean comedic vision encapsu-
> lates truth in a metaphysics of foolishness and failure.

Lentricchia also professes to find in Burkean comedy "a mandarin cool-ness" whose basic stance is *"noli me tangere*, for I belong to despair." Far from being a *praxis* aimed at constructive social change, in Lentricchia's interpretation Burkean comedy "would, in its 'wise' counsel of 'resigna-tion' and 'fear,' uphold the status quo." Comic *praxis* is just one form of political quietism (65–66).

Lentricchia's reading clearly misrepresents Burke's position. Burke makes no claim—directly or "in effect"—that comedy represents hu-man being as it really is. No metaphysical claim, no encapsulation of truth, can be found anywhere in his discussion. Rather, as we have seen, he contends only that the comic attitude is the best for approaching human relations. *Praxis* requires cooperation, and cooperation requires toleration and *caritas*. How, then, shall we encounter our enemies, espe-cially those who seem to us intolerant and wholly lacking in good will? Loving them may be asking too much, but at least we can take those who oppose our best efforts for constructive change as mistaken rather than vicious, and be wise enough to see ourselves as also prone to error. Otherwise we fall into misanthropy and arrogance; otherwise we fore-close on *praxis* and project an *ethos* certain to alienate.

Burke's justification for comedy is not metaphysical, but pragmatic. The comic attitude gets results and gets them without demonizing the enemy, without requiring a sacrificial victim. Burke's justification is also utopian: Far from contending that comedy represents human being as it really is—a foolish or naive position that evidence from any edition of a newspaper can refute—Burke holds that comedy represents us *as we could be*. A comic society should be our goal, our "no place" toward which *praxis* can continually strive.

As for Lentricchia's contentions about despair and political quietism: The paths to both are the frames of rejection, pushed to logical conclusions. Schopenhauer's pessimism and his attraction to Buddhism, rejection and the desire for nirvana, belong together. Here indeed is the mandarin coolness that doesn't want to be touched. Lentricchia apparently misses the mildly paradoxical nature of acceptance as presented in *Attitudes Toward History*: "Since both tragedy and comedy . . . promote, in Burke's terms, attitudes of social acceptance and accommodation, . . . quietism . . . is almost a foregone conclusion" (Lentricchia 66). Not at all. If we do not accept—that is, attach value to—"this life," this world, to human beings and human effort, there can be no *praxis*; negativism as a totalizing attitude makes *selective* rejection of *some* aspects of a given historical state of affairs nugatory. To reject in a way meaningful for *praxis* requires acceptance. That is why Burke wants us to understand rejection as derivative, as implied by acceptance.

Lentricchia *does* misread Burke—and egregiously at that. But why should so capable and otherwise friendly a critic thus shoot so wide of the mark? When it is easy to show that a reading has gone seriously wrong, something not so easy to detect must be disturbing the aim.

More than comedy *per se*, what Lentricchia objects to is a closely related notion that Burke calls "bureaucratization of the imaginative." By "the imaginative" Burke has in mind creative solutions to problems, innovative ways to live or govern, the visionary or prophetic, and so forth—all the ways, in sum, by which change is conceived and made appealing. He is thinking of *ingenium*, the process by which new paradigms (including but not limited to the scientific) suddenly leap into being, usually the work of one brilliant person or a small group of gifted people. "Bureaucratization" designates, in contrast, the necessary if uninspiring work of the ants—"normal *praxis*," by analogy to Kuhn's normal science. "An imaginative possibility (usually at the start Utopian) is bureaucratized," Burke explains, "when it is embodied in the realities of a social texture." "The bureaucratized" is the idea implemented, *ingenium* made routine.

Burke makes two points (amounting almost to the same point) about bureaucratization of the imaginative, both among the hard lessons of mature experience. "No imaginative possibility can ever attain complete bureaucratization" (e.g., contrast the "heresy" of St. Francis with the order founded in his name after its "domestication" by the Church); and "[i]n bureaucratizing a possibility, we necessarily come upon the necessity for compromise" (*ATH* 225)—without compromise, the Franciscan innovation would have had very few devotees and no official status. The work of the ants is certainly a process of "translation," with all the perils to the original translation implies. But without translation, the readership is limited, the impact of the original forever restricted to cultural heights or margins. *Praxis*, in short, is a very imperfect business requiring "complete sophistication," part of which is the ability to cope in a reasonably good-humored way with the difference between what we wanted and what we got.

Burke claims that bureaucratization of the imaginative "names a basic process of history" (*ATH* 225), a proposition hard to doubt. For Lentricchia, however, it "sets up a critique of the everyday life of the historical process as the Calibanization of Ariel" and consequently manifests "thinly veiled scorn for any and all sociohistoric textures," and an "idealistic projection of human being as a precariously fortified essence that can only be soiled, distorted, and encumbered by all actual and possible modes of government, production, and property relations." "Burke has given us," Lentricchia concludes, "a portrait of historical life as an arena of constriction with no exit" (61).

History sometimes yields a Caliban for an Ariel, Hitler as Wagner's Siegfried, Stalin as Marx bureaucratized, but Burke is not reading history as travesty, nor claiming that the gap between the idea and the idea put into practice is always absurdly great. He is simply saying that there is a gap and we must expect it. Far from scorning social textures, Burke's bureaucratization of the imaginative respects "the given" so much that *praxis* for him is always constrained by its powerfully inertial, conservative force. It is precisely the "idealistic projection of human being as a precariously fortified essence" that Burke's formula is designed to avoid. As he remarks, "Many persons who scorn the very name of Utopia become wounded as the 'imperfect world' of bureaucratic compromise is revealed. They are simply Utopians-scorning-the-name-of-Utopian" (*ATH* 227). Burke would save us from such self-inflicted wounds and fortify us for getting out there and mixing it up with a world we accept in advance as imperfect.

What I hear in Lentricchia's critique is not, however, a utopian-scorning-the-name-of-utopia. I detect instead the Enlightenment faith that in some ways Marx himself exemplified better than anyone else. Marx believed passionately in the perfectibility of humankind—in both the power of theory to comprehend our affairs totally, and in the power of *praxis* to transform them totally. It is this faith that we are in control of our own destiny or could be if we were smart enough and strong willed enough, a faith dear to modernism in all of its manifestations, that Lentricchia's neo-Marxism cannot relinquish, and which Burkean comedy and bureaucratization of the imaginative would require him to relinquish. Burke counsels resignation and fear not because he was satisfied with the status quo of the 1930s (or the 1990s) but because his *praxis* is post (*not* counter) Enlightenment. He does not believe that theory can comprehend totally. He does not believe that *praxis* can transform totally. We are therefore to resign ourselves to limitations and fear the Enlightenment hubris that recognized none. We are not to give up either theory or *praxis*, as some whose counsel is despair would urge us to do now, but rather engage both comically, without pretense to godlike omniscience and without the terrible arrogance that turned so much of the Enlightenment's promise into a curse. Burke will have none of the deification of the human that attended the "death of God."

But if, on the one hand, Burkean comedy repudiates the Enlightenment faith that still has us overreaching, on the other hand, it also connects with Burke's understanding of democracy as, at its best, the institutionalizing of dialectic and dialogue. The message is not all the wormwood of limitation. We cannot know totally, but, pooling our insights, we can know partially, maybe even sometimes enough "for all practical purposes." We cannot alter completely, only, when we cooperate with one another, somewhat, but maybe enough sometimes to make a significant difference. Above all comedy keeps before us the image of an *inclusive* society, a utopia of pragmatic freedom, of people sharing in festivity, of obsession, compulsion, and pretension overcome—hardly, I submit, a bitter vision to guide an energetic *praxis*.

Logology: Critical Theory for the Linguistic Turn

The veil of Maya is woven of the strands of hierarchy.

—Kenneth Burke, *A Rhetoric of Motives*

If we read Burke as I have read him throughout this study, in the context of postPhilosophy, his "comic attitude" makes immediate sense. The comic shares the central assumption of post-Enlightenment thought, human finitude. Its emphasis on society and the joys of festive association implies rejection of the Cartesian isolated consciousness. In cohering so well with the high value Burke allots to democracy and dialogue, it belongs to the postPhilosophical aspirations we find expressed, for example, in Rorty's postPhilosophical society. Indeed, the comic attitude might well represent the emerging *ethos* of contemporary philosophy. Burke claimed in the thirties that *the best* of Marx, Veblen, and Freud was high comedy. How many outstanding minds *as a whole* can now be claimed for it? The list would be very long, but certainly Bakhtin, Rorty, and Habermas, to match his three with three very diverse minds of almost equal influence sixty years later. Much of the complex phenomenon we call postmodernism amounts to the flowering of the comic attitude, especially the aspiration for pragmatic freedom, as against the ideals of certainty, totality, utter predictability, and technological mastery characteristic of modernism.

The comic attitude coheres—not only with Burke's thought as a whole but also with the spirit of a later time, ours. Logology also coheres in both ways, as I shall in a moment attempt to show. But first we should ask, What exactly is logology?

At its point of origin, in *The Rhetoric of Religion* (1961), it designates a method in the sense of the Greek words from which method derives: a *meta+hodos*, "after" + "a way"—that is, conscious reflection on a practice that makes more articulate that which was implicit in the practice itself. It is the difference, for example, between interpreting and having a theory of interpretation.

What characterizes Burke's *metahodos*? First, it is traditionally humanistic in the sense of reflecting primarily on mainstream Western texts, but not centrally on "literature" as humanists usually understand the word. Rather than poetry or fiction, logology concentrates on religious documents and philosophical-theological texts. Why?—because Burke is interested not in texts as such or in texts as aesthetic objects but rather in what texts reveal about human motivation, in particular the motives that only a symbol-using animal can have. Biblical narratives (for example) engross him because they expose the recurrent motives of human beings as they cluster around issues of dominion and power, hierarchy and mystery; identity, difference, and action; prohibition, sin, and sacrifice; concepts of history and human relation to "the transcendent"; and so on. Philosophy and theology concern him because they use language with maximum *thoroughness* (*RR* vi)—that is, they "think things through," as we say, with conscious attention to consistency and coherence—and because, among other contributions to intellectual life, they make explicit what is only implicit in our cultural narratives and in the languages by which they are told and translated.

In logology *mythos* meets *logos* again, but not as the triumph of the latter over the former, rather as a continuous, open-ended interaction. Burke moves from the formative stories of our culture to philosophical-theological reflections on them, the "timeless truths" that our ancestors tried to extract from them, and back again, playing the one off against the other, in search of transhistorical truths that concern logology—an understanding of the symbol-using, misusing, and used animal. Logology is a quest for self-understanding, a contemporary, language-centered version of "Know thyself," humanistic, as I argued in the essay on philosophical anthropology, but not Humanist (see my discussion, pp. 141–44).

The logological *metahodos*, then, has nothing to do with method as either Philosophy or science typically understands the term. Burke is not concerned with method as logic, with evaluating propositions, nor with issues of experimental design, control, replication, and so forth. As the Cartesian tradition understands method, it is not method at all. But it is also not *anti*-methodical in the sense of Feyerbend's *Against Method*. It is only *non*-methodical. Logology does not bother to quarrel with method's self-understanding; as so much postPhilosophy does, it simply works around it, preferring the surprise of *ingenium* and the insight of disciplined speculation to method's self-constriction.

From a Cartesian perspective non-methodical, logology is nevertheless, from postPhilosophy's more inclusive view, recognizably a method—or actually several methods working together. Burke is an outstanding textual phenomenologist, as tireless in his detailed study of individual texts as he is in patient comparison of several. Logology is phenomenological in the sense of seeking no underlying or "deep" structure for language but rather generalizing from comparative study of texts, often of texts more conventional minds would not think of juxtaposing.

But Burkean phenomenology is not purist. Whereas most phenomenology eschews theory as much as possible, Burke's exists entirely to refine, extend, deepen, and apply his theory of language as symbolic action and his philosophical anthropology, his theory of human being as the symbol-using animal (see my discussion of the former, pp. 75–76, and of the latter, pp. 151–53). Burke's phenomenology is theory-driven; this means, of course, that it passes beyond comparative study of texts *per se* and has a critical dimension or depth hermeneutical function that phenomenology *qua* phenomenology lacks.

Logology is phenomenological-*cum*-theoretical—or probably truer to the case, theoretical-*cum*-phenomenological. Basically, Burke wants to preserve a continuous tension between "vertical" integration (theory) and "horizontal" inclusion (respect for the integrity of "this text before us now," as well as other texts that manifest similar motivational ingredients, and can therefore be related to it).

Finally, as one might surmise given some of the comments above and Burke's unconditional commitment to dialectic and dialogue (see my discussions, pp. 97–99 and 175–79), logology is also a dialectical method. It is so in several ways. Like Hegel, Burke *courts* the paradoxes, contradictions, and tensions inherent in the concepts and logic of natural language. He seeks to expose and reflect upon them because they reveal *motivational* paradoxes, conflicts, and tensions in an animal whose purposes derive in large part from language. Unlike Hegel, Burke does not strive to surmount tensiveness, but to live with it; part of complete sophistication is acceptance of life as too complex and contradictory for a totalizing synthesis. But logology is certainly in notable respects Hegelian in its dialectical method.

It is also, minus the Ideas (i.e., minus the metaphysics), reconstructively Platonic. Burke retrieves Plato as a valuable contribution to the philosophy of language. Why? We have noted before Burke's contention that the study of human being should begin from theories of transcendence rather than from the naturalistic reductionism of laboratory experiment (see my discussion, p. 122). Language is inherently transcendent in that words for things are not the things named and behave in ways wholly unlike the behavior of things. To say that humans are symbol-using animals is to say that we are transcending animals. We can do nothing but "rise above" the conditions of speechless nature, and transcendence is inherent in our linguistic strategies (our symbolic actions) for coping with the world. We "rise above" our differences through identification with a common cause or by shared membership in a corporate body, such as a church or nation; we "rise above" adversity by seeing it as necessary to the development of character. Hence, Burke's high regard for Plato as the origin of thought about one of the key motives inherent in language.

Logology not only studies transcendence but also is itself designed to transcend certain human motivations through better understanding of their symbol-driven nature. For example, in the opening of *A Rhetoric of Motives*, Burke the phenomenologist is comparing the imagery of killing, being killed, and killing one's self across a number of texts. Burke is concerned with this imagery because it figures so prominently in the tragic *mythos* that his comic perspective would transcend.

But how do we "rise above" our fascination with "the kill" in all its forms, active, passive, and reflexive? By realizing that "the so-called 'desire to kill' a certain person [including one's self] is . . . . analyzable as a desire to *transform the principle* which that person *represents*" (13, Burke's emphasis). We "rise above" the satisfactions of blood sacrifice by abstraction to a "higher" category, the imagery of transformation in general. From there we see better that the physical act of killing as such is not the point; the point for human beings is what the kill represents, its symbolic value. We also see that there might be other ways to transform the principle besides killing the person (e.g., argument, persuasion) and that, in fact, killing someone has no dependable effect on the principle s/he represents. Killing Jesus of Nazareth, for example, had exactly the opposite effect intended by its perpetrators, to be rid of him. Whether we believe his body came back from the dead or not, his meaning certainly did, and in a form that would prove even more persuasive than he was when alive. Likewise, the suicide may escape the pain of existence, but s/he cannot, simply by taking poison, transform what s/he represents to her/himself and to friends, family, and so forth.

In sum, then, as a *metahodos*, logology may be characterized as follows:

- Theory-driven, a means of developing Burke's theory of

language as symbolic action and his theory of human
being as the typically symbol-using animal

- Phenomenological, centered in the comparative study of
symbolic acts as revelatory of human motivation

- Dialectical, both hegelian and platonic

To these characterizations I would add one more:

- Oriented toward praxis, in general designed to help
us cope with ourselves as symbol-using animals, in
particular designed to reflect upon other critical theories

Later in this section we will see what this last phrase means in more detail.

To understand the place of logology in Burke's thought, we need to
recall the program he announced near the end of *Permanence and
Change*: To "return through symbolism to a philosophy of *being*" (163,
Burke's emphasis). This phrase, I have argued, expresses the central intent of Burke's philosophy as a whole, which depends ultimately on the
notion I called "*praxis* Being" in Part One (see my discussion, pp. 101–3).
Instead of Nietzsche's theory of the "eternal recurrence of the same,"
Burke argues for the *approximate* recurrence of "the same" within a
conventionally Western, linear sense of time.

Logology is the fruition almost three decades later of Burke's decision to resist philosophies of becoming by reflection on two relatively
permanent (i.e., transhistorical) sources of human motivation, the body
and language. More than anything else, it is the pursuit of the approximately recurrent that unites the postPhilosophy of *Permanence and
Change* with, for instance, the "Dictionary of Pivotal Terms" in *Attitudes
Toward History* and with the theories that successively dominate his
later thought, symbol action, Dramatism, and logology. Nietzsche had
said that we cannot think without being, and this is certainly true in the
sense that we cannot think without language, and language "makes being" in that it makes categories and concepts possible. But while Burke
accepts Nietzsche's linkage of thought and being, his stress is elsewhere:
We cannot *act* without being—or more to the point of his philosophy
and the theme of this chapter, *praxis* is impossible without at least an
implicit norm, without a utopia or stable notion of the good life. Philosophies of pure immanence cannot provide the "ought-to-be" necessary for *praxis*.

But *praxis* Being alone is not enough. We must have some more or
less adequate idea of human motives, what drives us toward and away

from the good life. We must also know what can be changed as against what can only be accepted as the limitations of finitude. As a critical hermeneutic, logology serves both these epistemic functions indispensable to *praxis* and therefore indispensable to Burke's *praxis* philosophy. Thus, while we can link *praxis* Being to logology, we must in doing so recognize that logology moves beyond retrieving Being for *praxis* to answering a question that preoccupied Burke from *Permanence and Change* on, What is malleable in human affairs and what not? We will take up part of Burke's answer to this question shortly.

Linking logology to Burke's quest for a philosophy of Being based in symbolism is equivalent to understanding how it coheres with Burke's thought as a whole. But how does it cohere with philosophy now, more than thirty years after *A Rhetoric of Religion*?

To understand this we need to recall Thomas McCarthy's point, cited in Part One: "[T]he 'linguistic turn' . . . is no longer an issue. The question now is where that turn leads" (6). In Part One we discovered that Burke's linguistic turn took him in a direction shared by many contemporary philosophers—toward the pragmatics of natural language, language *in use*, rather than toward Cartesian linguistics, the scientific study of language as a self-contained, abstract system (see my discussion, pp. 66–67). As the study of religious and theological texts, logology clearly belongs to Burke's pragmatic approach. But I want to advance a special claim for it: *Logology is critical theory for the linguistic turn*, and therefore of special interest for anyone hoping to see the linguistic turn lead toward a viable contemporary *praxis*.

What we now call critical theory originated on the edge of—just prior to—the linguistic turn. Nietzsche is closest to a language-centered critical theory, with Freud, because of his interest in the symbolism of dreams, just behind him, and Marx last because of his tendency to reduce language and culture in general to an epiphenomenon of productive forces. But none of the great originators of critical theory had quite made the linguistic turn. For each there was something deeper, more fundamental than symbols—power, libido, class struggle—in short, mostly nonconscious or unconscious motivation independent of language which, prior to the theories, language could only darkly figure forth.

Hence it is not surprising that when the linguistic turn did come about, many students committed to critical theory began to reread their masters from a language-centered perspective. Lacan's work with Freud is, depending on one's point of view, a famous or infamous example, but there are many more, including Burke's effort to synthesize Freud and Marx around symbols of authority in "Twelve Propositions" (*PLF* 305–13). From the standpoint of philosophy after the linguistic turn, the most interesting work in critical theory since the thirties has come out of the struggle to reconceive Nietzsche, Freud, and Marx for symbol-centered thought. Now it is commonplace to take power, libido, and class struggle as always already entangled in language beyond extrication.

It is one thing, however, to reread early critical theory in the spirit of the linguistic turn, quite another to create an original, symbol-centered theory of one's own and employ it as a critique of critical theories. The former is an aspect of Burke's work, mainly in the thirties, represented by "Twelve Propositions" and other essays, such as "Freud—and the Analysis of Poetry" (*PLF* 258–92); the latter, though strongly foreshadowed in Burke's critique of Marx in *A Rhetoric of Motives*, emerges only in the early sixties as logology. Drawing mainly on his own rereadings of ancient and medieval theology, Burke's logology owes little to Nietzsche, Marx, or Freud but rather takes up a perspective "outside" their work from which these earlier critical theories can be assessed.

Another important difference between the Burke that reread Marx and Freud and the Burke of logology is that the latter, excepting the motives that arise from bodily existence, recognizes nothing "deeper" than language itself. Class and class consciousness, for example, depends on an animal that can classify more fundamentally than it does on an economic substructure. Alter the means of production and class structure will change too, but the only way to eliminate class is to eliminate the classifying animal.

Furthermore, while we can certainly doubt, for example, that Freud's psychosexual drama of the family actually exists—that is, we can call any claim to "depth insight" into question—we cannot doubt that Freudian theory and all its neo-Freudian variants are word constructs, and thus open to logological reflection, to the use of language to comment on language. Even the skeptic willing to entertain the possibility that Freud was talking about nothing must concede that Burke is talking about something, Freud's terminology, and telling us things about it that Freudian theory itself cannot disclose.

More than any theory before or since, logology is critical theory for the linguistic turn. We should therefore be more than casually interested in its implications for *praxis*, to which we will now turn.

Whereas the Dramatism of *A Grammar of Motives* was a genuine pluralism, a principled organization of philosophical stances around the implications of its key term "action," logology represents Burke's point of view, his voice in the conversation of history, his critical theory. Consequently, whereas Marx had a unique place among the scene-centered (i.e., materialistic) philosophies discussed in *A Grammar of Motives*, with the advent of logology Marx represents a competing theory that logology challenges as an adequate guide for *praxis*. We must address what this move from Dramatism to logology means for our postPhilosophical understanding of Burke's thought as a whole, but first let's consider part of Burke's critique of Marxist theory as developed in his treatment of mystery and hierarchy in *A Rhetoric of Motives.*

"Mystery," of course, is a negative term for Enlightenment philosophy in general, and especially so for Marxism, which associates it with mystification, the rhetorical resources by which ideology eludes or deflects critique. In contrast, "mystery" in Burke's language-centered philosophy is a much more inclusive term. "Mystery arises at that point where different *kinds* of beings are in communication. In mystery there must be *strangeness*; but the estranged must also be thought of as in some way capable of communion" (115).

We need nothing more than this definition to sense the direction of Burke's thought. Mystery is not only or simply a tactic employed by a priestly class to protect its and the upper class's vested interests; it derives rather from language, from the symbol-using animal's "spontaneous realism," our capacity to categorize, to distinguish kinds of beings. That is, the estrangement between kinds of beings necessary for mystery runs deeper than class-based alienation in the Marxist sense; we have also, as Burke points out, "the mystery of sex relations . . . grounded in the communication of beings *biologically* estranged." Such bodily kinds of difference, which have their source in what we are, symbol-using *animals*, may be "greatly accentuated by the purely *social* differentiations which, under the division of human labor, can come to distinguish the "typically masculine" from the "typically feminine" (115, Burke's emphasis).

Burke recognizes what everyone must recognize after Marx that there are purely social distinctions rooted in the divisions of labor characteristic of economic systems. But what *The German Ideology* called the "substructure" has itself a substructure, the body and language. Mystery cannot exist at all without the dialectic of strangeness and communion, neither of which is possible without a *symbol-using* animal, since both the capacity to conceptualize kinds of beings and to communicate beyond grunts, squeaks, and howls require symbols in general and natural language in particular. Furthermore, *some* kinds of difference derive not from social but bodily sources; in addition to the mystery of sex relations, we have also, for example, the mystery of generational difference, which, though at times "greatly accentuated" by cultural conditions, nevertheless is as natural as reproduction and the aging process.

There can be no question what Burke is claiming for logology as against Marxist theory: Logology "digs deeper." Burke traces the "roots of ownership" not to some economic dispensation but rather to "the *individual centrality of the nervous system* . . . the *divisiveness* of the individual human organism" (130, Burke's emphasis). Beneath "norms identified with social classes which are differentiated by property"—beneath the level of the Marxist analytic—there is an "underlying biological incentive towards private property" (130). A few pages later Burke claims that ideology cannot be flatly identified with capitalism:

> Ideology cannot be deduced from economic considerations alone. It also derives from man's nature as a "symbol-using animal." And since the "original economic plant" is the human body, with the divisive centrality of its particular nervous system, the theologian's concern with Eden and the "fall" come close to the heart of the rhetorical problem. For, behind the theology, there is the perception of generic divisiveness which, being common to all [people], is a universal fact about them, prior to any divisiveness caused by social classes. (146)

"Generic divisiveness"—in mythical terms created when Adam was made, with his potential to obey or disobey God—"comes close to the heart of the rhetorical problem" because persuasion strives to mitigate or surmount difference. As Burke expresses it elsewhere in A *Rhetoric of Motives*, "Identification is compensatory to division. If [people] were not apart from one another, there would be no need for the rhetorician to proclaim their unity" (22).

Divisiveness is also close to the heart of the *praxis* problem not only because *praxis* requires cooperation and therefore rhetoric but also because how we seek to cope with difference is at the heart of *praxis* itself. Marx read history as a process that would eventually eliminate difference: Class structure, along with the state, would wither away. In sharp contrast, logology takes difference as transhistorical, rooted in human being, *both* in bodies that are separated from one another by individuation into distinct central nervous systems, *and* by language, by a symbol-using animal that perceives individuals, not nominalistically, as individuals, but realistically, as representing this or that *kind* of being (e.g., man, woman, child, American, middle class, conservative, or liberal, etc.). It follows that for Burke, as for postmodernism generally, difference cannot be eliminated, nor therefore can mystery. Class structures will wither away, as feudalism gave way to capitalism, but class structure *of some sort* will remain so long as symbol-using animals exist.

Does logology leave us, then, in the grim position of accepting change by denial that anything has really changed? Lentricchia is right when he says that such an attitude toward history passes for sophistication among some intellectuals (40, 51). But Burke's "complete sophistication" does not vitiate *praxis* by denying the reality of change. Part of the task of *praxis* in Burke is to assess "the relative value of [existing] institutions . . . *pragmatically* . . . on their fitness to cope with the problems of production, distribution, and consumption that go with particular conditions peculiar to time and place" (*RM* 279). Not only does logology encourage the critical hermeneutical function, but also the creative one— imagining new orders less inequitable, exploitive, and destructive, and working toward their realization.

But logology does not allow us to think that the hierarchic principle can crumble, taking with it mystery itself in some final, glorious enlightenment and yielding complete equality. "The intensities [and] morbidities . . . of mystery come from institutional sources" and these are subject to change; "but the aptitude comes from the nature of . . . a symbol-using animal" (*RM* 279) and will not alter so long as our species endures. Thus, there is the kind of sophistication represented by Marxist historicism, which teaches us that current hierarchies are not natural, inevitable, or decreed by God. But "complete sophistication" requires "kinds of contemplation and sufferance that are best adapted to the recognition and acceptance of a social form inevitable to social order" ("Human Behavior" 294). The classless society is just as mythic as Eden. Hence, the *praxis* of complete sophistication might concede that "the slogan of 'no property' may be rhetorically effective in a given historical situation," but it must insist that the slogan "will be made effective only insofar as backed by organizational means that allocate properties all along the line" ("Human Behavior" 279).

Logology does dig deeper than Marxism—and because it does, it reveals better what is malleable in Being and what is not. That which is not we can nevertheless cope with better via an attitude of contemplation and sufferance, via, that is, a comic attitude that transmutes the limitations on *praxis* into something more positive, self-understanding, itself part of *praxis*. Thus, attitude and critical method, comedy and logology, come together. The insight of the latter secures the necessity of the former—or was it the former that opened the way to the insights of the latter? Who can tell? What matters is that they cohere with each other and offer a way distinct from, on the one hand, mere acquiescence to current institutional arrangements and, on the other, the unrealistic expectations of revolutionary *praxis*. And while logology is fully as language-centered as poststructuralism, it does not lead us into what William Rueckert aptly called the "sadomasochistic double-binding ironies" ("Some" 8) of Derridean semiotics. We can believe in and struggle for constructive change, even as we recognize that hierarchy and mystery will always be with us. There is irony enough in logology for a sophisticated *praxis*, but not the sort of irony that hamstrings *praxis*.

Before we turn to ecology in Burke's *praxis*, I would offer two concluding comments about logology. Recall Raymond Geuss's definition of critical theory: "a reflective theory which gives agents a kind of knowledge inherently productive of enlightenment and emancipation" (2). Logology, I have shown, is critical of critical theories; it is also critical of *the idea* of a critical theory. Logology certainly aims to enlighten and emancipate, but, as Burke's reflections on mystery and hierarchy confirm, the enlightenment is limited, the emancipation incomplete.

Consequently, while Burke does claim a greater depth for logology as compared with Marxist theory, logology does not represent an abandonment of Dramatistic pluralism nor a return to Philosophy. Burke does not say: "Now that we have logology, we can dispense with the Marxist analytic." Logology challenges but does not seek to replace Marxist thought as part of the knowledge we need to guide *praxis*. The same can be said about the relation of logology to Nietzschean or Freudian theory, or for that matter, to any critical theory. For all the vigor with which Burke argued for it and applied it, logology does not preempt. It claims truths, but it does not purport to deliver certainty and totality, Truth itself. The move from Dramatism to logology, then, while certainly significant in Burke's development and more significant for critical theory and *praxis* generally, is finally only part of a larger body of thought that assumes that Philosophy is over.

Ecology and the Struggle with Counter-Nature

Our question now is, How does ecology align with our emerging understanding of Burkean *praxis*? We know already that "ecology" and "ecological balance" became part of Burke's lexicon as early as 1937, in *Attitudes Toward History* (see my discussion, pp. 112–13). Already, too, ecology and comedy are connected in Burke's thinking, for he contends that

> [a] comic frame . . . show[s] us how an act can "dialectically" contain both transcendental and material ingredients, . . . both "service" and "spoils." . . . It also makes us sensitive to the point at which one of these ingredients becomes hypertrophied . . . A well-balanced ecology requires the symbiosis of the two. (167)

That is, whereas a sacrificial, revolutionary *praxis*, such as classical Marxism, seeks to *eliminate* "spoils," ecological balance seeks only to *restrain* self-seeking motives within a collectivistic regard for "service," the common good.

Ecology linked with comedy is well established in Burke's thought decades before logology emerges with equal explicitness. The roots of ecology can actually be followed back still further. If we can trace logology to Burke's decision to pursue a symbol-centered philosophy of Being in *Permanence and Change*, we can trace ecology to the same passage. To opt for Being entails replacing the metaphor of progress (and its bitter corollary, decadence) with the metaphor of a *norm*, the notion that at bottom the aims and genius of [hu]man [beings] have remained fundamentally the same, that temporal events may cause [us] to stray far from [our] sources but that [we] repeatedly struggle to restore, under new particularities, the same basic patterns of the "good life." (163, Burke's emphasis)

Burke's "metaphor of a norm" clearly has affinities with an ecosystem, dynamic in that species are always mutating and the environment always changing, sometimes gradually, sometimes suddenly, catastrophically, but "struggling" nevertheless to maintain, "under new particularities," the integrity and equilibrium of the whole. Perhaps instead of speaking of eras in human history, we might think in terms of "ecologies." In any case, once Burke rejected "up" or "down" metaphorics in favor of his dialectical metaphor of a "norm," ecology "had to" come next.

But we still need to ask, What does logology, as the study of verbal systems, have to do with ecology, the study of natural systems? In this regard, we must recall a point emphasized in Part One: that Burke was never tempted by the currently fashionable "semiotic reduction," that is, to the thesis that language is all there is. If we reduce Being in this way, language and ecology cannot be connected, for ecology is collapsed into sign systems.

For Burke, however, language was not semiotic but rather symbolic action, requiring a scene as action in a play requires a scene. Furthermore, the symbol-using animal evolved from nonsymbol-using species. Speechless nature was therefore for Burke the "ground" of language, both as part of the *context* of all speaking and as the *source* of all speakers.

But the "text" is not identical with its context, nor the symbol-using animal with its speechless ancestors. The difference is the Burkean dualism, nonsymbolic motion versus symbolic action. Logology and ecology are, therefore, not just different for Burke but radically different. He had to connect them, since reducing the latter to the former was not an option.

How, then, do these fundamentally different systems connect? In two ways primarily. First, if we are symbol-using *animals*, *bodies* that learn language, we remain dependent on ecosystems, even if we have fallen out of them through heavy dependence on a symbol-elaborated culture. Second, language makes elaborate tool-using possible, and when tool-using becomes elaborate enough, it yields high technology, which connects with ecology drastically, as the Destroyer.

All human beings, to recall a clause from Burke's "Definition of [Wo/]Man," are "separated from [our] natural condition by instruments of [our] own making" (*LASA* 16), by a culture of some kind and its accompanying *techne*. But the degree of separation matters a great deal. Native Americans, even in the high civilizations they developed in Central and South America, remained in tune with nature. In residence for tens of thousands of years before Columbus, their ecological impact was relatively minimal, well within the earth's amazing ability to tolerate human exploitation. Western culture and *techne*, however, amounts to a difference in degree great enough to become a difference in kind. In only five hundred years we have managed to disrupt the ecology not only of the Americas but also, through global hegemony, of the entire earth. What began as the local development we call the industrial revolution, limited mainly to Western Europe and North America initially, became the worldwide scramble for high tech we now call the information age.

This difference in kind between a *techne* that supplements nature versus one that seems driven to supplant it is what Burke means by Counter-Nature. Rueckert explains the "basic irony" of Counter-Nature as follows: "That in perfecting [ourselves] by means of [our] technological genius, [we] will destroy our essential dualism and grounding in nature [as symbol-using *animals*], *under the delusion [we] have transcended to a higher level of being*" ("Logology" 184, my emphasis). The delusions of Counter-Nature are all around us, to my mind most notably in the uncritical confidence that somehow technology can solve the ecological problems that technology itself has largely generated.

But what exactly *is* the problem with Counter-Nature? How does Burke lead us to understand it? Basically, in this way: The motives that arise from the body have a natural rhythm about them, a curve of rising desire culminating in fulfillment, satiation, and a falling off toward contented quiescence. They have, so to speak, "inner checks." Even an elephant can only eat so much in a day of foraging, and the species as a whole is checked by the availability of forage, a relatively low rate of reproduction, disease, and so on. But the motives that arise from symbolusing have no inner check. There is always more to say or write. Every idea leads to still more ideas. "Of the making of books there is no end."

The problem with our tool-using, our technology, is that it is symbol-driven. It is consequently, to recall yet another clause from Burke's definition of human being, "rotten with perfection." There are certain species of birds that snap off twigs to help in extracting grubs embedded in tree trunks too deep for their bills to reach. But when the grub is extracted, or when enough grubs are extracted to satisfy its hunger and feed its young, the twig is discarded. In any case, the "*techne*" doesn't elaborate. So it is with all tool-using in nonsymbol-using animals; even with our near-kin, the chimpanzee, tool-using goes so far and no further. But with us the elaboration of tools and of tools for making tools goes on and on, like the making of our books. The kind of attention to things language makes possible also makes the elaboration of tools possible; detailed preservation of knowledge, itself an elaborate *techne*, first of mass-produced books and now internets, sustains the whole high-tech enterprise.

Furthermore, technology, for all of its materiality, glows with symbolic appeal. To have it is to have power, status. Technology is symbol-driven and rotten with perfection. It has no inner check. It belongs to no ecology of balance and equilibrium. It is constrained by time and competition for resources, rarely by any sense of *restraint*.

What, then, can be done about the blind excelsior mentality inherent in *techne*? If, as Burke claims, our "entelechy is technology," is there really anything to be done beyond assuming the attitude toward it he calls "Neo-Stoic resignation" (*GM* 442)? Are we simply to await the inexorable closing in of fate, like the ancient Greek audience who knew before they entered the theater what would happen to Oedipus?

I called attention earlier to Burke's struggle throughout his career to maintain a comic attitude amid the claims he himself pushed forward for tragedy as a privileged representation of human motives and history. The development of logology coupled with his meditations on Counter-Nature threatened the comic fundamentally because they threatened even Burke's modest estimation of the human capacity to act, and hence to have faith in *praxis* itself. Logology and Counter-Nature converge in emphasizing the *compulsiveness* of symbol-using and of everything quasi-symbolic and driven by symbols. Logology shows us that what we call thinking is largely a spinning out of the implications of our vocabularies. Our destiny is caught up in the *logos* of how we characterize ourselves and the world. Counter-Nature reveals that the pride we take in technological manipulation and control of nature conceals how technology manipulates and controls us. The instrument has become the agent. Anyone seeking confirmation of Heidegger's assertion that when we speak it is not we who speak but Language will find ample support in Burke's philosophy from 1961 on.

Yet Burke never abandoned his comic *praxis*. If what we will become is largely implicit in our interpretations now, then *praxis* must work on the interpretations. We must create a new vocabulary with different implications: not *homo sapiens*, "wise man," given dominion over the earth but only the symbol-using, misusing, and used animal, "goaded by the spirit of hierarchy" and "rotten with perfection," imperiled by our own facility with words. If the problem is that we have been taught to measure everything by notions of progress, we can be taught other metaphors, such as the ecological "norm" Burke would substitute for it. If the problem is that we have been taught to think of human societies as apart from nature, then we can be taught to think otherwise, in *terms* of the biosphere and the society of all living things. If the problem is that we have been taught to admire sheer technical expertise too much, we can be taught to think beyond it, in terms of the far greater expertise we will need to overcome (this last?) idolatry.

Clearly there is work to be done—the teaching, admonishing function Burke represented so well, and in which he had a limited but unwavering faith. We *are* doomed if we cannot alter how we characterize ourselves and the world—but Burke held that we can, that we can get "beyond language" in the sense of critique and reconstruction of our current vocabularies. The task may be slow to yield fruit and the harvest far from what we had hoped, but whatever the frustrations, it is worth doing.

We may move "beyond language" in at least one other way. It no doubt sounds impressive and profound to say that Language speaks us. If such a claim helps us to pass beyond the delusion of delusions afflicting modernity, mastery of ourselves, the cultural world we have created, and the natural world we did not create, perhaps it could even prove useful. But the truth is probably less impressive and hardly profound: Language speaks for the most part rather than us because we do not think much either about what we are saying or about language itself. We just "go about our business," unconscious of the implications in our terms, unaware of the medium of communication itself. But language can speak about itself, and when this capacity to reflect comes to the fore, language no longer speaks us. Even if it still "has" us beyond all escaping, we can speak about it.

But what should we say? The scientific study of language before and after the linguistic turn has not told us what we need to know most—the motives inherent in symbol-using, without which we can never understand adequately the claim that "Language speaks." "Language speaks" means that we are driven by the motives only a symbol-using animal can have. Burke reveals these motives better than anyone else and develops his understanding into a critical theory open to general use. Above all else, this is why his work matters for *praxis* and amounts to a new *praxis* for the linguistic turn.

Beyond Hope and Despair

If we resist Burkean *praxis*, I doubt that our resistance is based on what he advocates. That is, despite all daily irritations, impatience, and animosities, despite feeling justified sometimes in holding that people really are vicious, we know that *praxis* requires comic patience, shrewdness, and charity.

Despite thinking that Language speaks us too much for any reflective theory to make any difference, and despite doubts about whether the linguistic turn really has a pay-off commensurate to the investment, we know that critical theory must be or become logological, language and symbol centered. Despite the difficulty of thinking beyond our own little, but self-absorbing projects, despite doubts about whether we really understand ecology or can alter human motivations enough to save the planet, we know that any *praxis* lacking an ecological context will not be good enough for our purposes.

In sum, a *praxis* of comedy, logology, and ecology makes sense—certainly not beyond quarreling, not a self-evident kind of sense, but far beyond any casual wave of dismissal. We know that *praxis* now requires a more complete sophistication, say, than Marxism was able to provide.

Rather than resistance to its substance, what I suspect we doubt about Burke's *praxis* is its practicality. We think it won't work; we think it is too difficult for us.

And it may be. Burke was hardly himself sanguine about the probabilities. But if hope seems a little naive and despair useless, if enlightenment seems all-too-limited and emancipation from our symbol-driven quandaries an impossibility, yet we can still reflect on what Burke calls the "troublous genius of our symbolism." Furthermore,

> if we are trained, for generation after generation, from our first emergence out of infancy, and in ways ranging from the simplest to the most complex, depending on our stage of development, to collaborate in spying on ourselves with pious yet sportive fearfulness, and thus helping to free one another of the false ambitions that symbolism so readily encourages, we might yet contrive to keep from wholly ruining this handsome planet and its plenitude. (cited by Rueckert, *Drama* 162)

It isn't out of the question. Improbable perhaps, but not impossible. History is full of epoch-transforming events that few could imagine until they happened. We should leave it at that. It's enough to keep us at work for a long time.

Conclusion: Who Do You Say That I Am? Burke's PostPhilosophical Identity

Few people truly alive intellectually enjoy being labeled—and the greater the mind the greater the resentment at being "fixed with a phrase." It violates our sense of inner richness; it closes things off; it claims to know what it has not earned.

"Are you a postmodernist?" someone asked Burke, who deflected the whole question of his identity with characteristic humor, saying in reply only "I hope not" (Blakesley 16). I doubt that Burke felt any special desire to dissociate himself from postmodernism. He probably would have given much the same reply had the question been, Are you a critical theorist? Are you a hermeneutical theorist? and so forth.

We understand the resentment. At the same time, Burke himself taught us much about the inevitability of "decreeing essence," about the never-ending human struggle with identity and identifications. The identity question cannot be forever deferred with "I hope not." It has been answered already in many ways, and no doubt will be answered in many more. How we answer it matters, for it has practical consequences. Who reads him, how he is read, what conversations his thought enters into—all of this and more largely hinges on the question of identity.

No doubt the safest answer is Rueckert's: There are many Kenneth Burkes ("Some" 1). It is also true in at least two senses: in the sense Rueckert had in mind, that Burke himself performed in many roles (literary critic, rhetorical theorist, philosopher, poet, etc.); and in the sense that his thought, or aspects of it, have been taken up by students representing virtually every humanistic or social science discipline. But while I do not dispute the *accuracy* of Rueckert's characterization, I wonder about how *functional* it is. In practical terms, doesn't it leave us in much the same condition as Burke's "I hope not"? Dispersing identity is no better than dodging the identity question. "I am legion" has something sinister about it, threatens our will to truth.

I do not claim to have uncovered here "the real Kenneth Burke." I wouldn't know how to make sense out of such a claim. I do claim not to have deferred the question of identity, nor given an answer that scatters it. Nor have I attempted to *appropriate* Burke, as Southwell does in his attack on deconstruction, as Nelson does in his post-humanistic reading of Burke as a deconstructionist, or as Lentricchia does in arguing for Burke as a Western Marxist. Axes are always a-grinding, but the sound in these cases of too-narrow identifications is too intrusive, like Sir Gawain waiting for the Green Knight to strike off his head.

What I have tried to do is work a dialectic. On the one hand, I want to reaffirm what many of his best critics have held or implied—that Kenneth Burke is irreducibly, even stubbornly "Other," a figure that defies assimilation. On the other hand, I want to identify him with a very important convergence of minds we can track back to Kierkegaard and Nietzsche and forward through Heidegger to most contemporary European thought and through American pragmatism to contemporary philosophers like Richard Rorty—namely, the antimodernist movement away from Philosophy, away from metaphysics and epistemology, the effort to live and think without foundational Truth.

More specifically, I want to identify him with those contemporary philosophers who believe that philosophy is possible and worthwhile after Philosophy, which means dissociating him from those who think that philosophy died, or should have died, with the end of foundationalism. Burke belongs to the conversation going on now among hermeneuticists and critical theorists, not to poststructuralism or to the movement I have called radical postmodernism. The vital opportunities for extensive dialogue are, for example, between Burke and Bakhtin, Burke and Buber, or Gadamer, or Ricoeur, or Habermas, or Taylor, or Blumenberg, and so forth—not so much between Burke and Lyotard, or Derrida, or Foucault, or even Rorty to the extent that his brand of neo-pragmatism has brought him too close to a deconstructive position. My hope is that this book will help to get these dialogues underway.

But no useful dialogue can go on if we cannot grasp Kenneth Burke's Otherness. I have sought above all to stake out a *philosophical* identity for him by treating some of his major ideas in the context of postPhilosophy. Since this intent resulted in a fairly complicated argument—actually many arguments converging in the philosophy after Philosophy thesis—it might be useful to set down my understanding of his philosophical identity here in a few words.

Burke is a skeptic *in a specifically postPhilosophical way.* He does *not* hold that highly probable, strongly warranted claims to knowledge are impossible. He does hold that claims to Truth, the *whole* Truth and *nothing but* the Truth, are always doubtful. He also doubts that human beings can desist from telling metanarratives about the Truth. Our metaphysics are implicit in our orientations, our horizons of meaning, especially in our morality. We can and should be quizzical enough to explore the implications of our terminologies, including their metaphysical implications, but we need not claim Truth for them. It is best to say that we cannot avoid the Big Question any more that we can answer it.

From skepticism many roads lead—sometimes to fideism, sometimes to nihilism, even sometimes, as Descartes's case shows, to foundationalism. In Burke's case it led away from *theoretical* philosophy in the classical sense—contemplation of the eternal—to *practical* philosophy, a wholly secular reflection on human action, achievements, compulsions, failures, contradictions, and so forth.

Burke is a practical philosopher.

He is also a humanist (emphatically small "h").

Pinning matters down still further: From the time (1935) that he could say that he was seeking an "art of living," he was a *praxis* philosopher. That is why he returns again and again to the two great Philosophers of *praxis*, Aristotle and Marx, both of whom he reads postPhilosophically. That is why his question of questions is, Why do people do what they do? and why his ultimate concern is what can (and can't) be done to improve the human condition.

Still more specifically, Burke is a *praxis* philosopher *for the linguistic turn*. We do not have to adapt his thinking for language-centered inquiry; it is there already. If we want a nonviolent contemporary *praxis* designed for helping each other to cope with our symbol-driven ambitions, while struggling for constructive social change, we should at least attend carefully to Burke's. His *pragmatic* critique of current institutions combined with his *symbol-centered* critique of human motives offer a potent combination indeed.

But what, exactly, is his philosophy? To the extent that we can distinguish a project from a body of thought that underpins it, how might we identify his philosophy?

In turning away from metaphysics Burke turned toward what he called "metabiology," which led eventually to extensive reflection on human beings as "typically symbol-using animals," or "bodies that learn language." Burke's philosophy, then, is a *philosophical anthropology*. He contributes to a question that we can trace in modernism back to Kant, in classicism to Aristotle, and which engaged many minds in Burke's generation and not a few now: Who are we? What is a human being?

How might we characterize Burke's philosophical anthropology? Most importantly, as against Derrida and poststructuralism generally,

Burke holds that the question can be answered—at least, in practical terms. We do not know, perhaps cannot know, exactly how and from what our species evolved; and we have nothing but guesses about our future. We can no longer, then, tell a narrative about the Truth of human being; after Darwin the traditional, ontological question is either anachronistic or, as Derrida would say, undecidable.

Nevertheless, answers to the question of human being are always at minimum implicit in our ideologies or horizons of meaning, including the terminologies of our disciplines of study. In various ways we will "decree essence" for ourselves. And what we say we are matters, for it has practical consequences. Thus Burke argues that we must treat one another as *persons*, as beings capable of *choice* and *action*—not because we can prove such a claim beyond reasonable doubt but because otherwise society and morality become impossible. Dramatistic human being is implicit in language *as addressed*, as rhetoric, for we do not bother to appeal to beings without the ability to *respond*, who lack response-ability.

Furthermore, while we may doubt that there is anything permanent or eternal about human being, we can generalize about ourselves as we are now, from what we know about our past, and from what we can imagine we might become. We can discover a *relative permanence* good enough, if not for classical *theoria*, at least for "all practical purposes." We are animals. We also use symbols, especially as natural language. No other being we know of can make this claim (or for that matter, lacking symbols, any claim at all). "Symbol-using animals," therefore, may well suffice as a working definition.

From "symbol-using animal" a host of implications follow, but so far as Burke's philosophical anthropology is concerned, what counts the most is its capacity to steer clear of two metaphysical reductionisms. On the one hand, we have idealism, or the *Logos* reduction, which takes human being as essentially mind, or spirit, or, in the quasi-idealism of contemporary linguistic reductionism, language, Language, or signs. Against this reduction Burke advances the body, the total dependence of speech and writing on muscle, organ, and nerve, and the fact that we are embodied agents in a material world. On the other hand, we have naturalism, or the scientistic reduction, which takes human being as just another species, a complicated rat, a blond beast, a creature of deficiencies. Against this reduction Burke advances language and everything language enables, including the technology and culture of Counter-Nature. In sum, Burke's anthropology is neither the honorific conception of the past, *zoon echon logon* or *homo sapiens*, nor the often humiliating conception of the present we encounter in fashionable biologisms. In Burke's view we are indeed something special; the problem is that our specialness, our very aptitude with symbols, is ambivalent, both "angelic" and "demonic" in about equal proportions, and sometimes both at the same time. The question for human being as Burke's anthropology poses it is not, Are we distinctive? but rather, Can we cope better with what makes us distinctive?

And so, as we think Burke's philosophical anthropology through, we return to his project as a philosopher, to create a new *praxis* for the linguistic turn. The relationship is seamless, without being too pat or self-satisfied. What is so appealing about Burke's philosophy is that it encourages us to be critical, even suspicious of our thinking without falling into despair about the value and power of thought. What we once knew as Philosophy is over; but in Burke at least philosophy is not only alive and well but gainfully employed.

Works Cited

Index

Works Cited

Baynes, Kenneth. "Introduction to Charles Taylor." *After Philosophy: End or Transformation?* Ed. Kenneth Baynes, James Bohman, and Thomas McCarthy. Cambridge: MIT P, 1987. 459–63.

Bernstein, Richard J. *Praxis and Action: Contemporary Philosophies of Human Activity.* Philadelphia: U of Pennsylvania P, 1971.

Black, Max. "A Review of *A Grammar of Motives.*" *Critical Responses to Kenneth Burke, 1924–1966.* Ed. William H. Rueckert. Minneapolis: U of Minnesota P, 1969. 89–96.

Blakesley, David. "So What's Rhetorical about Criticism? A Subjective Dialogue Featuring Kenneth Burke and Fredric Jameson." *Textuality and Subjectivity: Essays on Language and Being.* Ed. Eitel Timm, Kenneth Mendoza, and Dale Gowen. Columbia, SC: Camden House, 1991. 14–20.

Blumenberg, Hans. "An Anthropological Approach to the Contemporary Significance of Rhetoric." *After Philosophy: End or Transformation?* Ed. Kenneth Baynes, James Bohman, and Thomas McCarthy. Cambridge: MIT P, 1987. 429–58.

Booth, Wayne C. *Critical Understanding: The Powers and Limits of Pluralism.* Chicago: U of Chicago P, 1979.

———. *Modern Dogma and the Rhetoric of Assent.* Notre Dame, IN: Notre Dame UP, 1974.

Brown, Richard Harvey. *Society as Text: Essays on Rhetoric, Reason, and Reality.* Chicago: U of Chicago P, 1987.

Bultmann, Rudolf. "The *New Testament* and Theology." *Kerygma and Myth.* Ed. Hans Werner Bartsch. London: SPCK, 1957. 1–44.

Burke, Kenneth. *Attitudes Toward History.* 3rd ed. Berkeley: U of California P, 1984.

———. *Auscultation, Creation, and Revision. Extensions of the Burkeian System.* Ed. James W. Chesebro. Tuscaloosa: U of Alabama P, 1993. 42–172.

———. *Collected Poems, 1915–1967.* Berkeley: U of California P, 1968.

———. *Counter-Statement.* Berkeley: U of California P, 1968.

————. *A Grammar of Motives*. Berkeley: U of California P, 1969.

————. "On Human Behavior Considered Dramatistically." *Permanence and Change: An Anatomy of Purpose*. 2nd ed. Indianapolis: Bobbs-Merrill, 1965. 274–94.

————. *Language as Symbolic Action: Essays on Life, Literature, and Method*. Berkeley: U of California P, 1966.

————. "(Nonsymbolic) Motion/(Symbolic) Action." *Critical Inquiry* 4 (1978): 809–38.

————. *Permanence and Change: An Anatomy of Purpose*. 2nd ed. Indianapolis: Bobbs-Merrill, 1965.

————. *The Philosophy of Literary Form: Studies in Symbolic Action*. 3rd ed. Berkeley: U of California P, 1973.

————. "Poem." *The Legacy of Kenneth Burke*. Ed. Herbert W. Simons and Trevor Melia. Madison: U of Wisconsin P, 1989. 263.

————. *A Rhetoric of Motives*. Berkeley: U of California P, 1969.

————. *The Rhetoric of Religion: Studies in Logology*. Berkeley: U of California P, 1970.

————. "Theology and Logology." *Kenyon Review* 1 (1979): 151–85.

————. "Variations on 'Providence.'" *Notre Dame English Journal* 13 (Summer 1981): 15–83.

Cassirer, Ernst. *An Essay on Man*. New Haven: Yale, 1944.

Clark, Katerina, and Michael Holquist. *Mikhail Bakhtin*. Cambridge: Belknap P of Harvard UP, 1984.

Cooper, David E. "Rhetoric, Literature, and Philosophy." *The Recovery of Rhetoric: Persuasive Discourse and Disciplinarity in the Human Sciences*. Ed. R. H. Roberts and J. M. M. Good. Charlottesville: UP of Virginia, 1993. 193–202.

Cowley, Malcolm. "Prolegomena to Kenneth Burke." *Critical Responses to Kenneth Burke, 1924–1966*. Ed. William H. Rueckert. Minneapolis: U of Minneapolis P, 1969. 247–50.

Crusius, Timothy W. "Kenneth Burke's *Auscultation*: A 'De-struction' of Marxist Dialectic and Rhetoric." *Rhetorica* 6 (1988): 355–79.

————. "Neither Trust nor Suspicion: Kenneth Burke's Rhetoric and Hermeneutics." *Studies in the Literary Imagination* 28 (1995): 79–90.

————. "Orality in Kenneth Burke's Dialectic." *Philosophy and Rhetoric* 21 (1988): 116–30.

Damrosch, David. "The Rhetoric of Allegory: Burke and Augustine." *The Legacy of Kenneth Burke*. Ed. Herbert W. Simons and Trevor Melia. Madison: U of Wisconsin P, 1989. 224–38.

Davidson, Donald. "The Method of Truth in Metaphysics." *After Philosophy: End or Transformation?* Ed. Kenneth Baynes, James Bohman, and Thomas McCarthy. Cambridge: MIT P, 1987. 166–83.

Davies, Paul. *The Mind of God: The Scientific Basis for a Rational World*. New York: Simon and Schuster, 1992.

De Man, Paul. *Allegories of Reading: Figural Language in Rousseau, Nietzsche, Rilke, and Proust*. New Haven: Yale UP, 1979.

Derrida, Jacques. "The Ends of Man." *After Philosophy: End or Transformation?* Ed. Kenneth Baynes, James Bohman, and Thomas McCarthy. Cambridge: MIT P, 1987. 125–58.

———. *Of Grammatology*. Trans. Gayatri Chakravorty Spivak. Baltimore: Johns Hopkins UP, 1976.

———. "Structure, Sign, and Play in the Discourse of the Human Sciences." *The Critical Tradition: Classic Texts and Contemporary Trends*. Ed. David H. Richter. New York: St. Martin's P, 1989. 959–70.

Foucault, Michel. *Power/Knowledge: Selected Interviews and Other Writings*. Ed. Colin Gordon. New York: Pantheon, 1980.

Freccero, John. "Logology: Burke on St. Augustine." *Representing Kenneth Burke*. Ed. Hayden White and Margaret Brose. Baltimore: Johns Hopkins UP, 1982. 52–67.

Frye, Northrop. *Anatomy of Criticism: Four Essays*. Princeton: Princeton UP, 1957.

Gadamer, Hans-Georg. *Hegel's Dialectic: Five Hermeneutical Studies*. Trans. P. Christopher Smith. New Haven, CT: Yale UP, 1976.

———. *Philosophical Hermeneutics*. Trans. and Ed. David E. Linge. Berkeley: U of California P, 1976.

———. "Rhetoric, Hermeneutics, and the Critique of Ideology: Metacritical Comments on *Truth and Method*." *The Hermeneutics Reader: Texts of the German Tradition from the Enlightenment to the Present*. Ed. Kurt Mueller-Vollmer. New York: Continuum, 1989. 274–92.

———. "On the Scope and Function of Hermeneutical Reflection." Trans. G. B. Hess and R. E. Palmer. *Hermeneutics and Modern Philosophy*. Ed. Brice R. Wachterhauser. Albany: State U of New York P, 1986. 277–99.

———. *Truth and Method*. 2nd ed. Trans. Garrett Barden and John Cumming, rev. trans. Joel Weinsheimer and Donald C. Marshall. New York: Crossroads, 1989.

———. "What Is Truth?" Trans. Brice R. Wachterhauser. *Hermeneutics and Truth*. Ed. Brice R. Wachterhauser. Evanston, IL: Northwestern UP, 1994. 33–46.

Gell-Mann, Murray. *The Quark and the Jaguar: Adventures in the Simple and the Complex*. New York: W. H. Freeman, 1994.

Geuss, Raymond. *The Idea of a Critical Theory: Habermas and the Frankfurt School*. Cambridge: Cambridge UP, 1981.

Glicksberg, Charles I. "Kenneth Burke: The Critic's Critic." *Critical*

Responses to Kenneth Burke, 1924–1966. Ed. William H. Rueckert. Minneapolis: U of Minnesota P, 1969. 71–79.

Grassi, Ernesto. *Rhetoric as Philosophy: The Humanist Tradition.* University Park: Penn State UP, 1980.

Gunn, Giles. *The Culture of Criticism and the Criticism of Culture.* New York: Oxford, 1987.

Gusfield, Joseph R. "The Bridge over Separated Lands: Kenneth Burke's Significance for the Study of Social Action." *The Legacy of Kenneth Burke.* Ed. Herbert W. Simons and Trevor Melia. Madison: U of Wisconsin P, 1989. 28–54.

Habermas, Jurgen. *Legitimation Crisis.* Trans. Thomas McCarthy. Boston: Beacon P, 1975.

———. "Philosophy as Stand-In and Interpreter." *After Philosophy: End or Transformation?* Ed. Kenneth Baynes, James Bohman, and Thomas McCarthy. Cambridge: MIT P, 1987. 296–315.

———. "A Reply to My Critics." *Habermas: Critical Debates.* Ed. John Thompson and David Held. London: MacMillan, 1982.

———. "A Review of Gadamer's *Truth and Method.*" Trans. Fred Dallmayer and Thomas McCarthy. *Hermeneutics and Modern Philosophy.* Ed. Bruce P. Wachterhauser. Albany: State U of New York P, 1986. 243–76.

———. *Theory and Practice.* Trans. John Viertel. Boston: Beacon, 1973.

Havelock, Eric. *Preface to Plato.* Cambridge: Belknap P of Harvard UP, 1963.

Heath, Robert L. *Realism and Relativism: A Perspective on Kenneth Burke.* Macon, GA: Mercer UP, 1986.

Heidegger, Martin. *Being and Time.* Trans. John Macquarrie and Edward Robinson. New York: Harper and Row, 1962.

———. "Building Dwelling Thinking." *Poetry, Language, Thought.* Trans. Albert Hofstadter. New York: Harper and Row, 1971. 145–61.

———. "Dialogue on Language." *On the Way to Language.* Trans. Peter D. Hertz. New York: Harper and Row, 1971. 1–54.

———. "Letter on Humanism." *Martin Heidegger: Basic Writings.* Ed. David Farrell Krell. New York: Harper and Row, 1977. 193–242.

———. "The Turning." *The Question Concerning Technology and Other Essays.* Trans. William Lovitt. New York: Harper and Row, 1977. 36–49.

Hook, Sidney. "The Technique of Mystification." *Critical Responses to Kenneth Burke, 1924–1966.* Ed. William H. Rueckert. Minneapolis: U of Minnesota P, 1969. 89–96.

IJessling, Samuel. *Rhetoric and Philosophy in Conflict: An Historical Survey.* The Hague: Mouton, 1976.

Isocrates. "Antidosis." *The Rhetorical Tradition: Readings from Classical Times to the Present*. Ed. Patricia Bizzell and Bruce Herzberg. Boston: Bedford, 1990. 50–54.

James, William. "Pragmatics and Radical Empiricism." *The Writings of William James*. Ed. John J. McDermott. Chicago: U of Chicago P, 1977. 311–17.

Jameson, Fredric R. *The Political Unconsciousness: Narrative as a Socially Symbolic Act*. Ithaca: Cornell UP, 1981.

———. "The Symbolic Inference; or, Kenneth Burke and Ideological Analysis." *Representing Kenneth Burke*. Ed. Hayden White and Margaret Brose. Baltimore: Johns Hopkins UP, 1982. 68–91.

Johnson, Mark, and George Lakoff. *Metaphors We Live By*. Chicago: U of Chicago P, 1980.

Kant, Immanuel. *The Critique of Judgement*. Trans. J. C. Meredith. Oxford: Oxford UP, 1973.

Kelbey, Charles A. "Translator's Introduction." *Paul Ricoeur: Fallible Man*. Rev. Trans. Charles A. Kelbey. New York: Fordham UP, 1986. xxxiii–xxxvii.

Kinneavy, James L. "*Kairos*: A Neglected Concept in Classical Rhetoric." *The Contribution of Classical Rhetoric to Practical Reasoning*. Ed. Jean Dietz Moss. Washington, DC: Catholic U of America P, 1986. 79–105.

Langer, Susanne K. *Mind: An Essay on Human Feeling*. Vol. 1. Baltimore: Johns Hopkins UP, 1967.

Lentricchia, Frank. *Criticism and Social Change*. Chicago: U of Chicago P, 1983.

Levinas, Emmanuel. "Martin Buber and the Theory of Knowledge." *The Levinas Reader*. Ed. Sean Hand. Oxford: Basil Blackwell, 1989. 60–74.

Levine, Norman. *Dialogue Within the Dialectic*. London: George Allen and Unwin, 1984.

Lyotard, Jean-Francois. "The Postmodern Condition." *After Philosophy: End or Transformation?* Ed. Kenneth Baynes, James Bohman, and Thomas McCarthy. Cambridge: MIT P, 1987. 73–94.

MacIntyre, Alasdair. *After Virtue: A Study in Moral Theory*. 2nd ed. Notre Dame, IN: Notre Dame UP, 1984.

Marx, Karl. "Capital." *Karl Marx: Selected Writings*. Ed. David McLellan. Oxford: Oxford UP, 1977. 415–507.

———. "On James Mill." *Karl Marx: Selected Writings*. Ed. David McLellan. Oxford: Oxford UP, 1977. 114–23.

McCarthy, Thomas. "General Introduction." *After Philosophy: End or Transformation?* Ed. Kenneth Baynes, James Bohman, and Thomas McCarthy. Cambridge: MIT P, 1987. 1–18.

McKeon, Richard. "The Uses of Rhetoric in a Technological Age: Architectonic Productive Arts." *Rhetoric: Essays in Invention and Discovery*. Ed. Mark Backman. Woodbridge, CT: Ox Bow, 1987. 1–24.

McPhail, Mark Lawrence. "Coherence as Representative Anecdote in the Rhetorics of Kenneth Burke and Ernesto Grassi." *Kenneth Burke and Contemporary European Thought*. Ed. Bernard L. Brock. Tuscaloosa: U of Alabama P, 1995. 76–118.

Mead, George Herbert. *Mind, Self, and Society from the Standpoint of a Social Behaviorist*. Chicago: U of Chicago P, 1934.

Megill, Allan. *Prophets of Extremity: Nietzsche, Heidegger, Foucault, Derrida*. Berkeley: U of California P, 1985.

Michelfelder, Diane P., and Richard E. Palmer, eds. *Dialogue and Deconstruction: The Gadamer-Derrida Encounter*. Albany: State U of New York P, 1989.

Nelson, Cary. "Writing as the Accomplice of Language: Kenneth Burke and Poststructuralism." *The Legacy of Kenneth Burke*. Ed. Herbert W. Simons and Trevor Melia. Madison: U of Wisconsin P, 1989. 156–73.

Nietzsche, Friedrich. *On the Genealogy of Morals and Ecce Homo*. Trans. Walter Kaufman. New York: Vintage, 1968.

———. *The Will to Power*. Trans. Walter Kaufmann and R. J. Hollingdale. New York: Vintage, 1967.

Ong, Walter J. *The Presence of the Word: Some Prolegomena for Cultural and Religious History*. Minneapolis: U of Minnesota P, 1981.

Oravec, Christine. "Kenneth Burke's Concept of Association and the Complexity of Identity." *The Legacy of Kenneth Burke*. Ed. Herbert W. Simons and Trevor Melia. Madison: U of Wisconsin P, 1989. 174–95.

Parkes, Henry Bamford. "Kenneth Burke" (Review of *Attitudes Toward History*). *Critical Responses to Kenneth Burke, 1924–1966*. Ed. William H. Rueckert. Minneapolis: University of Minnesota P, 1969. 109–22.

Peirce, Charles Sanders. "The Principles of Phenomenology." *Philosophical Writings of Peirce*. Ed. Justus Buchler. New York: Dover, 1955. 74–97.

Perelman, Chaim, and L. Olbrechts-Tyteca. *The New Rhetoric: A Treatise on Argumentation*. Trans. John Williamson and Purcell Weaver. Notre Dame, IN: Notre Dame UP, 1969.

Ransom, John Crowe. "An Address to Kenneth Burke." *Critical Responses to Kenneth Burke, 1924–1966*. Ed. William H. Rueckert. Minneapolis: U of Minnesota P, 1969. 141–58.

———. "Mr. Burke's Dialectic." *Critical Responses to Kenneth Burke, 1924–1966*. Ed. William H. Rueckert. Minneapolis: U of Wisconsin P, 1969. 159–62.

Ricoeur, Paul. *Fallible Man*. Rev. Trans. Charles A. Kelbey. New York: Fordham UP, 1986.

———. *Freud and Philosophy: An Essay on Interpretation*. Trans. Denis Savage. New Haven: Yale UP, 1970.

———. "Hermeneutics and the Critique of Ideology." *Hermeneutics and the Human Sciences*. Ed. John B. Thompson. Cambridge: Cambridge UP, 1981. 63–100.

———. *Interpretation Theory: Discourse and the Surplus of Meaning*. Fort Worth: Texas Christian UP, 1976.

———. *Lectures on Ideology and Utopia*. Ed. George H. Taylor. New York: Columbia UP, 1986.

Rorty, Richard. "Pragmatism and Philosophy." *After Philosophy: End or Transformation?* Ed. Kenneth Baynes, James Bohman, and Thomas McCarthy. Cambridge: MIT P, 1987. 26–66.

Rueckert, William H., ed. *Critical Responses to Kenneth Burke, 1924–1966*. Minneapolis: U of Minnesota P, 1969.

———. *Kenneth Burke and the Drama of Human Relations*. 2nd ed. Berkeley: U of California P, 1982.

———. "Kenneth Burke's Encounters with Walt Whitman." *Encounters with Kenneth Burke*. Urbana: U of Illinois P, 1994. 185–221.

———. "Poetry, Logology, Technology, Admonology: Kenneth Burke in 1981—from Counter-statement to Counter-nature." *Encounters with Kenneth Burke*. Urbana: U of Illinois P, 1994. 180–84.

———. "Rereading Kenneth Burke: Doctrine Without Dogma, Action with Passion." *The Legacy of Kenneth Burke*. Ed. Herbert W. Simons and Trevor Melia. Madison: U of Wisconsin P, 1989. 239–61.

———. "Some of the Many Kenneth Burkes." *Representing Kenneth Burke*. Ed. Hayden White and Margaret Brose. Baltimore: Johns Hopkins UP, 1982. 1–30.

Selzer, Jack. *Kenneth Burke in Greenwich Village: Conversing with the Moderns, 1915–1931*. Madison: U of Wisconsin P, 1996.

Simons, Herbert W., and Trevor Melia, eds. *The Legacy of Kenneth Burke*. Madison: U of Wisconsin P, 1989.

Southwell, Samuel B. *Kenneth Burke and Martin Heidegger, with a Note Against Deconstruction*. Gainesville: U of Florida P, 1987.

Taylor, Charles. "Overcoming Epistemology." *After Philosophy: End or Transformation?* Ed. Kenneth Baynes, James Bohman, and Thomas McCarthy. Cambridge: MIT P, 1987. 464–68.

———. *Sources of the Self: The Making of Modern Identity*. Cambridge: Harvard UP, 1989.

Vickers, Brian. *In Defence of Rhetoric*. Oxford: Clarendon P, 1988.

Warren, Austin. "The Sceptic's Progress." *Critical Responses to Kenneth Burke, 1924–1966*. Ed. William H. Rueckert. Minneapolis: U of Minnesota P, 1969. 51–60.

Weber, Max. "Religious Rejections of the World and Their Directions."
    From Max Weber: Essays in Sociology. New York: Oxford UP, 1958.
    323–59.

Wess, Robert. *Kenneth Burke: Rhetoric, Subjectivity, Postmodernism.*
    Cambridge: Cambridge UP, 1996.

Williams, David Cratis. "Under the Sign of (An)Nihilation: Burke in the
    Age of Nuclear Destruction and Critical Deconstruction." *The
    Legacy of Kenneth Burke.* Ed. Herbert W. Simons and Trevor Melia.
    Madison: U of Wisconsin P, 1989. 196–223.

Wittgenstein, Ludwig. *Philosophical Investigations.* Trans. G. E. M.
    Anscombe. Oxford: Basil Blackwell, 1953.

Index

Timothy W. Crusius is an associate professor of English at Southern Methodist University, where he teaches courses in rhetoric and composition at all levels of the curriculum. He has also published books on discourse theory, philosophical hermeneutics, and argumentation. His current project is *The Mayfield Guide to Writing*, a comprehensive textbook for first-year writing courses.